The Guinness Dictionary of

jokes

Nigel Rees

HA
HA
HA
HA
HA

GUINNESS PUBLISHING

This Publication copyright © Guinness Publishing Ltd, 1995
33 London Road, Enfield, Middlesex.

Reprint 10 9 8 7 6 5 4 3 2 1 0

Design and layout by John Rivers.

Typeset by Ace Filmsetting Ltd., Frome, Somerset.
Printed and bound in Great Britain by Cox & Wyman Ltd., Reading.

A catalogue record for this book is available from the British
Library.

ISBN 0-85112-666-9

INTRODUCTION

To call a book a dictionary of jokes is a bit of a joke in itself. But that is what it is – a book to which the reader can refer in order to find jokes listed under category or key-word headings. More importantly, it tries to do something a little unusual: wherever possible (though only in a minority of cases) it seeks to provide a source. Having been engaged for twenty years in the business of finding origins and sources of quotations and popular phrases, I have now been tempted to try to do the same thing for jokes: to start the archaeology of humour by recording where I first encountered a particular story or gag, and by pointing out the fact whenever a funny or witty line has become detached from its original speaker or writer or popularizer.

And this is a bit of a joke, too. It is a truism to say that there is no such thing as a new joke, only old ones which are endlessly recycled. It is even more true to say that most attempts to find the originators of jokes are doomed to failure because, in this area of folklore, that is something quite impossible to achieve. The same joke may occur to more than one person at the same time, in different places, so who would be foolish enough to claim to have originated a particular joke?

But I thought it was worth the attempt. Even if I managed to scratch no more than the surface, I believe it to be an interesting and worthwhile activity, though ultimately futile. As to the ascriptions and attributions that I have included, let me say very clearly that these are not intended to suggest that they are the origination of a joke. In most cases, they are merely an early published appearance. Any information of earlier use will naturally be welcomed for inclusion in future editions.

The collection is, equally, not intended to be comprehensive. It consists in the main of jokes that I have found funny (or interesting in some way) and doesn't consist of jokes inserted simply for their own sake.

In attempting to date some of the material, I have, for the most part, been shooting blindfold. When I have mentioned where I first encountered a particular joke, I have sometimes credited the person who first told it to me. I am not, of course, suggesting for a moment that that person invented the joke or even that version of it. Wherever I have tactfully pointed out that a joke told to me as though it was an incident involving the teller, was actually a joke already well-established elsewhere, the purpose is not to expose the teller. It has not been my intention to ridicule or humiliate such tellers of jokes by pointing out that the stories they fondly believe to be their own – or in which they involve their own relatives, friends or ancestors – are in fact as old as the hills. But, rather, it is just a reminder of the way in which so many joke-tellers do personalize their jokes in order to make them more immediate and compelling. When the comedian says, 'My mother-in-law's so fat she . . .' or 'my wife doesn't understand me. The other day . . .', we understand that he is not talking about his actual mother-in-law or wife, but using the persona in order to deliver a humorous message.

Where do jokes come from?

This is the central conundrum of this book. The short answer is, nobody knows. The slightly longer answer is that the minting of most jokes of the type with which this book is concerned, is very much bound up with the nature of language, especially the English language. Old jokes recur endlessly in an infinite variety of guises. The reason for this lies not so much in the speed of modern communications as in the nature of the English language itself. Because of its richness and variety, the language lends itself to playfulness. Many (some would say too many) of the jokes in this book are based on puns or other forms of word play. Wherever English is spoken, the same kinds of joke arise. It is as if the jokes are lying there within the words waiting for a form of spontaneous combustion to set them off, or for the circumstances and context to shift and trigger them into a joke. An example I like to give is of a joke I first heard in Australia in 1981. It was said that the then Prime Minister, Malcolm Fraser, 'does the work of two men . . .' Pause for admiration. '. . . Laurel and Hardy.' A month later, back in Britain, someone said of the then British Prime Minister, '. . . that Margaret Thatcher, you know, she does the work of two men . . . Laurel and Hardy.' Either one of these jokes may have been an adaptation of the other, but the fact is that the simple pun was waiting in the language – waiting for the right circumstances to arise – so that the joke could ignite.

How many basic jokes are there?

In seeking to prove that there is no such thing as a new joke, several – largely humour-free – people have attempted to enumerate the types. One popular suggestion is that there are only *five* basic jokes (just as there are sometimes said to be a mere six basic plots). On the other hand, Richard Janko in his book *Aristotle on Comedy* (1984) claims to have unearthed the Greek philosopher's long-lost classification of *eight* basic jokes. On the other hand, again, Sully Prudhomme (French poet and winner of the first Nobel Prize for Literature) in his 1902 'Essay on Laughter' identified *twelve* 'Classes of the Laughter-Provoking', which may amount to much the same thing:

1) Novelties
2) Physical Deformities
3) Moral Deformities and Vices
4) Disorderliness
5) Small Misfortune
6) Indecencies
7) Pretences
8) Want of Knowledge or Skill
9) The Incongruous and Absurd
10) Word Play
11) The Expression of a Merry Mood
12) Outwitting or Getting the Better of a Person.

Yet further, Robert Graves, in his pamphlet *Mrs Fisher, or the Future of Humour*, wrote of his tutor at Oxford who used to say that there were *forty-three* recognizable degrees of humour. Now degrees of humour may not be quite the same as jokes, but this is a delightfully eclectic number to plump for. According to Graves, 'he began with (1) laughter at deformities, (2) the rapidly drawn-away chair, (3) cheese, (4) mothers-in-law, (5) people without a sense of humour; and so on, up to the rarefied forty-third degree which was 'God'. Here, I think, he erred: to laugh at God after passing the forty-second degree (which was 'Shakespeare') is to make a bad throw at the finish of the snakes-and-ladder game and to slide back to degree five; for God has no sense of humour and that's all there is to the matter.' (All this and more was reprinted in Graves's *Occupation: Writer*, 1974.)

Humour theorists might do better to ponder the view that, in fact, there is really only *one* basic joke. It was defined best in the line attributed to Mack Sennett: 'An idea going in one direction meets an idea going in the opposite direction.'

Apart from being humour-free, such speculations are pretty pointless and one certainly does not want to end up in the position of the legendary German professor, recalled by J.R.R. Tolkien, who 'wrote a large book on Das Komische. After which, whenever anyone told him a funny story, he thought for a moment, and then nodded, saying: "Yes, there is that joke"' – (No. 232 in *The Letters of J.R.R. Tolkien*, 1981).

Indeed, if any reader of this collection is inclined to mutter 'old joke' or even accuse me of garnering yet more 'old rope', I can only reply, 'But that's the whole point!' Among the ancient war-horses of the joke-teller's trade there must be one or two lines here which readers have not encountered before. These are put in especially for them!

What is a joke?

When I was compiling *The Guinness Book of Humorous Anecdotes* (1994) – to which I very much hope this is a complementary and companion volume – I defined an anecdote as a story which (even if not true) *said* something about a particular personality or type of person. Inevitably some straightforward jokes crawled under the wire in the light of this definition. But, as I said in the first book, it had never been my intention to police the difference with any vigour.

Dealing now with straightforward jokes (which barely bear definition – 'a joke is a joke is a joke'), I have allowed some anecdotal material to creep in. I have also included a fair number of what might be described not so much as jokes but as 'humorous quotations'. I have done this because I have encountered these lines without any kind of accompanying attribution and thought that the originators deserved to be credited where they were known. In fact, a 'quotation' may be no more than a joke which has a very specific provenance. It comes not from that mysterious black hole from which most jokes come but from an identifiable source, which may in fact be the actual originator of the line.

The only definition of a joke is something that makes you laugh out loud or which (more quietly) amuses you by its wit, insight or just plain silliness. These are the jokes that I find – or have found – funny and thought worth recording with a modest amount of footnote and source material. It could be argued that there is no real point in proving that what Person A thinks is newly-minted wit was, in fact, being laughed at by Person Z eighty years ago in a fast-fading copy of *Punch*. But this matter, however abstruse, has a certain salutary purpose. Apart from which, I have to say *I* enjoy doing it, so that's as good a reason as any.

Did you hear about the politically-correct comedian?
He never managed to tell a single joke.

One of the most interesting areas of joke collection (I won't say 'study') is when a large number of jokes focus on one theme or category. I am not quite sure why some of these themes or joke types have endured longer than others, but I thought it was important to examine chicken jokes, elephant jokes and waiter jokes among others. Then there are the more questionable jokes about groups of people – minorities of one sort or another – Irish jokes, Polish jokes and light-bulb-changing jokes, to name but a few.

The fairly recent vogue for jokes about minorities, where a specific group within a nation or community is singled out and ridiculed for its supposed stupidity or outstanding characteristics, is in the tradition of jokes aimed at other nationalities. 'There was an Englishman, a Welshman and a Scotsman' is the traditional beginning of this kind of joke which usually goes on to express a clichéd – but not particularly unkind – view of national characteristics. The Scotsman is gently ribbed about his meanness, the Welshman about his deviousness, the Englishman about his stiff upper lip, and so on.

It was but a short step to turn these national jokes into minority jokes. The English jokes about the Scots were soon being told by the Scots about Aberdonians. Canadians have 'Newfie' jokes – about people in Newfoundland. Bulgarians have Armenian jokes. Minority jokes told by Americans have included Polish jokes, Aggie jokes, Mexican jokes, Black jokes, Valley Girl jokes . . . and others too humorous to mention. In a sense, light-bulb-changing jokes and blonde jokes and Essex Girl jokes are also minority jokes, though the subjects selected tend to be on the basis of jobs, professions and types rather than of ethnicity or nationality. By including such jokes, I run the risk of being condemned to eternal damnation by the politically-correct. Yet although the provoking of what has been termed 'inappropriate laughter' by the telling of racist and sexist jokes has been a central plank of political correctness – on the basis that it often demeans the subject persons by projecting stereotypes or by straightforward humiliation – the case against such humour is not proven. It may in fact have a healthy effect in releasing feelings which otherwise might take a more direct and violent form.

Besides, the subjects of minorities jokes may not entirely disapprove of the process themselves. The Irish who, famously, are the butt of many jokes told by the British are perfectly capable of telling them against themselves – as well as singling out their own minority – people from County Kerry – upon which to inflict the same type of cutting jest. It can be argued that though Jews tell some of the best Jewish jokes – against themselves – similar jokes become racist when told by non-Jews, but this may be to lose sight of the humour. A joke is a joke and, as I say, may be a way of containing or relieving inevitable feelings and prejudices that all people have in one direction or another.

The special categories of joke contained in this *Dictionary* are as follows:

ACRONYMS	DO IT JOKES
AGGIE JOKES	DUMB MEN JOKES
ANAGRAMS	ELEPHANT JOKES
BLONDE JOKES	ESSEX GIRL JOKES
BLOOPERS	FEMINIST JOKES
CHICKEN JOKES	FOOT-IN-MOUTH DISEASE

FREE —— JOKES
GOD'S INTENTIONS
GOLDWYNISMS
GOOD NEWS/BAD NEWS
  JOKES
GREAT MAN JOKES
INITIALS
INSURANCE CLAIMS
IRISH JOKES
JEWISH JOKES
JUST FANCY THAT
KERRY JOKES
KNOCK-KNOCK JOKES
LADA JOKES
LAWS, JOKE
LIGHT-BULB JOKES
LIMERICKS
MALAPROPISMS
MENU MISTAKES
MISPRINTS
NEWSPAPER HEADLINES
NURSERY RHYMES
OLD —— NEVER DIE. . .
OWL AND PUSSYCAT JOKES
POLISH JOKES

PROVERBS
PUNS
QUESTION AND ANSWER
  JOKES
RADIO ARMENIA JOKES
—— RULES OK
RUSSIAN JOKES
SCHOOLBOY HOWLERS
  (also under GEOGRAPHY,
  HISTORY, SCIENCE)
SHE WAS ONLY THE
  ——'S DAUGHTER
SMIRNOFF JOKES
SONG TITLE JOKES
SOVIET JOKES
SPOONERISMS
STICKERS (including
  BUMPER STICKERS,
  BUTTON JOKES,
  LAPEL BADGE JOKES,
  T-SHIRT JOKES)
TITANIC JOKES
TRANSLATIONS
VAN DER MERWE JOKES
WAITER JOKES

Acknowledgements

My special thanks for allowing me to dig deep in their humour banks
or to tap their thoughts on humour and its origins go to: John M. Cone;
John Gray; Raymond Harris; Donald Hickling; Sir Antony Jay;
Valerie Grosvenor Myer; Mark English; David Cottis. I would also like
to thank especially everybody who has sent me jokes over the years.
Wherever possible, I have tried to acknowledge these contributions in
the text.

NIGEL REES
London, 1995

AARDVARK
1 **It's aardvark, but it pays well.**
Included in John S. Crosbie, *Crosbie's Dictionary of Puns* (1977).

ABSINTHE
1 **Absinthe makes the tart grow fonder.**
A piggy-back joke. In Sir Seymour Hicks's *Vintage Years* (1943) it is given as a toast proposed by one Hugh Drummond. It rides on the back of 'Absinthe makes the heart grow fonder', the original pun on the proverb, which I have heard ascribed (inevitably perhaps) to Oscar Wilde, but also to Addison Mizner, the American architect (1872–1933) and so quoted in *The Treasury of Humorous Quotations*, ed. by Evan Esar & Nicolas Bentley (1951).

ABSTINENCE
1 **Abstinence is the thin end of the pledge.**
Recorded in *Graffiti Lives OK* (1979).

ACCIDENTS
1 **Be security conscious – because 80% of people are caused by accidents.**
Contributed by D.R. to *Graffiti Lives OK* (1979).

2 **Mum, you know that vase you were worried I might break?**
Yes, what about it?
Well, your worries are over.

ACCORDIONS
1 **An accordion is a bagpipe with pleats.**

See also GENTLEMEN 1.

ACCOUNTANTS *See under STATISTICIANS.*

ACRONYMS

1 BURMA

As everyone must know by now, BURMA is a lover's acronym for 'Be Upstairs Ready My Angel', the sort of thing that correspondents used to put in their letters when trying to get sexy things past the eyes of military censors in time of war.

2 NORWICH

Means, famously, '(K)Nickers Off Ready When I Come Home'.

Attempts have been made to revive this splendid custom. A *New Statesman* competition is remembered as having produced the following suggested acronyms:

3 EDINBURGH

'Erection Definitely Imminent Now, Book Usual Room, Grand Hotel', and:

4 LLANFAIR . . . GOGOGOCH

The start and the finish of the long Welsh placename were said to mean, 'Listen, Love, Accountancy's No Fun . . . God, Oh God, Oh God, Oh Christ, Hanky!'.

On 5 February 1994, the travel page of the *Independent* announced the results of a competition which produced these further offerings:

5 WALES

Meaning, 'Will Arrive Late Expecting Sex'.

6 NAMIBIA

'Nickers Arouse Me In Bed, I'm Afraid' and 'Not Action Man In Bed, I Agree'.

7 TODMORDEN

'Tonight Our Downstairs Maid Ought Really Dine Elsewhere (Noise!)'; 'Teeth Out, Dear, My Organ Requires Deflating 'Ere Night'; 'Turn Off Dictation Machine, Office Raver, Discretion Ends Now'.

ACTORS AND ACTING

1 Two old actors were reduced to thumbing a lift up the Thames on a barge which, as it happens, was carrying sewage. When

**they came to a lock, the lock-keeper asked the bargee what
he had on board.**
'A load of shit, and two actors,' he replied promptly.
'Ah,' murmured one of the actors, 'still not getting top
billing . . .'
Told by Martin Jarvis (1994).

2 **The secret of acting is sincerity — and if you can fake that,
you've got it made.**

A line usually attributed to the American comedian George Burns (as, for
example, in Michael York, *Travelling Player*, 1991). Fred Metcalf in *The Penguin
Dictionary of Modern Quotations* (1986) has Burns saying, rather: 'Acting is
about honesty. If you can fake that, you've got it made.' However, Kingsley
Amis in a devastating piece about Leo Rosten in his *Memoirs* (1991) has the
humorist relating 'at some stage in the 1970s' how he had given a
Commencement address including the line: 'Sincerity. If you can *fake that* . . .
you'll have the world at your feet.' So perhaps the saying was circulating even
before Burns received the credit. Or perhaps Rosten took it from him? An
advertisement in *Rolling Stone, c.* 1982, offered a T-shirt with the slogan
(anonymous): 'The secret of success is sincerity. Once you can fake that you've
got it made.'

3 **The ageing actor-manager had just led his company to the
conclusion of another performance of *Hamlet* in a small theatre
in the provinces. As the somewhat desultory applause died
away, he made a short speech informing the audience that the
following night the company would be giving a different play.
'I myself will be essaying the tragic role of Macbeth in the
Bard's play of that name, while my lovely lady wife will be
portraying Lady Macbeth.'**

**At this point, a voice from the gallery cried, 'Your wife's a
whore!'**

**Barely pausing to register the remark, the actor-manager
continued, '. . . *Nevertheless* she will be playing Lady Macbeth
tomorrow night.'**

Told by William Franklyn on BBC Radio *Quote ... Unquote* (8 August 1987).
Compare NEVERTHELESS.

4 **Alfred Lunt and Lynn Fontanne, the great American husband
and wife partnership, were appearing together in a play that
had run for many performances. Like so many actors and
actresses after a long run, their performance was, to say the
least, jaded. The producer called in and watched their
performance, then went and sent a telegram to the Lunts: 'I am**

standing at the back of the stalls. I'd like you to join me.'
Told by George Jean Nathan, drama critic of *Esquire* in his monthly feature
'First Nights and Passing Judgements', in c. 1937.

See also LIGHT-BULB JOKES 22, 23.

ADULTERY

1 **A class of girls at a convent school was asked to write an
essay on 'The Joys of Youth'. One little girl, having given a list
of the joys of youth, ended with the line: 'These are just some
of the Joys of Youth, but, oh, for the Joys of Adultery!'**
Traditional when I included it in *Babes and Sucklings* (1983). D.F. in his collection
of SCHOOLBOY HOWLERS has: 'Certainly the pleasures of youth are great
but they are nothing to the pleasures of adultery.'
   Compare: 'Adolescence is the stage between puberty and adultery' –
included in John S. Crosbie, *Crosbie's Dictionary of Puns* (1977).

2 **An Irish priest had his bicycle stolen – he thought by a member
of his flock – and went to ask his bishop what he should do
about it. The bishop advised caution but suggested a subtle
ploy. The priest was told to preach a sermon on the Ten
Commandments. When he got to 'Thou shalt not steal' he
should look round the church meaningfully and note if anyone
so much as moved, giving themselves away.**
   **A while later the bishop met the priest again and asked him
if the ploy had worked. 'Well, yes,' said the priest, 'but not
quite in the way you envisaged. I was going through the Ten
Commandments, one by one. And when I got to "Thou shalt not
commit adultery", I suddenly remembered where I left it.'**
This was told by Gay Byrne, host of Irish television's *Late, Late Show*, some time
in 1993. Miles Kington even wrote a column about this breath-taking event in
the *Independent* (21 February 1994). But it was a venerable joke even then. It
had been printed, for example, in *Pass the Port* (1976).

3 **Guns don't kill people; husbands who come home early kill
people.**
Told by Don Rose, American broadcaster, 1981 – quoted in Bob Chieger, *Was
It Good For You Too?* (1983).

4 **The travelling salesman came home unexpectedly in the middle
of the week. The phone rang late at night and a man's voice at
the other end asked, 'Is the coast clear?' 'How should I know?'
replied the salesman, 'That's three hundred miles from here.'**
Included in *The Best of 606 Aggie Jokes* (1988).

ADVERTISING

Lurking in almost every advertising copywriter's mind is a streak of iconoclasm and bad taste which gets subliminated in the telling of jokes about the lines they would love to have written about certain products if only they had dared . . .

1 **HAIL JAFFA – KING OF THE JUICE.**

2 **IT'S WHAT IT'S NOT THAT MAKES IT WHAT IT IS.**

3 **UN OEUF IS AS GOOD AS A FEAST.**

4 **TAMPAX . . . INSOFAR AS.**

This was in response to the tampon ad that had stated simply 'Modess . . . Because . . .'

5 **PEOPLE ARE STICKING TO KLEENEX.**

6 **HER CUP RUNNETH OVER.**

Suggested jokingly by American copywriter Shirley Polykoff to a corset manufacturer. He enjoyed it so much, 'it took an hour to unsell him', she recalls in her book *Does She . . . Or Doesn't She?* (1975).

7 **FOR SALE: Double bed and roller skates.
WANTED: Pram.**

This Personal Ad. appeared on a notice board at the sub-Post Office in Nursery Lane, Wilmslow in the 1950s. Recalled by Tim Norfolk (1994).

8 **'Every penny you spend will help the World Wildlife Fund's Tropical Rain Forest Campaign . . . '**

The World Wildlife Fund, as it was then called, had the bright idea of putting this slogan on wrappers. Contributed to BBC Radio *Quote ... Unquote* (9 November 1992) by Phyllis M. Teage of Devon.

9 *The following conversation was overheard in a northern supermarket: He:* **'I say, what was the name of the tea bags them monkeys talked about on the telly?'** *She:* **'PG Tips.'** *He:* **'I think we should get some – they spoke very highly of them.'**

As mentioned in *The Guinness Book of Humorous Anecdotes* (1994). I included this remark in my book *Eavesdroppings* (1981), following its broadcast on BBC Radio *Quote ... Unquote* (1980). It had been sent by Mrs Joan Scott of Burton. John A. Thornton of London SW11 sent me another version in 1992: 'I overheard a very English old lady in a smart chemist's shop in St James's, when offered the choice of two toothbrushes, say, "I will take that one; they speak very well of them in the advertisements."'

And then I noticed in David Ogilvy's introduction to *Confessions of an Advertising Man* (1963): 'My father used to say of a product that it was "very well spoken of in the advertisements". I spend my life speaking well of products in advertisements.' In fact, this sort of remark has become an oft-quoted example of amused comment on advertising influence. Recently I discovered this caption from a cartoon in the *Punch Almanack for 1911*: two women are being served in a chemist's shop and one, called 'Sweet Simplicity', is saying: 'And I'll have a bottle of that Dentifrine — I *must* try some of that. All the advertisements speak so well of it.'

ADVICE

1 **Never walk when you can ride, never sit when you can lie down.**

Helpful tips from Samuel Freeman who served in the US Supreme Court from 1862 to 1890. Claire Rayner, the British advice columnist, has a longer version which she received from the Sister Tutor who trained her as a nurse back in the 1950s: 'Nurse, never stand when you can sit, never sit when you can lie down, and never lie if there's any chance they might find you out.'

2 **Never be photographed with a glass in your hand, never pass up a free lunch, and never miss a chance to pee.**

The three secrets of public life, as also recalled by Claire Rayner, the last item possibly derived from:

3 **Never miss an opportunity to relieve yourself; never miss a chance to sit down and rest your feet.**

A piece of advice sometimes attributed to King George V. His son, the Duke of Windsor, was later to ascribe this remark to 'an old courtier', but it seems likely that it was said by George V. A correspondent who wished to remain anonymous told me in 1981 that a naval officer of her acquaintance who was about to accompany Prince George, Duke of Kent, on a cruise, was asked by George V to make sure that the Prince was properly dressed before going ashore. He also advised: 'Always take an opportunity to relieve yourselves.' Another correspondent suggested that King Edward VII had been the first to say something like this when he was Prince of Wales. On the other hand, even earlier, the Duke of Wellington had said: 'Always make water when you can.'

4 **Three rules for life for men over the age of 65:**
   1. Never pass up a chance to pee.
   2. Never trust a fart.
   3. Never waste an erection even if you're on your own.

Told to me in 1992 by Claire Rayner who had them from a well-known broadcaster (who shall remain nameless).

AGE AND AGEING

1 **It is a sobering thought . . . that when Mozart was my age he had been dead for two years.**
Tom Lehrer on the record album *That Was the Year That Was* (1965).

2 *Of a certain woman:* **'Pushing forty? She's clinging on to it for dear life!'**
Said by Ivy Compton-Burnett, the British novelist (1884–1969) Recounted by Julian Mitchell on BBC Radio *Quote ... Unquote* (5 January 1982).

3 **The distinguished actress had been so impressed by the flattering work of this particular photographer that she engaged him again to take her picture. 'Oh dear,' she remarked, looking at the new prints when they were finished, 'you make me look older than last time.'**
   The photographer was the quintessence of tact: 'Ah yes,' said he, 'but I was much younger in those days.'
Heard in April 1994. But who were the original participants?

4 *On being replaced in the Shadow Cabinet by a man four years his senior:* **'There comes a time in every man's life when he must make way for an older man.'**
Reginald Maudling, the British Conservative politician (1917–77), as reported in the *Guardian* (20 November 1976). He also said: 'I have never been sacked before. I was appointed by Winston Churchill and I am now being dismissed by Margaret Thatcher. Life goes on. The world changes.'

5 **A 102-year-old woman was asked whether she still had any worries. 'No, I haven't,' she replied. 'Not since my youngest son went into an old folks' home.'**
As mentioned in *The Guinness Book of Humorous Anecdotes* (1994). I now find that this version was contributed to BBC Radio *Quote ... Unquote* (19 June 1980) by Mrs V. Bedwell of Grays, Essex.

6 **Older women are best because they always think they may be doing it for the last time.**
Ian Fleming, British novelist and journalist (1908–64). Quoted in John Pearson, *The Life of Ian Fleming* (1966). Compare Benjamin Franklin's *Reasons for Preferring an Elderly Mistress* (1745): '8th and lastly. They are so grateful!'

7 **Just because there's snow on the roof, it doesn't mean the fire's out inside.**
What men say when their hair goes prematurely white. A relatively modern coinage, I think, and probably American. It is included in Mieder *et al*, *A Dictionary of American Proverbs* (1992).

AGGIE JOKES

An 'Aggie' is the sort of person who, in America, attends an 'agricultural and medical' college. He is not supposed to be very bright and so is the target of innumerable stupid person jokes. Texas A&M University, in particular, has given rise to a whole series of joke books devoted to the Aggie theme. They have been coming out since 1965. The publishers, The Gigem Press, state rather sweetly on the title page: 'It is not the intention of the publishers to ridicule or degrade any institution or individual. The purpose is to chronicle an important chapter in American humor.' Most of the jokes have also appeared, or have gone on to appear, in other collections of minority/stupid person jokes.

1 The definition of gross ignorance is quickly given as 144 Aggies.

2 When the marriage ceremony was over, the Aggie and his lovely bride went to a resort hotel to spend their honeymoon. Bedtime came and the bride retired, but the groom stood by the window gazing at the moon and stars.
   'Dear,' the bride called, 'why don't you come to bed?'
   Answered the Aggie, 'Mother told me that tonight would be the most wonderful night of my life, and I'm not going to miss a minute of it.'
   Included in *The Best of 606 Aggie Jokes* (1988). As also the following:

3 Did you hear about the Aggie who called his girlfriend to see if she was doing anything that night. She said she wasn't, so he took her out. Sure enough, she wasn't.

4 Then there was the Aggie who thought his sister was a very good girl when she came home from a weekend trip with a Gideon Bible in her handbag.

5 The Aggie in the pizza parlour, when asked by the waiter if he wanted his pie cut in six or eight pieces, replied, 'Six. I don't believe I can eat eight.'

6 Then there was the Aggie who threw himself on the floor and missed!

7 Did you hear about the Japanese Aggie who, on 7 December 1941 attacked Pearl Bailey?

8 An Aggie courting his girlfriend gazed into her eyes and said, 'I love you,' as he caressed her tummy. 'Lower, lower,' she murmured. 'I love you,' said the Aggie in tones an octave lower.

9 Did you hear about the Aggie who was so dumb he thought a bar stool was something Davy Crockett stepped in.

10 'Well, I'll be darned,' said the Aggie reading the deaths columns in the newspaper. 'It's amazing, the folks round here die alphabetically . . . .'

11 I broke my arm in three places.
   You ought to stay out of those places.

12 Did you hear about the Aggie skier with the frostbitten fanny? He couldn't figure how to get his pants on over the skis.

13 Before his first plane ride, an Aggie was told that chewing gum would keep his ears from popping during the flight. After finally landing he turned to his companion and said, 'The chewing gum works fine, but how do I get it out of my ears?'

14 A small Texas town purchased a new fire truck. The next time the council men met they discussed how to dispose of the old one. The Aggie council man suggested they keep it and use it for false alarms.

15 Did you hear about the Aggie who was such a poor reader that he belonged to the Page of the Month Club?

16 Do you know how an Aggie spells farm? E I E I O.

17 An Aggie went to an Aggie doctor to find out why urine is yellow and semen is white. 'So you can tell whether you're coming or going,' the Aggie M.D. told him.

See also BLONDE JOKES 5, 15; CEMENT 1; GOOD NEWS/BAD NEWS JOKES 2; LIGHT-BULB JOKES 5; NUDISTS 2, 3; ORAL SEX 4; SMOKING 3, 5.

AIRLINES

1 *British Airways transatlantic flights:*
BREAKFAST IN LONDON.
LUNCH IN NEW YORK.
– Luggage in Bermuda.

Graffito addition to airline advertisement. Contributed to BBC Radio *Quote ... Unquote* (14 June 1978) by William Alexander of Shoreham, Sevenoaks, Kent.

2 ALITALIA
Many airline names have been interpreted as acronyms, usually with derogatory effect. Hence, this one means: 'Always Late In Take-off, Always Late In Arrival'; 'Aircraft Landing in Tokyo, All Luggage In Australia.'

See also ALITALIA.

3 BCAL (British Caledonian Airways)
'Best C*** Aloft.'

4 BOAC (British Overseas Airways Corporation)
'Better On A Camel'; 'Bend Over Again, Christine.'

5 BWIA (British West Indian Airways)
'Better Walk It Alone.'

6 CPA (Canadian Pacific Air)
'Can't Promise Anything.'

7 EL AL
'Everything Lousy, Always Late.'

8 PAL (Portuguese Airlines)
'Pick Another Line.'

9 PAN AM (Pan American Airways or 'Pandemonium Scareways')
'Pilots Are Normally All Maniacs.'

10 PIA (Pakistan International Airlines)
'Please Inform Allah.'

11 QANTAS (Queensland And Northern Territories Aerial Services)
'Queer And Nasty, Try Another Service'; 'Queers And Nancies Together As Stewards.'

12 SABENA (*Société Belge d'Exploitation de la Navigation Aérienne*)
'Sodomy And Buggery Endanger Natural Appetites'; 'Such A Bloody Experience, Never Again.'

13 SAS (Scandinavian Airlines System)
'Sweet and Sexy.'

14 TAP (Tap Air Portugal)
'Take Another Plane.'

15 TWA (Trans World Airlines)
'Travel Without Arrival'; 'Try Walking Across.'

ALDERSHOT
1 PASSENGERS ARE REQUESTED NOT TO USE THE TOILET
WHILST THE TRAIN IS STANDING IN A STATION.
— except at Aldershot.
Amendment to traditional British railway notice. Contributed to *Graffiti Lives OK*
(1979).

ALERT
1 BE ALERT.
— your country needs lerts.
Graffito contributed to BBC Radio *Quote ... Unquote* (26 June 1979) by Mrs
Howes of Snitterfield, Warwickshire.

2 BE ALOOF. BRITAIN HAS ENOUGH LERTS.
— no really, be a lert, there's safety in numbers.
Graffiti with additions, observed near the A30. Included in *Graffiti 3* (1981).

ALICE
1 *Doctor:* 'I am afraid that you are suffering from Alice.'
Patient: 'What's that?'
Doctor: 'We don't really know, but Christopher Robin went
down with it.'
Graffito from Leeds Hospital Medical School. Included in *Graffiti 3* (1981).

ALIMONY
1 Alimony is like buying oats for a dead horse.
Arthur Baer, American columnist and writer (1897?–1969) — quoted in Bob
Chieger, *Was It Good For You Too?* (1983).

2 Alimony is the screwing you get for the screwing you got.
In Haan & Hammerstrom *Graffiti in the Southwest Conference* (1981). Compare
Lana Turner's comment on her lover Johnny Stompanato's use of her money in

1958: 'I wonder if the screwing I'm getting is worth the screwing I'm getting' — quoted in Bob Chieger, *Was It Good For You Too?* (1983).

3 **Paying alimony is like having the TV on after you've fallen asleep.**

ALITALIA
1 **Q. How can you tell it's an Alitalia plane?**
A. By the hairs under its wings.
Told by Alan Nixon (1982).

2 **Genitalia is not an Italian airline.**
Graffito from Carlton, Victoria. Quoted in Rennie Ellis & Ian Turner, *Australian Graffiti Revisited* (1979).

See also AIRLINES 2.

ALPHABET
1 **Q. How many letters are there in the alphabet?**
A. No, not 26 — 24, because ET went home.

2 **Q. How many letters are there in the alphabet?**
A. 19. ET went home, JR got shot, the angels sang no L, the B buzzed off back to its hive — and there's P running down your leg.
British school kids, quoted by Caroline St John-Brooks in *New Society* (2 June 1983).

AMATEURS *See under PROFESSIONALS.*

AMBIDEXTERITY/AMBIDEXTROUSNESS
1 **I'd give my right arm to be ambidextrous.**
Graffito contributed to BBC Radio *Quote ... Unquote* (29 January 1979) by R. Jamieson of Chapel-en-le-Frith, but an old chestnut even then. Hence the variations and emendations:

2 **— You can have mine, I'm left-handed.**
Included in *Graffiti 2* (1980).

3 **I'D GIVE MY RIGHT ARM TO BE AMBIDEXTRUSS.**
– and my left arm to be able to spell it.
Contributed to HTV *All Kinds of Everything* (7 May 1981).

AMBITION

1 **The egotistical surgeon is like a monkey: the higher he climbs the more you see of his less attractive features.**
Anonymous saying applied to anyone in any profession who has achieved high rank. On BBC Radio *Quote ... Unquote* (29 March 1994), John Oaksey recalled that his father, Geoffrey Lawrence (Lord Oaksey; 1880–1971) had said the same sort of thing about judges and other high-ups in the legal profession, drawing a parallel rather with orangutans. Perhaps there is some connection with the proverbial saying, 'The higher the monkey climbs the more he shows his tail,' discussed in *Notes and Queries* (1887).

AMERICA

1 **America is a nation that conceives many odd inventions for getting somewhere but can think of nothing to do when it gets there.**
Will Rogers, American humorist (1879–1935), quoted in *The Treasury of Humorous Quotations*, ed. by Evan Esar & Nicolas Bentley (1951).

ANAGRAMS

1 **Did you know Spiro Agnew is an anagram of 'grow a penis'?**
From Edinburgh University, included in *Graffiti 2* (1980).

2 **'I'm an evil Tory bigot' is an anagram of Virginia Bottomley.**
Current by 1992 by which time she was Secretary of State for Health in the British Conservative Government. On 31 May, the *Observer* reported that she was 'attracting some less than favourable thoughts from anagram lovers. "I obey, I'm a loving tart"; "I'm a bile voting Tory"; "I'm an evil Tory bigot"; "I live to train my gob"; and "O! Bite my vital groin" – these are just some of the anagrams on her name which are scurrilously being bandied around the Department of Health.'
  The search for acronymical jokes in political names is an old one. *Punch* (17 February 1877) revealed that 'The Earl of Beaconsfield' (Benjamin Disraeli) was 'The real Face of Old Ben'.

3 **'Stifle' is the only word which is an anagram of itself.**

See also ELIOT, T.S. 2.

ANARCHISTS
1 **Anarchists drink bad tea because all proper tea is theft.**

2 **Vote anarchist.**
Included in Reisner & Wechsler, *Encyclopedia of Graffiti* (1974).

3 **ANARCHY NOW**
   – pay later.
Slogan and graffitoed addition in Oxford Circus tube. Contributed to BBC
Radio *Quote ... Unquote* (28 August 1979) by Becky Cecconi of New Ash Green,
Kent.

ANDREWS, JULIE
British-born actress (1935–).
1 **Working with her is like being hit over the head by a**
   Valentine's Day card.
Said by Christopher Plummer after they had made *The Sound of Music* (1965).
Quoted in Leslie Halliwell, *The Filmgoer's Book of Quotes* (1973).

ANGOLA
1 **GET OUT OF ANGOLA**
   – who's she?
Graffito and addition, in Haan & Hammerstrom *Graffiti in the Big Ten* (1981).

ANIMAL LOVERS
1 **Calling all animal lovers – we wish to inform you that your**
   habits are illegal.
Included in *Graffiti 2* (1980).

See also BESTIALITY 2.

APATHY
1 **Last Tuesday's meeting of the Apathy Society has just been**
   cancelled.
From North London, contributed by D.R. to *Graffiti Lives OK* (1979).

2 **I couldn't care less about apathy.**
Included in *Graffiti 2* (1980).

3 **Not enough is being done for the apathetic.**
From Clifton, Bristol, included in *Graffiti 2* (1980).

4 **THIS COUNTRY IS BEING SCREWED BY APATHY.**
– what apathy?
– I don't know and I don't care.
Included in *Graffiti 2* (1980).

5 **Sock it to me with apathy.**
Included in Reisner & Wechsler, *Encyclopedia of Graffiti* (1974).

APHORISM
1 **Aphorism is the death-rattle of the revolution.**
Graffito from the wall of Balliol College, Oxford, in 1968/69.

APPEARANCES
1 **He looks as if someone has just poured cold porridge into his Wellingtons.**
Anon., of Fyfe Robertson, the gaunt Scots TV interviewe of yesteryear (1903–87).

ARCHAEOLOGY
1 *The reported remark of Sir Arthur Evans on finding a fragment of pottery at an excavation in Crete:* **'An ill-favoured thing, but Minoan.'**
Related by Sir Antony Jay (1995).

ARDEN, ELIZABETH
Canadian-born American beautician (c. 1880–1966).

1 **Q. What made Elizabeth Arden?**
A. When Max Factor.
From Folkestone. Included in *Graffiti 2* (1980).

ARMED FORCES
1 **At this moment you are the only man in the Air Force who knows what he is doing.**
In the men's room, Westover Air Force Bass, Mass. Included in Reisner & Wechsler, *Encyclopedia of Graffiti* (1974).

2 **The Army works like this: if a man dies when you hang him, keep hanging until he gets used to it.**
Attributed to Spike Milligan by Richard Ingrams on BBC Radio Quote ... Unquote (4 May 1977).

3 **Join the army, meet interesting people, and kill them.**
Graffito said to be from the 'loo at the Athenaeum', contributed by Terry Wogan to BBC Radio Quote ... Unquote (22 January 1979).

ARMS
1 **ARMS FOR AFGHANISTAN.**
– legs for Tito.
Mona Vale, New South Wales, Australia (1981).

2 **THE AVERAGE BRITISH FAMILY SPENT £16 A WEEK ON ARMS LAST YEAR.**
– if they didn't this poster would be in Russian.
Contributed to Graffiti 4 (1982) by S.J. Williams, Portishead, Bristol.

ARROWS, RED See RED ARROWS.

ART
1 **Art is what you can get away with.**
Graffito at the Walker Art Gallery, Liverpool, recounted by Paula Yates (1982).

2 **Ars Longa, Vita Sackville-West.**
Anonymous observation, recorded in Quote ... Unquote (1978).

ARTIFICIAL INSEMINATION
1 **Practise artificial insemination – keep your hand in.**
Quoted in Bruce Ridley (ed.), Wall Flowers: A Collection of Australian Graffiti (1981).

ASBESTOSIS
1 **My uncle Fred died of asbestosis – it took six months to cremate the poor devil.**
From Southsea, included in Graffiti 2 (1980).

ASTAIRE, FRED
American dancer, actor and singer (1899–1987).

1 **Q. What's old and wrinkled and smells of ginger?
A. Fred Astaire.**
Graffito from Covent Garden, London (1982).

ASS
1 **Q. What do you get when you cross a donkey with an onion?
A. A piece of ass that will make your eyes water.**
In Haan & Hammerstrom *Graffiti in the Southwest Conference* (1981).

ASTROLOGY
1 **I was born under Taurus the Bull. Quite what Taurus the Bull thought about it, I never heard.**
By the 1960s.

ATHEISTS
1 **I was an atheist until I realised I was God.**
Graffito from Brighton Beach, New South Wales, Australia (1981).

2 **An atheist is a man who has no invisible means of support.**
Saying attributed to John Buchan (later Lord Tweedsmuir), British politician and writer (1875–1940), in H.E. Fosdick, *On Being a Real Person* (1943).

AUDIENCES
1 *On his own stage début:* **The secret is perseverance. At the end of that night, I had the audience with me all the way. But I shook 'em off at Catford.**
Les Dawson, British comedian, quoted in the *Independent* (9 April 1990). According to *The Goon Show Companion* (1976), Harry Secombe once sent a telegram to Michael Bentine (in the late 1940s), saying, 'Audience with me all the way. Managed to shake them off at the station.'

2 **A story variously told concerns – in one version, at least – the British melodramatic actor Tod Slaughter (1885–1956) who used to tour the provinces with plays like *Sweeney Todd* and *Maria Marten*. In the latter, he had just killed the girl,**

the police whistles were sounding and he was busy
asking rhetorically, 'What can I do? What shall I do with the
girl?'

Helpful as ever, a voice from the Gods called down, 'Shag
her while she's still warm!'

A politer version of this appears in *Roy Hudd's Book of Music-Hall, Variety and
Showbiz Anecdotes* (1993).

AU PAIRS

1 They used to treat their au pair just like one of the family. So
she left.

AUSTRALIA

1 Australians are living proof that aborigines screw kangaroos.

Graffito from The Old China Hand pub, Wanchai, Hong Kong, by John M.
Freeman (1983).

2 Australia: where men are men, and sheep are nervous.

In *Graffiti 4* (1982), photographed by Brian Robson. Has also been applied to
Yorkshire and South Dakota.

AUTHORS

1 Of a certain author it was said, 'A first edition of his work is a
rarity but a second is rarer still.'

Franklin Pierce Adams, American humorist (1881–1960), quoted in *The Treasury of
Humorous Quotations*, ed. by Evan Esar & Nicolas Bentley (1951).

AUTOGRAPHS

1 The writers Tennessee Williams and Truman Capote were
sitting talking together in a café one day when an over-
excited female fan came bustling up and invited Mr Capote to
sign her breast. Before he could oblige, her furious husband
rushed up, whipped out his penis and insisted that Mr Capote
sign that instead. Replied the writer, 'Well, I don't think I could
manage to put my whole signature on that – but I could initial
it.'

Recounted in the *Observer* (3 July 1994).

AYATOLLAH KHOMEINI
Iranian religious and political leader (1900–89)

1 **The Ayatollah is uncircumcised. There's no end to the prick.**
Graffito in Sydney, New South Wales, Australia (1981).

2 **Ayatollah Khomeini is a Shiite.**
Included in *Graffiti 2* (1980).

BABIES
1 **A small daughter approached her mother and remarked on the size of her tummy.**
'Ah, well, you see, darling, daddy has given me a little baby and it's inside there.'
After a pause to digest this information, the girl rushed to where her father was.
'Daddy,' she cried, 'did you give mummy a little baby?'
'Well . . . er . . . yes I did,' said the father.
'Oh, well,' said the daughter resignedly, 'she's eaten it!'
Recounted in *Pass the Port* (1976).

2 **Definition of a baby: A loud noise at one end and no sense of responsibility at the other.**
Generally attributed to Ronald Knox, British priest and writer (1888–1957).

BACHELORS
1 **A bachelor never quite gets over the idea that he is a thing of beauty and a boy forever.**
Helen Rowland, American columnist and writer (1875–1950) in *A Guide to Men* (1922). Flann O'Brien (1911–66) commented on the supposed youthfulness of the Irish police force: 'A thing of duty is a boy forever.'

2 **A bachelor enjoys the chase but doesn't keep the game.**

3 **I belong to Bridegrooms Anonymous. Whenever I feel like getting married, they send over a lady in a housecoat and hair curlers to burn my toast for me.**

Dick Martin, American comedian, in *Playboy* (1969) — quoted in Bob Chieger, *Was It Good For You Too?* (1983). This ended up in Nan Tucket, *The Dumb Men Joke Book* (Volume II, 1994) as: 'They have something now called Marriage Anonymous. When you feel like getting married, you call somebody and they send over a man in a dirty t-shirt who hasn't shaved in three days, smells like beer and watches football.'

BAD LUCK

1 **Some day my ship will come in — and with my luck I'll be at the airport.**

Included in *Graffiti 2* (1980).

BAGPIPES

1 **Listening to the bagpipes is a fate worse than deaf.**

Glasgow graffito, quoted in the *Financial Times* (5 March 1984).

See ACCORDIONS.

BAIL

1 **Please do not ask for bail as a refusal often offends.**

Graffito in the dock at Willesden magistrates court. Contributed to BBC Radio *Quote ... Unquote* (26 June 1979) by Owen Wells, a probation officer of Ilkley.

BALDNESS

1 **The most delightful advantage of being bald — one can *hear* snowflakes.**

Saying of R.G. Daniels, British magistrate (1916–), quoted in the *Observer*, 11 July 1976.

BALLPOINT PENS

1 **EIGHT OUT OF EVERY TEN PEOPLE WRITE WITH A BALLPOINT PEN.**
— what do the other two do with it?

Contributed by Kenneth Williams to BBC Radio *Quote ... Unquote* (5 February 1979).

BALLS

1 **A group of people were being shown round a stately home in Shropshire. On entering a particularly large room, the guide turned to his audience and said: 'This is where his lordship holds his balls and dances.'**

Contributed by Ian Burrow of Taunton to BBC Radio *Quote ... Unquote* by 1982.

BARRISTERS

1 **Is a lady barrister without her briefs a solicitor?**

From University College, London, and included in *Graffiti* 2 (1980).

BASTARDS

1 **ALL POLICEMEN ARE BASTARDS.**
– but some have birth certificates which show they ain't.
– yes, clever bastards.

Graffito observed by P.S.B. in Solihull (1983),

BATHS

1 **When a body is immersed in water . . . the phone always rings.**

One of life's immutable laws, included in Granada TV *Cabbages and Kings* (4 November 1979).

BATMAN

1 **If Batman is so smart, why does he wear his underpants outside his trousers?**

Contributed to BBC Radio *Quote ... Unquote* (19 April 1978) by Germaine Greer.

BAUHAUS

1 **Dada wouldn't buy me a Bauhaus.**

Graffito by students at local art college spotted by Finlay Bates of Norwich (1981).

BBC

1 **The BBC has always been 50 years old.**

Graffito at the time of the BBC's 50th anniversary celebrations in 1972, included in Reisner & Wechsler, *Encyclopedia of Graffiti* (1974).

2 **Radio 4 over-fortifies the over forties.**
Observation, c. 1978.

BEATLES, THE
British pop musicians and composers fl. 1962–70.

1 **When Ringo Starr was asked what was the greatest threat to the Beatles – the H-Bomb or dandruff – he answered: 'The H-Bomb. We've already got dandruff.'**
Quoted in Michael Braun, *Love Me Do: the Beatles' Progress* (1964).

BEDS
1 **On double beds v. single beds: 'It is not the wild, ecstatic leap across that I deplore. It is the weary trudge home.'**
Anonymous observation, quoted by Ronald Fletcher on BBC Radio *Quote ... Unquote* (4 May 1977).

BEER
1 **Don't complain about the beer – you'll be old and weak one day.**
Graffito from a pub in Oxford. Contributed to BBC Radio *Quote ... Unquote* (1 December 1981) by Francis D. Glenister of Withington, Manchester.

2 **You don't buy the beer in this pub – you only rent it.**
Graffito contributed by Martin Jarvis to Granada TV *Cabbages and Kings* (4 November 1979).

BEETHOVEN, LUDWIG VAN
German composer (1770–1827).

1 **Beethoven was so deaf, he thought he was a painter.**
Graffito on an Intercity train between Newcastle and Sheffield. Contributed to BBC Radio *Quote ... Unquote* (19 February 1979) by Pete and Kathy Weslowski of South Gosforth.

2 **Having listened to a performance of an opera by a somewhat lesser composer, Beethoven turned to him and said: 'I like your opera – I think I will set it to music.'**
Contributed to BBC Radio *Quote ... Unquote* (1984) by Mrs Kathleen Newell of Chigwell.

BEGGING

1 The beggar approached the smart man wearing a pin-stripe suit and carrying a rolled umbrella. 'Sixpence for a cup of tea, guv?' The man duly fished out a sixpence from his pocket and gave it to the beggar.

    After waiting patiently for a short while, the man asked: 'Any sign of that tea I paid for yet?'

Oxford revue 'quickie' sketch, c. 1965.

2 A man was walking along the street minding his own business when another man with a microphone went up to him. 'Excuse me for troubling you, sir,' he said, 'I'm from the BBC.'

    The other man frowned momentarily and then sighed. Taking some coins out of his pocket and giving them discreetly, he walked on.

Oxford revue 'quickie' sketch, 1965.

BEHAVIOURISM

1 Behaviourism is the art of pulling habits out of rats.

BESTIALITY

1 Bestiality — a poke in a pig?

Quoted in Bruce Ridley (ed.), *Wall Flowers: A Collection of Australian Graffiti* (1981).

2 He was into animal husbandry — until they caught him at it.

Tom Lehrer on record album, *An Evening Wasted with Tom Lehrer* (1953).

3 An Argentine gaucho named Bruno
Once said, 'There is something I do know:
A woman is fine
And a sheep is divine
But a llama is Numero Uno!'

G. Legman, *The Limerick* (1964/9) finds this by 1942–44.

See also FLOGGING.

BIBLE, THE

1 **The lion and the lamb shall lie down together, but the lamb won't get much sleep.**
Anonymous saying, quoted on Granada TV *Cabbages and Kings* (29 July 1979). Probably based on a saying of Woody Allen's.

BIGAMY

1 **If I were to marry two women at the same time, would that be bigamy?**
Yes, it would be extremely big of you.
This sounds as if it should have been in a Marx Brothers film — but was it ever?

2 **The maximum penalty for bigamy is two mothers-in-law.**
Attributed to Oliver Stainton. Also to Lord Russell of Killowen, a 19th-century judge.

BIOGRAPHY

1 **No innocent man buys a gun and no happy man writes his memoirs.**
Raymond Duff Payne, quoted in Garrison Keillor, *Lake Wobegon Days* (1985).

2 **Suggested title for Kylie Minogue's biography — 'Superstar — Jesus Christ!'**
From Barry Cryer on BBC Radio *Quote ... Unquote* (1989). But in an earlier programme (4 June 1986), Tim Rice, the lyricist of *Jesus Christ Superstar*, had jokingly offered it as the title of his autobiography.

BIRDS

1 **Q. What do you call a bird that has been run down by a lawn mower?**
A. Shredded tweet.
Told by Sascha Waring, Plymouth (1986).

BIRTH

1 **How was it that you were born in Scunthorpe?**
Well, you see, I thought it was important to be near my mother.
Probably based on the reply given by the American painter James McNeill Whistler (1834–1903) to the question why had he been born in such an

unfashionable place as Lowell, Massachusetts: 'The explanation is quite simple. I wished to be near my mother.'

BISEXUALITY

1 **I can't understand why more people aren't bisexual. It would double your chances for a date on Saturday night.**
Woody Allen, 1975 — quoted in Bob Chieger, *Was It Good For You Too?* (1983).

BISHOPS

1 **80% OF BISHOPS TAKE THE TIMES.
— the other 20% buy it.**
Slogan and graffitoed addition, contributed to BBC Radio *Quote … Unquote* (14 August 1979) by Michael Meadowcroft of Leeds.

BISON

1 **A water bison is what yer wash yer face in.**
In Roger McGough's *An Imaginary Menagerie* (1988). Another version: 'What's the difference between a buffalo and a bison? You can't wash your hands in a buffalo.'

BITTERNESS

1 **We are the unwilling, led by the unqualified, doing the unnecessary for the ungrateful.**
This is a slogan said to have been seen written on GI helmets in Vietnam. In the June 1980 issue of *Playboy* there was a slightly different version from 'the Ninth Precinct': 'We, the willing, led by the unknowing, are doing the impossible for the ungrateful. We have done so much for so long with so little, we are now qualified to do anything with nothing.' Somebody bitter about police salaries had amended the last line to read, 'To do anything for nothing'.

BLAME

1 **Ours is not to reason why . . . ours is to do and be blamed afterwards.**
One of life's immutable laws, included in Granada TV *Cabbages and Kings* (4 November 1979).

BLONDE JOKES

In the United States, there was a craze for these jokes about dumb, dumb blondes in 1991. Towards the end of the same year they appeared in Britain as ESSEX GIRL JOKES. Either way, they are definitely not a politically correct form of entertainment. From The Times *(London), 7 November 1991: 'Feminists are now denouncing the blonde jokes as "a manifestation of the new misogyny". Top of their hit-list is a television advertisement for beer which asks: "Why do gentlemen prefer blondes?" Answer: "Dumb Question". "They aren't politically correct," said Valerie Strauss, an editor at the* Washington Post. *"They are dumb woman jokes and there is nothing new about them".'*

1 **Q. Why do Blondes wear shoulder pads?**
   A. So they won't hurt themselves when they say, 'I don't know'.

   In the *Washington Post* (23 September 1991) this appeared as: 'Q: Why do Blondes wear shoulder pads? A. To keep their heads from falling over.'

2 **Q. How do you make a Blonde's eyes sparkle?**
   A. Shine a flashlight in her ear.

   Unless stated otherwise, all these Blonde Jokes were obtained in a consignment sent to me from a collector in Dallas, Texas, in 1991.

3 **Q. How do you make a Blonde laugh on Friday?**
   A. Tell her a joke on Monday.

4 **Q. What does a Blonde say after sex?**
   A. 'Say . . . who are you guys?'

5 **Q. Why do Blondes have 'TGIF' painted on their shoes?**
   A. 'Toes Go In First.'

   Earlier this had appeared in *The Best of 606 Aggie Jokes* (1988).

6 **Q. How does a Blonde turn on the light afterwards?**
   A. She kicks open the car door.

   In the *Washington Post* (23 September 1991) this appeared as: 'Q: What does a Blonde do after sex? A: Opens the car door.'

7 **Q. How are a turtle and a Blonde the same?**
   A. Once on their backs, they're both screwed.

8 **Q. What's the first thing a Blonde does after sex?**
   A. Goes home.

9 **Q.** How are Santa Claus, the Tooth Fairy, the Easter Bunny
       and a Smart Blonde alike?
   A. They're all Make Believe.

10 **Q.** How are Blondes and computers alike?
   A. You never fully appreciate them until they go down on you.

11 **Q.** Why does a Blonde laugh three times at a joke?
   A. (1) When you tell it.
       (2) When you explain the punch line.
       (3) When she gets it.

12 **Q.** What do you get when you put a dollar on a Blonde's
       head?
   A. All you can eat under a buck.

13 **Q.** Why do Blondes wear green lipstick?
   A. Red means stop.

14 **Q.** What do Blondes and beer bottles have in common?
   A. They're both empty from the neck up.

15 **Q.** Why do employers give Blondes only a half-hour lunch?
   A. Any longer and they'd have to retrain them.

   Earlier, this had appeared among AGGIE JOKES, included in *The Best* of 606
   Aggie Jokes (1988): 'They say that the reason they limit A&M graduate
   engineers to five-minute coffee breaks at electronic plants is that longer
   intervals require extensive retraining.'

16 **Q.** How many Blondes does it take to screw in a light bulb?
   A. Five. One to screw it in and four to say, 'I could have done
       that!'

17 **Q.** How many Blondes does it take to change a light bulb?
   A. One. She holds it up to the socket and waits for the world
       to revolve around her.

   Quoted in the *Washington Post* (23 September 1991) (or — 'Only one — we all
   know the whole world revolves around a Blonde!'

18 **Q.** What's the mating call of the Blonde?
   A. I'm soooOOOooo drunk!

   Same source.

19   **Q.** Why don't Blondes like vibrators?
     A. They chip their teeth.

20   **Q.** What do Blondes never die from?
     A. A brain tumour.

21   A brunette walked into a bar and asked the bartender for a
'W and W'. The bartender had never heard of it and asked
her what it was. She replied, 'Whiskey and water'.
     A redhead walked into the same bar and ordered an 'S
and S'. The bartender had never heard of that either and
asked her what it was. She replied, 'Scotch and soda'.
     A Blonde walked into the same bar and asked for a '15'.
The bartender had never heard of that one either and asked
her what it was. She replied: 'You know, 7 and 7!'

22   **Q.** What do you call a Natural Blonde?
     A. An endangered species.

23   **Q.** What do you call a Natural Blonde who dyes her hair
       black?
     A. Artificial intelligence.

24   **Q.** How are cowpats and Blondes alike?
     A. The older they get, the easier they are to pick up.

25   **Q.** What's the difference between a Blonde and the Suez
       Canal?
     A. One is a busy ditch.

26   **Q.** What do you call a brunette between two Blondes?
     A. An interpreter.

27   **Q.** What does a Blonde say after having sex for the first
       time?
     A. 'So, you guys are all on the same team, huh?'

28   **Q.** What do you do when a Blonde throws a grenade at you?
     A. Take out the pin and throw it back!

29   **Q.** If a Blonde and a brunette fall off the Empire State
       Building at the same time, which will land first?
     A. The brunette. The Blonde would have to stop to ask
       directions.

30 **Q.** If another Blonde and another brunette jump off the Empire
    State Building at the same time, which will land first?
    A. The brunette again. The Blonde would have to stop at each
    window to check herself out.

31 **Q.** What does a Blonde say after sex?
    A. Who was that Masked Man anyway?

32 **Q.** Why do Blondes buy coats with fur hems?
    A. To keep their necks warm.

33 **Q.** How do you drown a Blonde?
    A. Put a mirror in the bottom of your swimming pool.

34 **Q.** What do Bleached Blondes and 747s have in common?
    A. Black boxes.

35 **Q.** What does a Blonde say to her boyfriend when he blows
    in her ear?
    A. Thanks for the refill.

36 Did you hear about the Blondes who went to the drive-in and
    froze to death? They went to see 'Closed for the Season'.

BLOOPERS
*This is the name given in the US to broadcasting boobs – slips of the
tongue and worse. They date back to the more formal days of wireless
when any fall from grace appeared so much the greater. But as many come
from the excessive ad-libbing and informality of today.*

1 At the Wimbledon tennis championships, Billie Jean King was
  seen to toss the ball in the air and observe its movements. Dan
  Maskell, the BBC commentator, helpfully explained, 'Billie Jean
  has always been conscious of wind on the centre court.'
  Contributed to *Foot in Mouth* (1982), as also the following:

2 Also at Wimbledon, a BBC Radio commentator was waxing
  eloquent about a South American player: 'It's remarkable when
  you consider that in the whole of Paraguay there are only
  about two hundred tennis players. Victor Pecci is one of those.'

3 One of the most delicious radio boobs was not, alas, ever
  broadcast. A too-kind studio manager pointed out to the

distinguished academic who was introducing a BBC Radio discussion on aspects of British industry that it would be better if he rephrased the words he had used at rehearsal. The academic had planned to introduce the speakers and give their credentials and fields of specialisation, thus: 'Michael Clapham – Director of ICI – chemicals; Val Duncan – Managing Director of Rio Tinto Zinc – mining; R.D. Young – Deputy Chairman, Alfred Herbert – "The Biggest Machine Tool in Europe".'
In the 1970s?

4 In Australia there is a deadly spider called a funnel-web. A newscaster is reported to have announced: 'This afternoon in Sydney a woman was bitten on the funnel by a finger-web spider.'

5 Dan Maskell was providing the commentary of a Braniff Airways Mens Doubles tennis match in which David Lloyd and Mark Cox were participating. At one point he remarked: 'The British boys are now adopting the attacking position – Cox up.'

6 'A series of strikes at the Liverpool Royal Hospital has caused a lot of ill-feeling'.

7 'We are now to hear some Birdsong by Plain.'

8 'Police fired rubber bullocks . . . er, sorry, bullets.'

9 'Widespread fist and mog can be expected.'

10 'The trouble has been caused by unpatriotic elephants in the country.'

11 'There has been a heavy fall of rain here at Trent Bridge but fortunately it didn't touch the ground.'

12 'The unorganized conference . . . er, I'm sorry, the U.N.-organized conference . . .'

13 'Reports are coming in from Australia that Serbo-Croat extremists have attempted to sabotage the Sydney water supply by blowing up the pipes.'
Contributed to BBC Radio Quote ... Unquote (28 August 1979) by Peter E. Boorman of Littledean, Gloucestershire.

14 **On BBC news from Norwich, there was an item about an open day at Wisbech sewage farm which included the following passage: 'A spokesman for the East Anglian Water Authority said they considered a trip round the sewage works a unique and interesting day out. They were even laying on transport for people who wanted to go.'**

Contributed to BBC *Radio Quote ... Unquote* (5 June 1980) by Peter Petts of London SE1.

See also KURDS 1.

BORES

1 **A bore is a man who, when asked how he is, tells you.**

Almost a proverbial observation, but it is credited to Bert Leston Taylor in Allen Andrews, *Quotations for Speakers and Writers* (1969).

2 **To be a bore is to have halitosis of the mind.**

The *Daily Telegraph* (10 September 1994) credited me with this observation. Indeed, I had put it in my book *Best Behaviour* (1992), though with the rider, 'as someone should probably have said before me.'

BOSTON STRANGLER

Consider the history of a joke. Working backwards:

1 **'Denis Healey ... claimed to have tried to do for economic forecasters what the Boston Strangler did for door-to-door salesmen ...'**

From the *Sunday Times* (9 February 1992).

2 **'Shields introduced Hatch, the starched shirt of the Senate hearings, as "the man who has done for bipartisanship what the Boston Strangler did for door-to-door salesmen".'**

From the *Washington Post* (16 October 1991).

3 **'Mr Healey also had a pithy word for President Reagan: "He has done for monetarism what the Boston Strangler did for door-to-door salesmen".'**

From the *Independent* (20 January 1989).

4 **'Liberal David Steel said earlier this year: "Mrs Thatcher seems to have done for women in politics what the Boston Strangler did for door-to-door salesmen".'**

From *Today* (24 May 1987).

BRAINS

1 **The brain is a wonderful organ. It starts working the moment you get up in the morning, and does not stop until you get into the office.**

Attributed to Robert Frost, American poet (1874-1963). Sometimes rendered as '. . . until you get up to make a speech.'

BREAKING WIND *See FARTING.*

BREEDING

1 **When Alfred E. Smith, the American politician, was Governor of New York, he was told by the Mayor of Boston, 'Of course, up in Boston, we think breeding is everything!' Smith replied: 'Well, down here in New York, we think it's quite fun, too, but we don't think it's everything.'**

Told by Margaret R. Jackson, Chipping Campden (1994).

BRITISH RAIL

Since the British railway system was nationalized in 1948, it has been a stock target for jokes – especially on account of the catering. In January 1995, the British Prime Minister John Major said: 'I am not content with the service we have had from British Rail. I want to remove them for good from the stand-up comedian's joke book and turn them into the envy of the world.' But jokes about the railways in Britain long predated nationalization.

1 **The LNER (London and North Eastern Railway)**
The initials of the old private railways were reinterpreted just as AIRLINE ACRONYMS are today. Hence, the LNER was known as 'the Late and Never Early.'

2 **The LMS (London Midland and Scottish)**
''Ell of a Mess'; 'Let Me Sleep'; 'Lord's My Shepherd'.

3 **The GWR (Great Western Railway)**
'Go When Ready'; 'Great Way Round'; and, more complimentarily 'God's Wonderful Railway'.

4 **The LCD (London Chatham and Dover)**
'London, Smash'em and Do for 'em'; 'London Smashem and Turnover'.

5 The GC (Great Central Railway)
'Gone Completely'.

6 The MSL (Manchester Sheffield and Lincolnshire Railway)
'Money Sunk and Lost'; 'Muck, Sludge and Lightning'.

7 The MGN (Midland and Great Northern Railway)
'Muddle and Go Nowhere'.

8 The SE & C (South Eastern and Chatham Railway)
'Slow, Easy and Comfortable'.

9 BRITISH RAIL ADVISE THAT THIS RIGHT OF WAY IS NOT
DEDICATED TO THE PUBLIC.
– neither is British Rail.
Notice and amendment, included in *Graffiti 2* (1980).

10 My heart aches and a drowsy numbness drains my sense as
though of hemlock I had drunk. Signed: a British Rail tea victim.
Graffito from King's Cross station, London, contributed to BBC Radio *Quote ...
Unquote* (12 June 1980) by Margaret Etheridge of Bickley, Kent.

11 God made things that creep and crawl
But British Rail – it beats them all.
On Harrow station, included in *Graffiti 2* (1980).

12 Did you know that railway timetables may be found in Public
Libraries filed under 'fiction'?

13 The down trains will be delayed owing to the late arrival of
the up trains.
Station announcer at Waterloo, quoted in 1978.

14 On a list of British Rail sandwich prices following an increase in
VAT, there appeared the note: 'No increase in prices due to
VAT while stocks last.'
Contributed to BBC Radio *Quote ... Unquote* (25 December 1979) by Mr J.
Osborne of Canterbury.

BRITISH WORKMEN

1 You can tell a British workman by his hands. They're always in
his pockets.
Graffito at Westfield College, Hampstead. Contributed to BBC Radio *Quote ...
Unquote* (26 June 1980) by Ian Fisher of Brighton. Compare SOVIET JOKES 8.

BROADCASTERS

1 A woman found that she was unable to have a baby and so she went to see her doctor. 'Are you doing it?' was his first question to her. 'Well, no, not really,' she replied. 'I've been married three times. My first husband was 91 and he was past it. My second was gay, and didn't want to do it. And then I married a TV presenter.'

'Oh, really,' asked the doctor, 'and what's the problem there?'

'Well, all he does is sit at the end of the bed and say how good it's going to be.'

Told by Carol Vorderman (1994).

BUFFET

1 'Can you tell me where the buffet is?'

'It's over there — oh, and by the way, it's pronounced "buffay", the "t" is silent.'

'Not the way I drink it.'

BUMPER STICKER JOKES *See under STICKERS.*

BUSINESSES

1 The ultimate in business hard luck is contained in the proverbial Arab saying: 'We traded in shrouds; people stopped dying.'

Told by Anthony Thwaite on BBC Radio *Quote ... Unquote* (27 April 1993). Another version is: 'He was the world's worst businessman. If he was a florist, he'd close on Mother's Day.'

BUTLERS

1 Mrs Ronald Greville, chatelaine of the stately home, Polesden Lacey, had a 'house steward' who was prone to drink and lachrymosity. He was frequently intoxicated during her grand dinner parties and, on one occasion, Mrs Greville was forced to write him a note on the little silver pad she carried with her. It said: 'YOU ARE DRUNK. LEAVE THE ROOM IMMEDIATELY.' Accordingly, the man swayed across

the room and handed the note to one of Mrs Greville's guests.

Told by James Lees-Milne in his diary entry for 4 November 1942 (reprinted in *Ancestral Voices*, 1975 — where the guest is identified as Sir John Simon).

2 And then there was the butler who, as he was falling downstairs, replied to his master's inquiry as to what was going on: "Tis I, sir, rolling rapidly.' He was obviously a learned butler because, as he fell, he was punning on Thomas Campbell's poem 'Hohenlinden' (1802):

> On Linden, when the sun was low,
> All bloodless lay the untrodden snow,
> And dark as winter was the flow
> Of Iser, rolling rapidly.

I expect they don't employ butlers like that any more. W.W. Keen James of Providence, Rhode Island found the story in his great-grandfather's memoirs (1915–17).

BUTTON JOKES *See under STICKERS.*

CAMELS

1 **Q. What is grey, has four feet and a hump and is found in Alaska?**
A. A lost camel.

Told by Daniel Waring, Plymouth (1986).

CANNES FILM FESTIVAL

1 Cannes is where you lie on the beach and look at the stars — or vice versa.

Rex Reed, American film critic (1938–), quoted in *Playboy* (c. 1980).

CANNIBALS

1 The missionary asked the cannibal, 'Do you like beans?'
'Yes, I do!' replied the cannibal.
'What sort of beans do you like?'
'Human beans.'

See also QUESTION AND ANSWER JOKES 28.

CANNONBALLS

1 The human cannonball decided to quit the circus. The owner
was outraged. 'You can't quit!' he said, 'Where will I find
another man of your calibre?'
Told in A. Moger, *The Complete Pun Book* (1979).

CAPITALISM

1 Capitalism is the survival of the fattest.
Observed in Sheffield University Biology Department by Paul Smith (1982).

2 *Written in cultivated hand using fountain-pen on railway station
timetable poster:* 'Please help smash capitalism.'
Included in *Graffiti Lives OK* (1979).

See also RADIO ARMENIA JOKES 6.

CAR STICKER JOKES *See under STICKERS.*

CATS

1 Dogs come when you call. Cats have answering machines.

2 **Q.** Why did cats learn to see in the dark?
A. Because they can't reach the light switch.
Told to me by Caroline Lewis, Plymouth (1986).

CELEBRITY

1 A celebrity is one who works all his life to become well-known
and then goes through back streets wearing dark glasses so he
won't be recognized.
Attributed to Jane Powell, the American film actress (1929–). Also to Fred
Allen in *Treadmill to Oblivion* (1956).

CELIBACY

1 **Celibacy is not an inherited characteristic.**
   Contributed by D.R. to *Graffiti Lives OK* (1979).

CEMENT

1 **Drink wet cement and get really stoned.**
   Graffito contributed by Prunella Gee to Granada TV *Cabbages and Kings*
   (6 June 1979).

2 **There was the Aggie walking down the street who saw a sign
   that read 'WET CEMENT', so he did.**
   Included in *The Best of 606 Aggie Jokes* (1988).

CENSORSHIP

1 **F*** CENSORSHIP.**
   Lapel button, quoted in Rennie Ellis & Ian Turner, *Australian Graffiti Revisited* (1979).

CHARISMA

1 **He was so unimpressive I think he must have had a charisma
   bypass operation.**
   This remark was made about I can't remember who on BBC Radio *Quote ...
   Unquote* (31 October 1989) and I have always liked to believe that it was
   originated by Barry Cryer, the British comedian and scriptwriter. But apparently
   not. The earliest use of it I have found in the press is in the *Washington Post*
   (2 May 1986) concerning a Texas gubernatorial primary: 'When Loeffler started
   the campaign, his name recognition was well under 10% . . . . Part of the
   problem, according to one Republican consultant, is his rather plodding nature.
   "The guy is in desperate need of a charisma bypass," said the consultant. "But if
   he gets into the run-off against Clements, he might get some charisma in a
   hurry."'
       The following year the jibe was stuck on an Australian politician. From the
   Daily Telegraph (14 February 1987): 'Politicians fall victim to a quick swipe with
   a well-turned phrase, such as the "charisma bypass", which the unfortunate
   Premier of New South Wales is said to have undergone.'
       Since then, the insult has been levelled at almost anybody you can think of.
   From *Today* (25 November 1987): 'When Betty Ford slipped quietly into hospital
   for a heart operation, the surgeon told her he had carried out Richard Nixon's
   charisma bypass.' From the *Sunday Times* (11 December 1988): '[Of Steve Davis,
   snooker player] "Oh yes, we say he had a charisma bypass when he was 17,"
   said Barry Hearn [manager] last week, without bothering to get involved in any
   defence of his protégé.'

CHASTITY

1 **Chastity is its own punishment.**
From High Holborn, London, contributed to *Graffiti 2* (1980). Also included in Reisner & Wechsler, *Encyclopedia of Graffiti* (1974).

2 **Chastity: the most unnatural of the sexual perversions.**
Aldous Huxley, quoted in the *Sunday Times* (1973) — and re-quoted in Bob Chieger, *Was It Good For You Too?* (1983).

CHATTING UP

1 **A young and pretty typist was soon spotted by the office Romeo — a man of about forty. Adjusting his tie, he approached her and said, 'Hello, gorgeous, where've you been all my life?' To which she replied: 'Well, for most of it I wasn't born . . . '.**
Contributed to BBC Radio *Quote ... Unquote* (13 July 1985) by Mr F.G. Seabrook of Whetstone, North London. But a traditional put down?

2 **A tiresome man was boring a girl to tears in his efforts to make a conquest. 'Say, honey,' he asked her, leeringly, 'how do you like your eggs in the morning?' Came the reply: 'Unfertilised'.**
Current by 1987.

3 **Are you the kind of girl who parks with men on dark country roads?**
Not unless driven to it.
Performed on CBS TV *Rowan and Martin's Laugh-In* and included on the record album *Laugh-In '69* (1969).

CHICKEN JOKES

The basic chicken joke is, of course, 'Why did the chicken cross the road?' — 'To get to the other side.' One possible source for this series of jokes is mentioned below but Max Tiler, historian of the British Music Hall Society, suggested in a letter to the Daily Mail *(28 January 1994) that the jokes may have originated with the minstrel shows which came to the UK from America during the 1880s and 1890s. It is of a type known as a 'stump story' or 'stump riddle': 'The performers would sit in a semi-circle on the stage and the two corner men would ask and then answer questions. Other stump riddles include: "Who was that lady I saw you with last night?", "That was no lady, that was my wife"; and "My wife has gone to the West Indies", "Jamaica?", "No, she went of her own accord/ her own free will".'*

Chicken jokes suffered a revival in CBS TV's Rowan and Martin's Laugh-In *(1967–73), whence came the catchphrase 'Is that a chicken joke?' uttered by the likes of Goldie Hawn and Jo Ann Worley.*

1 **Q. Why did the one-eyed chicken cross the road?
A. He wanted to go to the birds' eye shop.**
Told by Daniel Waring, Plymouth (1986).

2 **Q. Why did the chicken cross the road?
A. Because he was stupid.**
Said to be 'the oldest joke in Belfast' (*Independent*, 17 June 1993) – where divisions between the communities are clearly signalled by colours painted on the pavements.

3 **There was this man whose brother was under the delusion that he was a chicken. 'Why don't you turn your brother in, then?' the man was asked. He replied: 'I need the eggs.'**
Attributed to Woody Allen. Told in the *Sunday Times* (8 September 1991).

4 **Q. How do you cook chicken socialist-style?
A. First, steal the chicken, then cook it any way you want.**
A joke critical of Spanish socialism when voters became disenchanted with many years of socialist government, a fading economic miracle, and a widening gap between the haves and have-nots. Told in *The Times* (5 June 1993).

5 **A: Why is an owl more intelligent than a chicken?
B: I dunno.
A: Well, how often have you see a Kentucky Fried Owl?**
Told in the *Sunday Times* (11 May 1986).

See also ELEPHANT JOKES 10.

CHILDREN
1 **'Oh Auntie, I'm so glad you've arrived, 'cos Dad said that your turning up today was just what he needed . . . .'**
The words of his small daughter, Wendy, contributed to BBC Radio Quote ... Unquote (26 June 1980) by Tom Westman of the Isle of Skye.

2 **A small boy was taken to tea at a neighbours' house. Also there was the neighbour's lodger. In spite of being told not to, the boy stared continuously at the lodger. When asked why, he replied: 'Well, I can't see that he drinks like a fish . . .'**

Contributed to BBC Radio *Quote ... Unquote* (9 February 1982) by Bob Wright of Coventry. An old chestnut? But none the worse for that.

3 **I love children — especially when they cry, for then someone takes them away.**

Attributed to Nancy Mitford, British novelist (1904–73), by John Law of Lock Eck, by Dunoon, Argyll, in BBC Radio *Quote ... Unquote* (26 April 1978).

CHINA AND THE CHINESE

1 **The Great Wall, I've been told, is the only man-made structure on earth that is visible from the moon. For the life of me I cannot see why anyone would go to the moon to look at it, when, with almost the same difficulty, it can be viewed in China.**

John Kenneth Galbraith, American economist (1908–), in an article for the *Sunday Times Magazine*, 23 October 1977.

2 **He is so ignorant of German literature that he thinks Kleist is the Chinese Messiah.**

3 **If you lay the Chinese end to end around the world, do you know that you'd drown half the buggers?
— BRODDY ENGRISH!**

Graffito and addition, reported from Bolton by James Darwell (1982), included in *Graffiti 5* (1986).

4 **2.30 — time to go to Chinese dentist.**

CHIVALRY

1 **Definition of chivalry: 'going about releasing beautiful maidens from other men's castles, and taking them to your own castle.'**

Henry W. Nevinson, English journalist (1856–1941), quoted in *The Treasury of Humorous Quotations*, ed. by Evan Esar & Nicolas Bentley (1951).

CHRISTMAS

1 **'Some years ago, a friend and I were looking into a card shop window at Christmas where we saw such cards as, "From my**

dog to your dog" and even "From my budgie to your budgie".
Another woman was also looking in the window and, on seeing
a Nativity Scene, she was heard to say, "Look at that – they
bring religion into everything nowadays."'

Told by Dorothy Knapp of Orpington, Kent in August 1994. Compare what
Richard H. Davies of London E13 contributed to BBC Radio *Quote ... Unquote*
(25 December 1979): he recalled a Christmas 'a year or two ago' when he was
on top of a bus outside Selfridges store in London where giant Christmas cards
depicting Biblical scenes were being used as the background to a window
display. Mr Davies heard one woman passenger remark to another: 'Look,
Mavis, now they're even dragging religion into Christmas.'

2 *Overheard on Christmas Eve:* 'I don't care who you are; get
those reindeer off my roof!'

3 **Christmas comes but once a year. Thank God I'm not Christmas.**

Graffiti reported from Luton, included in *Graffiti 2* (1980).

4 **My mother-in-law's been coming round to our house at
Christmas for the past seventeen years. This time we're thinking
of letting her in.**

Les Dawson, British comedian, in the 1980s.

5 **Go to church on Sunday now and avoid the Christmas rush.**

Contributed to BBC Radio *Quote ... Unquote* (28 August 1979) by Peggy Roper
of Clifton, Bristol.

CHUTZPAH

1 **The classic definition of chutzpah is the man who had killed his
parents and then threw himself on the mercy of the court on
the grounds that he was an orphan.**

So given in Leo Rosten, *The Joys of Yiddish* (1968).

CINDERELLA

1 **What did Cinderella say when her pictures didn't arrive?**
'Some day my prints will come . . .'

CIGARETTES *See SMOKING.*

CLASS

1 *When asked by a radio interviewer whether she thought British class barriers had come down:* **'Of course they have, or I wouldn't be sitting here talking to someone like you.'**

Attributed to Barbara Cartland, the British romantic novelist (1902–), by Jilly Cooper in *Class* (1979). The interviewer was Sandra Harris of the BBC Radio *Today* programme.

CLERGYMEN

1 **Margaret Diggle of Ringmer in Sussex recalls that many years ago she heard a sermon in the chapel of Girton College, Cambridge. Four years later the same clergyman was invited to Girton again, whereupon he gave out exactly the same text and preached exactly the same sermon. The text was, 'Ye have not passed this way heretofore.'**

Contributed to BBC Radio *Quote ... Unquote* (7 June 1978).

CLERIHEWS

1 **When questioned, E. Clerihew Bentley**
   Smiled gently.
   Said those who can write a good clerihew
   Are very few.

Contributed to BBC Radio *Quote ... Unquote* (7 June 1978) by the actor Peter Jeffrey.

CLICHÉS

1 **I used to use clichés all the time but now I avoid them like the plague.**

Contributed by Kenny Ball, the musician, to BBC *Radio Quote ... Unquote* (20 August 1983). The injunction 'All clichés should be avoided like the plague' is sometimes ascribed to Arthur Christiansen, an editor of the *Daily Express*. Keith Waterhouse in *Daily Mirror Style* (1981) attributes it rather to Samuel Goldwyn, probably in mistake for:

2 **Let's have some new clichés.**

Sam Goldwyn, quoted in the *Observer* (24 October 1948).

CLOTHES

1 **I didn't recognize you with your clothes on.**

An almost traditional joke from medical person to patient. Compare from the Marx Brothers film *Go West* (1940), Groucho saying: 'Lulubelle, it's you! I didn't recognize you standing up'. And compare: 'I was a District Nursing Sister and was attending a parents "do" at my son's school. A strange gentleman came across to me through the crowd greeting me like an old friend, saying, "You remember me — you came when I was out of hospital with a fractured leg." Light dawned and I replied rather loudly during a lull in the hubbub: "Oh, of course I know you. I'm so sorry, I would only know you in bed".' — Ruth Gale, Hinckley, quoted in *Foot in Mouth* (1982).

And compare a remark attributed to Tallulah Bankhead who said to a man who had failed to recognize her: 'Don't you recognize me with your clothes on?' (contributed by Glenda Jackson to BBC Radio *Quote ... Unquote*, 6 August 1983).

2 **She opened the door in her nightie.**
Funny place to have a door.

3 **What do you think would go well with these turquoise, pink and orange leggings?**
Thigh-length boots.

See also NUDISTS.

COLLINS, JOAN

British actress (1933–) All these jests were current in about 1984 when La Collins was at the height of her fame in the American TV series Dynasty *and other manifestations.*

1 **Nancy Reagan has had a face lift. Joan Collins uses a fork lift.**

2 **Joan Collins makes a movie a year. She's just started her 67th.**

3 **Joan Collins is a former has-been.**

4 **Joan Collins has discovered the secret of eternal middle age.**

5 **What do you get when you send a Joan Collins dress to an African laundry? Cinzano on the rocks.**

6 **I hope I look as good as Joan Collins when I get to her age.**

COMMITTEES

1 **A Committee is a group of men who, individually, can do nothing, but collectively can meet and decide that nothing can be done.**
Quoted in Prochnow & Prochnow, *Treasury of Humorous Quotations* (1969).
Winston Fletcher in *Meetings, Meetings* (1983) attributes something like it to the American radio comedian, Fred Allen (1894–1956).

See CONFERENCES 1.

2 **If you can avoid a decision, do so. If you can get somebody else to avoid a decision, don't avoid it yourself. If you cannot get one person to avoid a decision, appoint a committee.**
Attributed to Sharu S. Ragnekar in *The Art of Avoiding Decisions.*

3 **If you have enough meetings over a long enough period of time, the meetings themselves become more important than the problem they were intended to solve.**
'Hendrickson's Law', by Dr E.R. Hendrickson (1971).

4 **What is a committee? A group of the unwilling, picked from the unfit, to do the unnecessary.**
Richard Harkness in the *New York Herald Tribune* (15 June 1960).

5 **The average committee comprises eight executives, each of whom wishes that at least three of the other seven weren't on it.**
Quoted in a *Harvard Business Review.*

6 **A committee is a cul-de-sac down which ideas are lured and then quietly strangled.**
Sir Barnett Cocks in the *New Scientist* (8 November 1973).

7 **Nothing is ever accomplished by a committee unless it consists of three members, one of whom happens to be sick and the other absent.**
From Chapter XXXI of Hendrik Van Loon's *America* (1927). The idea has also been attributed to Lord Mancroft (died 1987) in some anthologies, but Hesketh Pearson ascribes it to Sir Herbert Beerbohm Tree (1853–1917) in his 1956 biography of the great actor-manager. On the other hand, *The Treasury of Humorous Quotations* (1951) has E.V. Lucas (1868–1938) saying, 'The best committee is a committee of two when one is absent.'

8 **When in doubt, never commit yourself – committee yourself.**

Attributed to a reactionary politician by Michael Barsley in *Common Man and Colonel Bogus* (1944).

9 **If Moses had been a committee the Israelites would still be in Egypt.**

Attributed to J.B. Hughes (untraced) or, in the form 'never would have got across the Red Sea', in 1965, to the late General Booth, founder of the Salvation Army.

10 **A camel is a horse designed by a committee.**

Anon. quoted, for example, in American *Vogue* (1958). This bears an interesting resemblance, surely, to 'A donkey is a horse translated into Dutch' – which Georg Christoph Lichtenberg (died 1799) had in his *Aphorisms*. John Le Carré included in the novel *Tinker, Tailor, Soldier, Spy* (1974), the observation, 'A committee is an animal with four back legs.' Anon. also said: 'A committee of one gets things done.'

COMPLAINERS

1 **'My father ran an industrial company aided, for many years, by the same secretary – so that he came to leave to her the composing and typing of replies to a whole range of letters that contained standard complaints or queries. The curious note he always pencilled on such letters originated with the manager of a hotel where a friend of his had stayed – and been bitten by bed bugs. His friend had then written to the manager to say that the hotel was a disgrace, that he would never stay there again and that he would warn off all his friends.**

'He received a prompt, profuse apology; such a bad thing had never happened before . . . the floor maid had been sacked . . . and so on. Somewhat mollified, he was just thinking, "Well, I suppose the best hotel can have the occasional lapse . . ." when he spotted his own letter still pinned to this reply. Across it was written in blue crayon: "WRITE THE USUAL BUG LETTER"'.

Related by D.F. of Shifnal, Shropshire (May 1994). But compare the story (told earlier, for example, in *Pass the Port*, 1976) of the distinguished gentleman – an ambassador, no less – who had an unfortunate experience when travelling on the Orient Express: he was bitten by bugs. Duly complaining to the travel company, he received a fulsome letter of apology back – 'unhappily, the clerk who dealt with the complaint, by inadvertence, attached to this reply the

Ambassador's original letter of complaint, across which someone had scribbled, "Usual bug letter, please".'

COMPLEXES
1 **I keep thinking I'm the Sydney Opera House.
You've got an edifice complex.**
Quoted in Bruce Ridley (ed.), *Wall Flowers: A Collection of Australian Graffiti* (1981).

COMPLIMENTS
1 *A woman said to the mother of a girl:* **'Oh, what a pretty little girl! Is your husband good-looking?'**
Contributed to BBC Radio *Quote … Unquote* (13 July 1985) by Mrs Miki Jakeman, a medical missionary, who recalls that it was said with regard to her when she was three years old. A cartoon in *Punch* (3 August 1904), however, makes the same put-down to a *man* regarding a child: 'What a very pretty woman your wife must be.'

COMPUTERS
1 **It was decided to ask a computer if there was a God. The Bible, the Koran, and all documents relating to every creed, every philosophical argument for and against, were duly fed in. The computer trundled away for a whole week and came up with the answer, 'THERE IS NOW!'**
Recounted by Valerie Grosvenor Meyer in *Folk Review* (November 1974), adding that this was an encapsulation of a science fiction story by Frederick Brown.

2 **Shown a computer which could answer all questions, a man asked it where his father was. It answered, 'Your father is playing a crap game in a saloon in Kansas City.' 'Wrong,' said the man. 'My father is dead and his body lies in the Baptist Cemetery in Columbus, Ohio.' 'You bastard,' replied the computer, 'your real father is playing a crap game in . . .'.**
Recounted by Valerie Grosvenor Meyer in the same *Folk Review*, as also the following:

3 **A patient whose doctor failed to diagnose his complaint watched fascinated while the details were fed into a computer. The patient and the doctor chatted while the machine rattled and banged. Finally, it spewed out a card. The patient, tense with excitement and suspense, asked, 'What**

does it say, doctor?' 'It says,' replied the doctor, squinting hard at the card, 'that there's a lot of it about.'

4 A computer was installed by the army. An officer asked it, 'How far is it from A to B?' '6,000', replied the computer. The officer fed in the question '6,000 what?' and the computer replied, '6,000, Sir!'

5 To err is human but to really foul things up requires a computer.

Anon., quoted in Granada TV *Cabbages and Kings* (11 August 1979). In 1982, B.R. Corbett of West End, Brisbane, Australia reported a graffito from a road bridge there: 'TO ERR IS HUMMAN.'

See also TRANSLATIONS 1.

CONCEIT

1 I used to be conceited — but now I'm absolutely perfect.

Graffito contributed to BBC *Radio Quote ... Unquote* (19 June 1979) by John Holmanm of Dartford, Kent.

CONFERENCES

1 A conference is a gathering of important people who singly can do nothing, but together can decide that nothing can be done.

Fred Allen, American comedian (1894–1956), quoted in *The Treasury of Humorous Quotations*, ed. by Evan Esar & Nicolas Bentley (1951).

See also COMMITTEES.

CONFIRMATION

1 The twelve-year-old accompanied his mother to the Communion rail in church to receive a blessing but as the priest did not know if the boy had been confirmed, he bent down and whispered something in his ear. Then, to the mother's consternation, the priest administered the sacrament. When later on his mother asked the boy what had been said, he replied: 'Well, he asked if I was Conservative and I said Yes.'

Contributed to BBC *Radio Quote ... Unquote* before 1982 by Kenneth Walker of Long Marston, concerning his grandson.

CONSERVATIVES

1 **A conservative is a man who will not look at the new moon, out of respect for that ancient institution, the old one.**

Douglas Jerrold, English humorist (1803–57), quoted in *The Treasury of Humorous Quotations*, ed. by Evan Esar & Nicolas Bentley (1951).

2 **A conservative is someone who believes that nothing should be done for the first time.**

This appears to be a development of the remark by the English academic Francis Cornford (1874–1943), 'Nothing should ever be done for the first time' in his *Microcosmographia Academica* (1908). The precise wording is: 'Every public action, which is not customary, either is wrong, or, if it is right, is a dangerous precedent. It follows that nothing should ever be done for the first time.'

CONSTIPATION

1 **Constipation is the thief of time. Diarrhoea waits for no man.**

Included in *Graffiti 2* (1980).

CONSULTANTS

1 **Those that can, do. Those that could, but now don't, consult.**

Compare TEACHERS 2.

2 **A consultant is someone who knows a hundred ways of making love but can't get a girl.**

CONTRACEPTIVES

1 **Contraceptives should be used on every conceivable occasion.**

Attributed to Spike Milligan. He speaks the line in his script for BBC Radio *The Last Goon Show of All* (1972). Also, from Michigan, in Haan & Hammerstrom *Graffiti in the Big Ten* (1981).

2 **The best contraceptive is a glass of cold water: not before or after, but instead.**

Anonymous Pakistani delegate at International Planned Parenthood Federation Conference. Quoted in *The Penguin Dictionary of Modern Quotations* (1971).

3 **I thought oral contraception was when you talked your way out of it.**

Anon.

4 **PLACE 50P IN SLOT AND PULL HANDLE
– if this is sex, it sounds extremely boring.**
Graffito addition to contraceptive vending machine instructions. Contributed to BBC Radio *Quote ... Unquote* (7 June 1978) by Kenneth Williams.

5 **Homes for retired semen.**
Graffito on machine, Piccadilly, London – included in *Graffiti 3* (1981).

6 **MADE IN THE UK.
ABSOLUTELY SAFE AND RELIABLE.
APPROVED TO BRITISH STANDARD BS 3704.
– so was the *Titanic*.**
Various graffiti and addition – included in *Graffiti Lives OK* (1979) and *Graffiti 3* (1981).

7 **My dad says they don't work.**
Graffitoed comment on machine, included in *Graffiti Lives OK* (1979).

8 **Insert baby for refund.**
On machine, Oxford, included in *Graffiti 3* (1981).

9 **BUY ME AND STOP ONE
– buy two and stay one jump ahead.**
Graffitoed comments on machine, included in *Graffiti Lives OK* (1979). The parody of the Walls ice-cream slogan ('Stop me and buy one') was also suggested as a slogan for Dr Marie Stopes, the pioneer of birth control (1880–1958).

10 **Condoms should be marketed in three sizes, because failures tend to occur at the extreme ends of the scale ... We should package them in different sizes and maybe label them like olives – jumbo, colossal, and supercolossal – so that men don't have to go in ask for the small.**
Barbara Seaman (sic), in testimony to a Select Committee on Population (1978) – quoted in Bob Chieger, *Was It Good For You Too?* (1983).

COUGHERS

1 **Did you know that people who cough loudly never go to the doctor – they go to the theatre.**

CREMATION

1 **Class distinction is only temporary. All men are cremated equal.**
Graffito, Chelsea, quoted in the *Financial Times* (27 September 1985).

2 **Save fuel – get cremated with a friend.**
Graffito from Liverpool, included in *Graffiti 2* (1980).

3 **THE CREMATION OF MR —— WILL TAKE PLACE AT GOLDERS GREEN CREMATORIUM AT 2.30.**
– please put him on a low light. Can't get there till four o'clock.
Addition to notice, Covent Garden, included in *Graffiti 2* (1980).

4 **'At my father's funeral, my step-mother had allowed one of father's friends to say "a few words" after the service was over. He started by saying that the last time he had been at the crematorium there had been some swallows flying about. He then went on to say how he had gone on bird-watching expeditions with my father, and so on. He ended (the cremation was taking place in early January) by saying: "Now Mr G— and the swallows have departed to a warmer climate".'**
Related by the Revd P.G., Oxford, before 1982.

CRICKET

1 **Why was the Ancient Mariner a poor wicket-keeper? Because, according to Coleridge's poem, he only 'stoppeth one in three'.**
Quoted in Granada TV *Cabbages and Kings* (20 June 1979).

CRIME

1 **Nationalize crime and make sure it doesn't pay.**
Graffito reported by Bernard Mattimore, Henley-on-Thames, included in *Graffiti 2* (1980).

2 **Crime doesn't pay, but the hours are good.**
Graffito from Staines police station, reported by Mrs L. Stokes, included in *Graffiti 2* (1980).

3 **The crime is so bad round where I live that even the muggers go around in pairs.**

CRITICS

1 **I am sitting in the smallest room of my house. Your notice is before me, it will shortly be behind me.**

In the London *Evening Standard* (30 January 1992), Milton Shulman referred to the sentiments of Noël Coward who wrote thus to a critic who had savaged one of his plays. In Ned Sherrin's *Theatrical Anecdotes* (1991), a similar retort had been reported from Oscar Hammerstein (grandfather of the lyricist) to a creditor: 'I am in receipt of your letter which is now before me and in a few minutes will be behind me.' One might also mention the revelation contained in the *Oxford Dictionary of Modern Quotations* (1991): that in 1906, Max Reger, the German composer, had written to the Munich critic, Rudolph Louis, in response to his review in *Münchener Neueste Nachrichten* (7 February 1906), 'I am sitting in the smallest room of my house. I have your review before me. In a moment it will be behind me'. This is quoted in N. Slonimsky, *Lexicon of Musical Invective* (1953), having been translated from the German.

But there seems every chance that the real first user of the remark was John Montagu, 4th Earl of Sandwich (the one who gave his name to the snack). N.A.M. Rodger in *The Insatiable Earl* (1993) suggests that when William Eden (later Lord Auckland) defected from Sandwich in 1785 he wrote him a letter. Says Rodger: 'Contemporaries repeated with relish Sandwich's terse reply . . . "Sir, your letter is before me, and will presently be behind me".' Rodger gives his source as J.H. Jesse, *George Selwyn* (1843–4) and adds, helpfully, 'Manufactured lavatory paper was not known in the 18th century.'

2 **A drama critic said of a certain insipid play that it 'left a taste in the mouth of warm parsnip juice'.**

Ascribed to Alexander Woollcott by Arthur Marshall on BBC *Radio Quote ... Unquote* (1 August 1987).

3 **He has Van Gogh's ear for music.**

Appearing on BBC Radio *Quote ... Unquote* in 1977, Kenneth Williams came up with a rather good showbiz story. He quoted the above as what Orson Welles had reputedly said of the singing of Donny Osmond (then a popular young star).

In fact, Orson Welles did not say it, nor was it about Donny Osmond, but the reasons why the joke had been reascribed and redirected are instructive. It was in fact Billy Wilder, the film director, who made the original remark. He has a notably waspish wit but is, perhaps, not such a household name as Orson Welles. He lacks, too, Welles's Falstaffian stature and his, largely unearned, reputation in the public mind for having said witty things. And Wilder said it about Cliff Osmond, an American comedy actor who had appeared in the film director's *Kiss Me Stupid*, *The Fortune Cookie* and *The Front Page*. As far as one knows, he is not related to Donny Osmond but, apparently, he had to be replaced in the anecdote because he lacked star status. The correct attribution was given in Gary Herman, *The Book of Hollywood Quotes* (1979).

CROCKETT, DAVY
American frontiersman (1786–1836).

1 **Q. How many ears did Davy Crockett have?**
A. A left ear, a right ear, and a wild frontier.
Childrens' joke by the summer of 1956. Recorded in Iona and Peter Opie, *The Lore and Language of Schoolchildren* (1959).

See also AGGIE JOKES 9.

CROP CIRCLES
1 **Beware makers of crop circles; they are cereal killers.**

CRABS
1 **I've got crabs — come upstairs and see my itchings.**
Quoted in Bruce Ridley (ed.), *Wall Flowers: A Collection of Australian Graffiti* (1981).

CUNNILINGUS
1 **Cunnilingus is a tongue-twister.**
Graffito quoted in Rachel Bartlett (ed.), *Off the Wall* (1982).

See also IRISH JOKES 2.

CUSTOMERS
1 **'I'd like to try on that dress in the window, please.'**
'I'm sorry, madam, you'll have to try it on in the changing rooms like everybody else.'

2 **A man walked into a bar and said, 'I want a crocodile sandwich — and make it snappy!'**
Told by Richard Ingrams on BBC Radio *Quote ... Unquote* (29 September 1984). He may have got it from Jeffrey Bernard.

3 **A young scouser was leaving a Liverpool off-licence loaded up with bottles, cans, and mixers, etc. The shop assistant called after him and kindly asked, 'Would you like a box?' But the customer said, 'Ta, luv, but I've got enough to carry already.'**
Contributed to BBC Radio *Quote ... Unquote* in the early 1980s, source not known.

4 At the cinema box-office, the ticket-seller pointed out: 'That's the sixth ticket you've bought, sir.'

   'I know,' said the customer, 'but there's a girl inside who keeps tearing 'em up.'

See also DOGS 5.

CYNIC

1 What is a cynic? A man who knows the price of everything and the value of nothing.
   Oscar Wilde, *Lady Windermere's Fan* (1892).

2 A cynic is man who looks at the world with a monocle in his mind's eye.
   Carolyn Wells, American writer (187?–1942), quoted in *The Treasury of Humorous Quotations*, ed. by Evan Esar & Nicolas Bentley (1951).

3 A cynic is something you do the washing-up in.
   Contributed by Charles Hemming to BBC Radio *Quote ... Unquote* (20 April 1993). Emily Malster of Ipswich's version was 'A cynic is where you put the tea-leaves.'

DANCING

1 Dancing is wonderful training for girls; it's the first way you learn to guess what a man is going to do before he does it.
   Christopher Morley, American writer and editor (1890–1957), quoted in *The Treasury of Humorous Quotations*, ed. by Evan Esar & Nicolas Bentley (1951).

2 Sorry about my dancing – I'm a little stiff from badminton.
   I don't care where you're from, it's my toes I'm worried about.

DEAFNESS

1 **At last I've got my new hearing aid.**
Does it work?
Nearly three o'clock, dear.
Something like this actually happened to my mother in the early 1960s. Coming out of church after a service she saw a deaf old lady that she knew and made polite conversation. 'That was a very good sermon, wasn't it?' she said. And Miss ——— replied, 'Yes, but I don't think I'd go there for a holiday again.'

DEATH

1 **It's not that I'm afraid to die, I just don't want to be there when it happens.**
Woody Allen, 'Death (A Play)', *Without Feathers* (1978).

2 **A famous joke concerning the Revd Spooner of SPOONERISMS fame was that he had inquired of an undergraduate at Oxford c. 1918), 'Now, tell me, was it you or your brother who was killed in the war?'**
Well, as related in *The Guinness Book of Humorous Anecdotes* (1994), Frank Muir in *The Oxford Book of Humorous Prose* (1990) cites this from John Taylor's *Wit and Mirth*: 'A nobleman (as he was riding) met with a yeoman of the country, to whom he said, "My friend, I should know thee. I do remember I have often seen thee." "My good lord," said the countryman, "I am one of your honour's poor tenants, and my name is T. I." "I remember thee better now," (saith my lord). "There were two brothers but one is dead. I pray thee, which of you doth remain alive?"' And the date of this version? 1630.

Mark English of Bradford wrote (1994), however: '"There were two brothers, one of whom died. On bumping into the survivor, an egghead asked, "Was it you who died, or your brother?" — that comes from Barry Baldwin's 1983 translation of *The Philogelos*, or *Laughter-Lover* which is an early Byzantine joke-book written between the 3rd and 10th centuries, and conventionally attributed to one Hierocles. It seems not to be dateable with certainty any more closely than that. There are many more very familiar jokes to be found there, hence the phrase "That one's as old as Hierocles" which was at one time much used by the classically-educated and ill-mannered.'

3 **I have never wanted to see anybody die, but there are a few obituary notices I have read with pleasure.**
Clarence Darrow, American lawyer (1857–1938) — quoted in *The Treasury of Humorous Quotations*, ed. by Evan Esar & Nicolas Bentley (1951).

4 **KEEP DEATH OFF THE ROADS**
– drive on the pavement.
Slogan and graffitoed addition. Contributed by B. Longthorne, Palmers Green, London to BBC Radio *Quote ... Unquote* (19 June 1979).

5 **Death is nature's way of telling you to slow down.**
A joke current in the US by 1960 (as in *Newsweek*, 25 April). It has been specifically attributed to Severn Darden (1937–), the American film character actor. It is capable of infinite variation: from *Punch* (3 January 1962): 'Some neo-Malthusians have been heard to suggest that the bomb is Nature's way . . . of checking . . . the over-spawning of our species.' In 1978, the American cartoon strip Garfield produced a bumper-sticker with the slogan: 'My car is God's way of telling you to slow down.'

6 **Death is just another way of saying, 'Yesterday was the last day of the rest of your life.'**

7 **A barrister who worked as legal adviser to a businessman whom he despised was rung up by the businessman's wife to inform him that her husband had died suddenly. 'The funeral's on Wednesday,' she said. 'Are you coming?' 'No,' said the barrister, 'I believe you.'**
Told by George Mikes on BBC Radio *Quote ... Unquote* (14 August 1979).

8 **Death is the best trip of all. That's why they save it up till the end.**
Slogan seen by Carlos Castaneda in San Francisco, quoted in *Say No More* (1987).

9 **'When my mother was a young girl in Grasmere, the family cat was run over by a coach (horse drawn!) and killed. The young members of the family gathered to give the cat a good funeral, but at the graveside none of them knew quite what to say until a visiting cousin said he knew because he had heard it in church. He solemnly held the dead animal by its feet, moving it backwards and forwards over the grave, chanting: "To God the Father and God the Son and into the hole he goes . . ."'**
Told by David Scott of Windermere (1994). However, his mother is not alone in experiencing this! David H. Walton of Crowland, Lincolnshire, contributed to BBC Radio *Quote ... Unquote* (10 August 1985) another version: 'The curate's children were playing in the garden with a small toy barrow and in it a teddy bear. They tipped the bear into a small hole with the words: "Into the Father, into the Son, and into the hole he goes . . ."'

10 The Scotsman had just lost his wife and went round to the local newspaper to put a notice in the deaths column. 'What would you like to say?' asked the clerk. 'Maggie's dead,' said the Scotsman. 'But you can put a bit more than that in, if you like,' said the clerk, 'and for absolutely no extra charge.' 'Ah, weel,' the Scotsman replied, 'then how about ". . . And second-hand Ford for sale"?'

A Spanish version of this joke, involving a similarly tight-fisted Catalan, was told in the *Observer* (16 December 1994).

DECISIONS, DECISIONS

1 The decision is maybe and that's final.

Graffito from Hawthorn, Victoria, Australia (1981).

DEFENCES

1 *On building site hoarding in Jamaica Street, Bristol:*
'CUT DEFENCES' — and mow de lawn.

Slogan and graffitoed addition, reported by E.R. Kermode, Bristol, March 1987. Jack Minnit of Kingston upon Thames reported a similar joke, also from Bristol, in 1993: 'DOWN WITH DEFENCE — and dig de garden.'

DEFINITIONS

1 **Q.** What is a bigamist
A. It's an Italian fog.

Included in John S. Crosbie, *Crosbie's Dictionary of Puns* (1977).

2 'Hebrew' — a male teabag.

From the John Gray 'taglines' collection, 1994.

3 **Q.** What's a Hindu?
A. Lays eggs.

Graffito from Newcastle upon Tyne (1982).

4 Define the word 'aftermath'.
It is what you do in the lesson that follows arithmetic.?

DE MILLE, CECIL B.
American film director (1881–1959).

1 This joke tells of the day when Cecil B. De Mille, the famed producer of biblical epics for the cinema, was directing a

battle scene which involved thousands of extras and animals and probably ended with the destruction of the set. Whatever the case, it would only be possible for there to be one 'take'. And so, C.B. covered himself by having the scene filmed by four cameras. When the action was completed, the destruction wrought, and any chance of repeating the matter had been lost for all time, Mr De Mille checked with each cameraman that he had filmed the scene successfully. 'No, I'm afraid not,' said the first, 'the film jammed in the camera.' 'No,' said the second, 'There's a hair in the gate'. 'No,' said the third, 'the sun shone into the lens.'

In desperation, De Mille director turned to the last cameraman who said brightly, 'Ready when you are, Mr De Mille!'

Presumably this joke is popular because it portrays innocence in the face of dire calamity. The punchline hangs in the air almost joyfully. *Ready When You Are, Mr McGill* became the title of a British TV play (by Jack Rosenthal, 1976) about how a TV production is ruined by an actor who can't remember his (two) lines.

DEODORANTS

1 *Boy:* 'Have you got any deodorant?'
Chemist's assistant: 'Would you like the ball type?'
Boy: 'No, it's for my armpits.'
Quoted in *Say No More* (1987).

DEPRESSION

1 Joseph Grimaldi (1779–1837) was known as the 'King of the Clowns' and changed the face of pantomime. But he had a tough life. Indeed. A man went to see his doctor complaining of depression. The doctor advised him to get out and about a bit more. 'Tell you what,' he said, 'a very good thing would be if you went to Sadler's Wells and saw Grimaldi the clown.'

'Ah, yes,' said the man, 'but I am Grimaldi the clown.'
Told in *Roy Hudd's Book of Music-Hall, Variety and Showbiz Anecdotes* (1993).

DESCARTES

1 I am, therefore I think. Is this putting Descartes before the horse?
Quoted in Bruce Ridley (ed.), *Wall Flowers: A Collection of Australian Graffiti* (1981).

DIARRHOEA

1 **Diarrhoea is hereditary, it runs in your jeans.**
In Haan & Hammerstrom *Graffiti in the Big Ten* (1981).

See also CONSTIPATION 1.

DICTIONARIES

1 **Who was it first said of the *Oxford English Dictionary* that, as books go, it had a fine vocabulary but not much of a plot?**

DIETS

1 **I'm on a seafood diet. Whenever I see food I eat it.**
Graffito, quoted in Rachel Bartlett (ed.), *Off the Wall* (1982).

DINING

1 **The best number for a dinner party is two: myself and a damn good head waiter.**
Nubar Gulbenkian, British industrialist and philanthropist (1896–1972) – quoted in the *Daily Telegraph*, 14 January 1965.

DIPLOMACY

1 **Diplomacy is the art of saying 'Nice Doggie!' till you can find a rock.**
Ascribed to Wynn Catlin by Laurence J. Peter, *Quotations for Our Time* (1977).

2 **Speak softly and carry a big mean Doberman.**
Graffito described on Granada TV *Cabbages and Kings* (29 July 1979).

3 **What is the difference between a diplomat and a lady? When a diplomat says 'yes', he means 'perhaps'. When he says 'perhaps', he means 'no'. When he says 'no', he is not a diplomat. When a lady says 'no', she means 'perhaps'. When she says 'perhaps', she means 'yes'. But when she says 'yes', she is no lady.**
Told by Lord Denning, a senior British jurist, in October 1982. Whether Denning claimed it as his own is not recorded, but in Hans Severus Ziegler's *Heitere Muse: Anekdoten aus Kultur und Geschichte* (1974), the passage appears in a

(possibly apocryphal) anecdote concerning Bismarck at a ball in St Petersburg. His partner, whom he had been flattering, told him, 'One can't believe a word you diplomats say' and provided the first half of the description as above. Then Bismarck replied with the second half.

DIRTY
1 *Written on a mud-covered Mercedes estate car seen in Tunbridge Wells:* **'Also available in blue.'**
Reported by Peggy Langdown, East Sussex (1989).

DIRTY OLD MEN
1 **He was such a dirty old man that people began to comment on the fact that he was always showing Boy Scouts over the road.**
Current by the 1960s.

DISARMAMENT
1 **DISARM TODAY**
– Dat arm tomorrow.
Slogan and graffitoed addition. Contributed to BBC Radio *Quote ... Unquote* (26 June 1980) by David Linford of Rugeley.

DISEASE
1 **Did you know, I've got Parkinson's disease. And he's got mine.**
A modern reworking of 'I've got Bright's disease and he's got mine.' A caption by S.J. Perelman, US writer (1904–79), to a cartoon in *Judge*, 16 November 1929.

DO IT JOKES
The '—— do it ——ly' joke craze flourished from about 1979 onwards. On 26 April of that year, the British Sun *newspaper was offering a variety of T-shirts with nudging 'do it' slogans inscribed upon them. The craze was said to have started in the US. Whatever the case, scores of slogans 'promoting' various groups with this allusion to performing the sexual act appeared over the next several years on T-shirts, lapel-buttons, bumper-stickers and car-window stickers.*

All this from simple exploitation of the innuendo in the phrase 'do it', which had perhaps first been exploited by Cole Porter in the song 'Let's Do It, Let's Fall in Love' (1928):

> *In shady shoals, English soles do it,*
> *Goldfish in the privacy of bowls do it . . .*

and then in a more personal parody by Noël Coward (in the 1940s):

> *Our leading writers in swarms do it*
> *Somerset and all the Maughams do it . . .*

Much later came the advertising slogan 'You can do it in an M.G.' (quoted in 1983).

In my Graffiti books (1979–86) I recorded some seventy, among them:

1 **Art majors do it with their brushes.**

2 **Artists do it with imagination.**

3 **Astronomers do it with one eye open/with a collapsible instrument.**

4 **Bankers do it with interest.**

5 **Bartenders do it on the rocks.**

6 **Booksellers do it over the counter.**

7 **Broadcasters do it with frequency.**

8 **Builders do it with erections.**

9 **Calligraphers do it at 45 degrees.**

10 **Campers do it in rows.**

11 **Charles and Di do it by Royal Appointment.**

12 **Chinese food lovers want to do it again after twenty minutes.**

13 **City planners do it with their eyes shut.**

14 **Civil servants do it in a minute.**

15 **Cyclists do it in the saddle.**

16 **Cyclists have it between their legs.**

17 **Debaters do it orally.**

18 **Divers do it deeper.**

19 **Dons do it in their sleep.**

Suggested by Walter Redfern, *Clichés and Coinages* (1989).

20 **Donyatt Dog Club does it with discipline and kindness.**
Reported from Somerset by Celia Haddon (1982).

21 **Elevator men do it up and down.**

22 **Epistemologists do it knowingly.**

23 **Farmers do it in wellies.**

24 **Fencers don't do it — they feint.**

25 **Firemen do it for anybody.**

26 **Footballers do it in the bath afterwards.**

27 **Geographers do it all over the world.**

28 **George does it best.**

29 **Glider pilots stay up longer.**

30 **Gordon does it in a flash.**

31 **Hancockians do it H-H-Half Hourly.**
A slogan of the Tony Hancock Appreciation Society.

32 **Hang gliders stay up longer.**

33 **Hang gliders do it quietly.**

34 **Historians do it looking back.**

35 **House of Commons can't do it in one sitting.**

36 **Kamikazes do it once.**

37 **Karajan does it with a little stick.**

38 **Lawyers do it in their briefs.**

39 **Linguists do it orally.**

40 **Lord Snowdon does it in soft focus.**

41 **Lumberjackers do it with their choppers.**

42 **Marathon runners keep it up for hours.**

43 **Microbiologists do it with culture and sensitivity.**

44 **Missionaries do it on their knees.**

45 **Monks do it habitually.**

46 **Morticians are dead keen on doing it.**

47 **Musicians do it by the score.**

48 Musicians do it with rhythm.

49 Nudists do it in the altogether.

50 Paris does it plastered.

51 Philosophers do it thoughtfully.

52 Photographers do it in the dark.

53 Piano tuners do it twice a year.

54 Piggot does it on the flat.

55 Politicians just talk about it.

56 Printers do it and don't wrinkle the sheets.

57 Procrastinators do it when they get round to it.

58 Psychiatrists do it in on the couch.

59 Publishers do it between covers.

60 Shotputters do it on one leg.

61 Skiers go down faster.

62 Skiers do it on the piste.

63 Skiers do it with both legs together.

64 Snooker players do it bending over.

65 Squash players do it against the wall.

66 Squatters do it sitting down.

67 Swimmers do it with the breast stroke.

68 Swimmers do it down under.

69 Teachers do it with class.

70 Tennis players do it with love.

71 Tommy Cooper does it just like that.

72 Torvill and Dean do it on thin ice.

73 Treorchy Male Voice Choir does it all through the night.

74 Trombonists do it in any position.

75 Vicars do it on Sundays.

76 Violinists don't do it but fiddle around at it.

77 **Waterskiers do it in rubber suits.**

78 **Waterskiers do it behind boats.**

79 **Wildlife biologists do it like animals.**

80 **Window cleaners do it up ladders.**

81 **Windsurfers do it standing up.**

DOBEDOBEDO

1 **To do is to be – Rousseau.**
To be is to do – Sartre.
Dobedobedo – Sinatra.

Contributed by Anna Morrell to Granada TV *Cabbages and Kings* (15 July 1979). A version is included in Reisner & Wechsler, *Encyclopedia of Graffiti* (1974).

DOCTORS

1 **It's amazing the little harm they do when one considers the opportunities they have.**

Attributed to Mark Twain, but unverified.

2 **The doctor came and sat on the patient's bed to break him the bad news. 'I'm very sorry to have to tell you,' he said, as soothingly as he could, 'that you have only four minutes left to live.'**
'Gee, that's terrible, doc,' said the patient. 'There is really nothing you could do for me?'
'Well, I suppose I could boil you an egg.'

3 *Green young medical student to patient:* **'Nothing to worry about, just a little prick with a needle!'**
Patient: **'Yes, I know you are, but what are you going to do?'**

Exchange related by Dr Rob Buckman on BBC Radio *Quote ... Unquote* (22 January 1979).

4 **Nurse, please pay more attention. I said, 'Prick his boil . . .'**

5 **Doctor, I keep thinking I'm a pair of curtains.**
For heaven's sake, woman, pull yourself together.

6 A man walked into a doctor's surgery with a duck on his head. 'What seems to be the matter?' the doctor asked. The duck said, 'I've got this growth on my foot.'

DOGS

1 'My dog has no nose.'
'How does he smell?'
'Terrible.'
The quintessence of old joke.

2 Every day my dog and I go for a tramp in the woods. Does the dog enjoy it?
Yes, but the tramp's getting a bit fed up.

3 My dog's called Isaiah.
Fancy that! And, tell me, why is your dog called Isaiah?
Because one eye's 'igher than the other.

4 I was thinking of sending my dog to one of these pet psychiatrists — but the trouble is he knows he's not allowed on the couch.

5 *Customer in pet shop:* 'Have you got any dogs going cheap?'
Owner: 'No, all our dogs go "Woof!"'

DOORS

1 When is a door not a door? When it's ajar.
Seemingly one of the oldest punning riddles. *Punch* in its 'comic chronology' (17 December 1872, i.e its *Almanack for 1873*) has 'AD 1001 invention of the riddle "When is a door not a door?"'

DIVORCE

1 The happiest time of anyone's life is just after the first divorce.
John Kenneth Galbraith, American economist (1908–) — quoted in Bob Chieger, *Was It Good For You Too?* (1983).

DREAMS

1 I had this terrible dream the other night. I dreamt I had swallowed an enormous marshmallow. Then, when I woke up, I couldn't find my pillow.

DRESS

1 **Kindly adjust your dress before leaving – as a refusal often offends.**
Graffito contributed by Peter Cook to Granada TV *Cabbages and Kings* (4 November 1979). Also to BBC Radio *Quote ... Unquote* (31 July 1980) by Mrs D. Lawrence of Brighton.

2 **'Arrangements had been made for us to meet up with another couple to go out together. My wife, who was dressed up to the nines, blurted out, "We thought you'd get dressed up." There was an awkward silence and then one of them replied dismally: "We thought we had . . . ".'**
Contributed to BBC Radio *Quote ... Unquote* (31 July 1980) by Peter Nelson of Hull.

3 *Asked whether she dressed for men or women:* **'I dress for women and I undress for men.'**
Angie Dickinson, American actress (1931–).

DRINK AND DRUNKS

1 **Do you have a drink problem?**
– Yes, I can't afford it.
Contributed by Arthur Marshall to BBC *Radio Quote ... Unquote* (21 August 1979).

2 **One more drink and I'd be under the host.**
Dorothy Parker, American wit and writer (1893–1967) – quoted in John Keats, *You Might As Well Live* (1970).

3 **I saw a notice which said 'Drink Canada Dry' and I've just started.**
Brendan Behan, Irish dramatist (1923–64) – attrib., by 1980.

4 **The drunk was scrabbling around in the gutter underneath a lamp-post looking for his front door key when a policemam, helpfully and kindly, volunteered to help him look for it. After searching fruitlessly for a while, the policeman asked, 'And are you sure you dropped your key hereabouts?'**
'No, I dropped it in Church Street,' said the drunk.
'But if you dropped it in Church Street why are you looking for it here?'
'Because there are no lamp-posts in Church Street.'
Traditional. Could it have originated in a *Punch* cartoon?

5 *Defending his taste for alcohol:* **'I'm so holy that when I touch wine, it turns into water.'**
Aga Khan III, Muslim leader (1877–1957). Attributed by John Colville, *Footprints in Time* (1976).

6 **I've made it a rule never to drink by daylight and never to refuse a drink after dark.**
H.L. Mencken, quoted in the *New York Post*, 18 September 1945.

7 **I was in love with a beautiful blonde once – she drove me to drink – 'tis the one thing I'm indebted to her for.**
W.C. Fields, in the film *Never Give a Sucker an Even Break* (US, 1941).

8 **On the day the Japanese attacked Pearl Harbor, John Barrymore was visiting W.C. Fields at his home in Hollywood. When the news came in, Fields picked up the phone and ordered forty cases of gin from his liquor dealer. 'Are you sure that is going to be enough?' asked Barrymore. 'Yes,' replied Fields, 'I think it's going to be a short war.'**
Unverified. Told by Charles G. Francis (1994).

9 **Don't drink and drive – you'll spill it.**
Traditional, by 1988.

10 **One for the road could be the pint of no return.**
Contributed by Celia Haddon to Granada TV *Cabbages and Kings* (22 July 1979).

11 **A man went into a pub with a newt on his shoulder. 'That's a nice newt,' said the barman, 'what's he called?' 'He's called Tiny,' said the man. 'Why's he called Tiny?' asked the barman. The man replied: 'Because he's my newt.'**

DRINKING CHOCOLATE
1 **Eighteenth-century drinking chocolate was rococoa.**
Quoted in Bruce Ridley (ed.), *Wall Flowers: A Collection of Australian Graffiti* (1981).

DRIPPING

1 **Q. How do you annoy a butcher?**
A. Go into his shop and ask if he keeps dripping. If he says he does, then tell him to wipe his nose.

I was told this by my grandfather, so I expect he heard it about 1900 . . .

DUMB MEN JOKES

These were a brave but hardly successful attempt by an American publisher to turn the tide against BLONDE JOKES. The material is mostly the same as in FEMINIST JOKES. A British publisher attempted the same thing with 'Stupid Men' joke books in the early 1990s. A small selection:

1 **In England, a dumb man who doesn't do anything is called a gentleman. Here we call him a boyfriend.**

Included in *The Dumb Men Joke Book* (Volume II, 1994) by Nan Tucket. As also the following:

2 **A dumb man walks into an antique shop and says, 'What's new?'**

3 **My best friend just ran off with my husband. I'll miss her.**

Compare: 'My wife's run away with my best friend — gee, I miss him', an entry from an Australian graffiti competition (1981).

4 **Why don't dumb men drink coffee at work?**
It keeps them awake.

5 **A dumb man finds his wife in bed with another man.**
'What are you doing?' he yells.
'See,' she says to her lover, 'I told you he was dumb.'

6 **What's bleached blond, has huge breast implants, and lives in Sweden?**
Salman Rushdie (so he's not a dumb man . . .).

7 **If Roosevelt were alive today, he'd turn over in his grave.**

I have no idea how old this format is. This particular example has been ascribed to Samuel Goldwyn. I recall the idea being suggested as one of President Ford's idiocies in c. 1975 in the form: 'If Abraham Lincoln were alive today he'd be turning in his grave.'

8 A dumb man was ordered to take a paternity test.
'Were you the father?' asked one of his friends.
'They'll never find out,' he said. 'They took samples from my finger.'

9 Once a woman told a dumb man that they use alligators to make shoes.
Shaking his head he said, 'What will they teach them to do next?'

10 What's the quickest way to lose 180 pounds of ugly fat?
Divorce him.

11 We sometimes wonder if there are any limits to a man's laziness. One said, 'I'm thinking of going to Australia. The news says that someone's discovered a diamond mine in the Outback where they sit all over the ground. All you have to do is bend down and pick them up.'
The other guy looked at his friend and said, 'Bend down?'
Compare this from Arthur Marx, *Son of Groucho* (1973): 'One day Father called [George S. Kaufman] long distance and filled him full of glowing tales about the fantastic salaries Hollywood movie writers were pulling down every week . . . . "George," pleaded Father, hoping to persuade him with his fine choice of cliché, "the streets are paved with gold." There was a moment's pause, and then Kaufman said, "You mean, you have to bend over and pick it up?"'

DWARVES
1 Six-inch Chinese dwarf wishes to meet person with similar interests.
Graffito written five feet up a wall in the Bodleian Library, Oxford. Underneath was written a P.S.: 'This took considerable effort.' Reported by Humphrey Carpenter (1979).

ECONOMY
1 Due to the present financial situation, the light at the end of the tunnel will be turned off at the week-ends.
Graffito from Dublin. Reported by Darren Hickey, Leixlip, Co. Kildare, in 1987.

EDITORS

1 Editor: a person employed by a newspaper whose business it is to separate the wheat from the chaff and to see that the chaff is printed.
Elbert Hubbard, US writer and editor, in the *Roycroft Dictionary* (1914).

ELECTIONS

1 You can't fool all the people all of the time but, if you do it just once, it lasts for five years.
Graffito observed in the British Museum, included in *Graffiti 3* (1981).

2 At a state dinner, Eleanor Roosevelt was discussing democracy with an oriental ambassador. 'And when did you last have an election?' she asked. 'Before blekfast,' he replied.
Included in John S. Crosbie, *Crosbie's Dictionary of Puns* (1977).

See also GOVERNMENT.

ELEPHANT JOKES
Popular especially in the 1950s/60s.

1 WHY DON'T ELEPHANTS EAT PENGUINS?
– because they can't manage to take the wrapping paper off.

2 An elephant encountered a mouse. 'My,' said the elephant, 'you're a very small little thing, aren't you?' 'Yes,' agreed the mouse. 'but, you see, I haven't been very well . . .'.
Told in *Pass the Port* (1976). I remember a similar exchange in BBC Radio's *I'm Sorry I'll Read That Again* (c. 1968). *Doctor to patient:* 'Haven't seen you for a long time, Mrs ——'. *Patient:* 'Ah, well, you see, doctor, I've not been very well . . .'.

3 What did the elephant do when he was being charged by a herd of wild buffalo?
Made a trunk call and reversed the charges.
Told to me by Ben Waring, Plymouth (1986).

4 How do you make an elephant fly?
Well, first you take a gr-r-r-reat big zip . . .
Told by C. Gruner in *Understanding Laughter* (1978).

5 **Performing elephants were among the acts at the circus. They walked along a bench about a foot wide and a foot high. The four-year-old girl gazed at this for a while and then remarked scornfully: 'I could do that . . .'**

Contributed to BBC Radio Quote ... Unquote in the mid-1980s. Source unknown.

6 **One morning I shot an elephant in my pyjamas. How he got in my pyjamas I'll never know.**

Groucho Marx in the film Animal Crackers (1930). Script by Morrie Ryskind, from the musical by himself and George S. Kaufman.

7 *Sheriff:* **'Where are you going with that elephant?'**
Jimmy Durante: **'What elephant?'**

From the film Jumbo (US, 1962). The joke was specifically credited to Charles Lederer. The film was based on the 1935 Rodgers-Hart-Hecht-MacArthur stage show Jumbo in which Durante had delivered the same joke.

8 **How do you get an elephant into a telephone box?**
Open the door.

9 **What did the elephant say into the microphone?**
Tusking, tusking, one, two, three.

10 **Why did the elephant cross the road?**
To pick up the squashed chicken.

11 **What's the difference between an elephant and a banana?**
I don't know.
Have you ever tried to put an elephant in your fruit salad?

12 **How can you tell that an elephant has been in the refrigerator?**
You can see the footprints in the butter.

13 **How do you stop a herd of elephants from charging?**
Take away their credit cards.

14 **Why can't two elephants go into the swimming pool at the same time?**
Because they've only got one pair of trunks.

15 **Why do elephants hide behind trees?**
So that they can trip up ants.

16 **How do you get four elephants into a Mini?**
Two in the front and two in the back.

ELEVATORS *See LIFTS/ELEVATORS.*

ELIOT, T.S.
American-born British poet (1888–1965).

1 **When it was announced that Eliot had been awarded the Nobel Prize for Literature In 1948, he was making a lecture tour of the United States. A Mid-Western reporter asked him if he had been given the prize for his great work** *The Waste Land.* **'No,' replied Eliot, 'I believe I have been given it in recognition of my whole corpus.' Accordingly, the journalist wrote: 'In an interview with our airport correspondent this morning, Mr Eliot revealed that the Swedish Academy had given him the Nobel Prize not for** *The Waste Land* **but for his poem** *My Whole Corpus.'*
Told by Philip French in the *Observer* (17 April 1994). A slightly different version – with the work entitled *The Entire Corpus* – had appeared earlier in David Wallechinsky & Irving Wallace, *The People's Almanac 2* (1978).

2 **T.S. Eliot is an anagram of toilets.**
Graffito from Leicester University, included in *Graffiti Lives OK* (1979).

ENDS
1 **The ends justify the jeans.**
In *Graffiti 4* (1982).

ENEMAS
1 **With friends like mine, who needs enemas.**
Quoted in Bruce Ridley (ed.), *Wall Flowers: A Collection of Australian Graffiti* (1981).

ENGAGEMENTS
1 **A friend of mine, who worked in the circus, got engaged to a lady contortionist. But I'm afraid she broke it off.**

ENGINEERS

1 **Yesterday I couldn't spell engineer – now I are one.**
Graffito on the walls of Loughborough University. Contributed to BBC Radio Quote ... Unquote (8 January 1979) by S.L. Colledge of Newton-le-Willows, Merseyside.

ENGLISH, THE

1 **They tell me that the English are a people who travel all over the world to laugh at other people.**
Anonymous Spaniard, quoted by Gerald Brenan, The Face of Spain, 1950.

2 **Englishmen hate two things – racial discrimination and Irishmen.**
Reported from Dublin, 1988.

3 **Continental people have sex life; the English have hot-water bottles.**
George Mikes, Hungarian-born writer (1912–87). From How To Be An Alien (1946).

4 **Most Englishmen can never get over the embarrassing fact that they were born in bed with a woman.**
Reported from Ireland, 1988.

5 **ENGLISHMEN MAKE THE BEST LOVERS – and the Japanese make them smaller and cheaper.**
From Thames TV, The Benny Hill Show, by 1981.

6 **'At a promotional evening for the Berlin Tourist Board, I was asked by a German official, "Have you ever been to Berlin?" Without thinking, I heard myself answer: "No, but my father often flew over it during the war".'**
Contributed to BBC Radio Quote ... Unquote (22 December 1981) by Len Eden, Birmingham.

7 **An Englishman, even if he is alone, forms an orderly queue of one.**
George Mikes, How To Be An Alien (1946).

ENTERTAINMENT

1 **A new variety act went along to a theatrical agent and did an audition. The man simply waved his arms about, flew up to**

the ceiling, swooped about the room a bit and then neatly landed just in front of the agent.

'So, you're a bird impersonator,' said the agent. 'Do you do anything else?'

2 **Don't clap too hard — it's a very old building.**
John Osborne, *The Entertainer* (1957). But an old music-hall joke.

EPISTEMOLOGY
The theory of knowledge.

1 **Can one really know about epistemology?**
Quoted in Bruce Ridley (ed.), *Wall Flowers: A Collection of Australian Graffiti* (1981).

See also DO IT JOKES 22.

EPITAPHS

1 **A man of much courage and superb equipment.**
Suggested epitaph for Brigham Young, the Mormon leader (1801–77) who died leaving seventeen wives and fifty-six children. Contributed to BBC Radio *Quote ... Unquote* (1977) by Mr Lee Etchells of Southsea.

2 **Died at the age of 98, shot by a jealous husband.**
His own hoped-for epitaph by the British comedian Ted Ray — who, in fact, died in 1977 at the age of 68. Recalled by Roy Hudd on BBC Radio *Quote ... Unquote* (19 April 1994).

3 **Ars longa, vita brevis.**
Suggested epitaph for one Thomas Longbottom who died young. Contributed to BBC Radio *Quote ... Unquote* (17 May 1978) by Harry Miller of Prestwich, Manchester.

4 **Under this sod lies another one.**
All-purpose epitaph for those one dislikes. Contributed to BBC Radio *Quote ... Unquote* (8 June 1977).

5 **There was a man whose parents named him 'Amazing', but he did nothing in his life to live up to that name. He stayed on the family farm and remained married to the same woman for sixty years. Because of his name, however, he was the butt of**

countless jokes – so much so that he said that, when he died, he did not want his name put on his gravestone – certainly not his first name.

In due course, when he died, his widow duly buried him – but she did not want to leave the gravestone entirely blank so, instead of putting his name, she caused to be inscribed the words, 'Here lies a man who was faithful to his wife for sixty years.'

Unfortunately, whenever people now pass the gravestone, they read the inscription and exclaim, 'That's amazing!'

Told in *Executive Speeches* (December 1994/January 1995).

6 **By and by**
God caught his eye.
An epitaph on a waiter, credited to the American poet David McCord (1897–), from *Bay Window Ballads* (1935).

7 **He was literally a father to all the children of the parish.**
The obituary for a much-loved vicar which is supposed to have appeared in the *Church Times* – recalled by B.W.H. Taylor, Chalfont St Giles, Buckinghamshire (1979).

8 **In this grave here do lie**
Back to back my wife and I
When the last trump the air shall fill
If she gets up, I'll just lie still.
Epitaph remembered by Dr A.J. Nimmo, London SE22 (1982).

9 **I told you I was sick.**
Epitaph on a hypochondriac – from the southern US – remembered on BBC Radio *Quote ... Unquote* (22 December 1981). In January 1994, it was reported that the dying wish of Keith Woodward of Shrivenham, Wiltshire, had been to have a tombstone bearing the joke 'I told them I was ill'. However, parish councillors ordered the message to be removed.

10 **Lord she is thin.**
It is said that this epitaph appears at the bottom of a Tasmanian tombstone. The 'e' is on the back, the stonemason not having left himself enough room to carve it on the front. Is there a source for this much-told tale?

11 **She sleeps alone at last.**
Epitaph for an unnamed movie queen, suggested by Robert Benchley (1889– 1945).

12 **Here lies James Burke
    A decent man entirely.
    We bought this tombstone second-hand —
    And his name's not Burke, it's Reilly.**
    Told by Roy Hudd on BBC Radio Quote ... Unquote (5 April 1994). A joke
    apparently taken from a song.

13 **Down the lanes of memory
    The lights are never dim
    Until the stars forget to shine
    We shall remember . . . her.**
    Quoted by Alan Bennett from 'a Lancashire newspaper' on BBC Radio Quote ...
    Unquote (26 January 1982). He had earlier included the lines in 'The English
    Way of Death' in Beyond the Fringe (Broadway version, 1964).

    ERECTIONS
1   **An erection is like the Theory of Relativity — the more you think
    about it, the harder it gets.**
    Graffito from Liverpool University, included in Graffiti 2 (1980). Compare 'Life is
    like a penis — the more you think about it, the harder it gets', from elsewhere.

    See also ELECTIONS 2; SEX 28.

    ERRATA
1   **Erratum. This slip has been inserted by mistake.**

2   **Erratum. In my article on the Price of Milk, 'Horses' should have
    read 'Cows' throughout.**
    'Beachcomber' (J.B. Morton), included in The Best of Beachcomber (1963).

    ERRORS
1   **To err is human — but it feels divine.**
    Attributed to Mae West.

    See also COMPUTERS 5.

    ESKIMOS
1   **Eskimos are God's frozen people.**
    Included in Graffiti 3 (1981).

2 **Your Mum's an Eskimo, right? Where does she come from?
Alaska.
Never mind, I can ask 'er myself.**

3 **What song do Eskimos sing before they have their supper?
'Whale Meat Again.'**

See also FROZEN.

ESSEX GIRL JOKES
*There was a craze for these jokes in Britain in the Autumn of 1991 –
sample: 'How does an Essex Girl turn on the light afterwards? She kicks
open the car door.' As such, they were a straight lift of the BLONDE
JOKES that had been popular in the United States shortly before. The
British type was probably so named on the model of 'Essex Man' – a term
describing a prosperous, uncouth, uneducated person who did well out of
the Thatcher years and was identified as likely to be found dwelling in
Essex (a county just to the east of London). 'Not long ago, I worked very
briefly at [BBC] Radio 4, which is a terrifically politically correct sort
of place, and one day in the office I told an Essex Girl joke. A young
woman there turned on me as if I came from another, less advanced planet,
and, more in sorrow than in anger, said she didn't think what I'd said was
frightfully right-on ... [This] is the age of the joyless and the shrivelled.
Do your own thing has turned into not in my back yard' (Independent,
23 April 1992).*

1 **Q. What did the Essex Girl ask when told she was pregnant?
A. How do you know it's mine?**
Quoted in the *Independent* (5 November 1991). This is probably a version of
the earlier joke: 'Did you hear about the Irish girl who told her mother she was
pregnant? The mother replied, "Are you sure it's yours?"'

2 **Q. What's the difference between an Essex Girl and a
supermarket trolley?
A. The supermarket trolley has a mind of its own.**
Same source.

3 **Q. How can you change an Essex Girl's mind?
A. Blow in her ear.**

4 **Q. Why do Essex Girls wear panties?
A. To keep their ankles warm.**

5 **Q.** Why did the Essex Girl climb up on the roof?
A. She heard drinks were on the house.

6 **Q.** Why do Essex Girls love BMWs?
A. They can spell it.

7 **Q.** What do you call twenty-four Essex Girls floating down the River Thames?
A. The Isle of Dogs.

8 **Q.** What do you call an Essex Girl with half a brain?
A. Gifted.

9 **Q.** Why do Essex Girls wash their hair in the kitchen sink?
A. Isn't that where you wash vegetables?

10 **Q.** What do you call an Essex Girl with a balloon on her shoulder?
A. Siamese twins.

11 **Q.** Why don't Essex Girls eat pickles?
A. They can't fit their heads in the jars.

ESTATE AGENTS

1 Why don't estate agents look out of the window in the morning?
So they'll have something to do after lunch.
Told during the collapse of the British housing market during the early 1990s. Reported in the *Daily Telegraph* (10 January 1994).

ETIQUETTE

1 Etiquette is knowing how to yawn with your mouth closed.
Herbert V. Prochnow, American writer (b 1897), in Herbert V. Prochnow Snr & Jnr, *A Treasury of Humorous Quotations* (1969).

EUNUCHS

1 Eunuchs unite – you've nothing to lose.
Included in *Graffiti 2* (1980).

EUROPEANS

1 There have been many definitions of hell, but for the English the best definition is that it is a place where the Germans are the police, the Swedish are the comedians, and the Italians are the defence force, Frenchmen dig the roads, the Belgians are the pop singers, the Spanish run the railways, the Turks cook the food, the Irish are the waiters, the Greeks run the government and the common language is Dutch.
David Frost and Antony Jay, *To England with Love* (1967).

2 Heaven is an English policeman, a French cook, a German engineer, an Italian lover and everything organized by the Swiss.
   Hell is an English cook, a French engineer, a German policeman, a Swiss lover and everything organized by the Italians.

Compare FOOD 1.

EVIDENCE

1 Some circumstantial evidence is very strong, as when you find a trout in the milk.
Henry David Thoreau, American writer (1817–62), quoted in *The Treasury of Humorous Quotations*, ed. by Evan Esar & Nicolas Bentley (1951).

EXAGGERATION

1 I've told you for the fifty thousandth time, stop exaggerating.
From Imperial College, London, included in *Graffiti Lives OK* (1979).

EXAMINATIONS

1 Examinations – nature's laxative.
From the City of London Polytechnic, included in *Graffiti 2* (1980).

2 Avoid the end of the year rush – fail your exams now.
From a London teaching hospital, included in *Graffiti 2* (1980).

EXCALIBUR

1 I trust Excalibur doesn't choose this particular stretch of water to make his reappearance.
Graffito in the 'left-hand cubicle of the gents' in the Radcliffe Camera library,

Oxford. Contributed to BBC *Radio Quote ... Unquote* (7 June 1978) by Arthur J.
Durrant of Keble College, Oxford.

EXCUSES
1 **From a note to teacher: 'Please excuse Johnny from being
absent as I was having a baby — and it's not his fault!'**
Told by Isabel Lovett of the Isle of Skye, August 1994.

EXPERIENCE
1 *Quoting an anonymous Scotsman:* **'You should make a point of
trying every experience once, excepting incest and folk-
dancing.'**
Sir Arnold Bax, British composer (1883–1953) in *Farewell, My Youth* (1943).
Often wrongly ascribed to Sir Thomas Beecham or to Bax himself — but he was
quoting a 'sympathetic Scotsman'.

EYES
1 **My uncle's got a glass eye.
Did he tell you?
No, it just came out in the conversation.**

FACE LIFTS
1 *Joan Rivers on Gloria Vanderbilt:* **'I think she's had her face
lifted. Every time she crosses her legs, her mouth snaps open.'**
Attributed on BBC Radio *Quote ... Unquote* (1985). But Bob Chieger in *Was It
Good For You Too?* (1983) has Rivers saying about Sophia Loren: 'She's had it
fixed. You know how you can tell? When a woman sits down, crosses her legs,
and her mouth snaps open' (on NBC-TV's *Tonight Show*, 1981).

FAILURE
1 **Did you hear about the man who shot an arrow in the air —
and missed!**

FAIRY

1 I'm a fairy. My name is Nuff. Fairy Nuff.
Included in *Graffiti Lives OK* (1979)

FAMILIARITY

1 Familiarity breeds contempt — and children.
Mark Twain, included in *Mark Twain's Notebook* (1935) — quoted in Bob Chieger, *Was It Good For You Too?* (1983).

FAMILIES

1 A family reunion is an effective form of birth control.

2 THE FAMILY THAT PRAYS TOGETHER STAYS TOGETHER
— thank God my mother-in-law's an atheist.
Slogan and addition, included in *Graffiti 3* (1981).

3 Hamlet is the tragedy of tackling a family problem too soon after college.
Tom Masson, American humorist (1866–1934), quoted in *The Treasury of Humorous Quotations*, ed. by Evan Esar & Nicolas Bentley (1951).

FAMOUS LAST WORDS
Suggested death-bed utterances of the famous, all taken from the first series of BBC Radio Quote ... Unquote *(1976), and by various hands:*

1 Princess Anne (1950–) would say: 'One flew over the cuckoo's nest'.

2 John Logie Baird (1888–1946), Scottish inventor of television: 'I think I will just turn over and see if there is anything on the other side.'

3 Mrs Beeton (1836–65), household and cookery writer: 'I think I am just about done now.'

4 Alexander Graham Bell (1847–1922) would have said: 'Dead, dead . . . and never called me mother!'

5 Cleopatra (69–30 BC) would have said: 'It's the biggest asp-disaster in the world'.

6 General Franco, the Spanish dictator (1892–1975) should have said: 'Yes, we have no *mañanas*.'

7 Lenin (1870–1924) should have said: 'I was born under a squandering Tsar.'

8 William Pitt (1759–1806) should have said: 'Oh God! I think I have just eaten one of Bellamy's veal pies.'

He is usally credited with having said, 'I think I could eat one of Bellamy's veal pies'. This emendation was contributed to BBC Radio *Quote ... Unquote* (17 May 1978) by Charles Goulding of Maidenhead.

9 King Richard III (1452–85) should have said: 'A hearse, a hearse . . . my kingdom for a hearse!'

10 The Marquis de Sade (1740–1814) should have said: 'This is going to hurt me more than it hurts you.'

11 Madame Tussaud (1761–1850) should have said: 'Once I was waxing, now I am waning.'

12 Queen Victoria (1819–1901) should have said: 'The Empire's decision is funereal.'

FAMOUS MEETINGS

1 What would cricketer W.G. Grace (1848–1915) have said to Casanova?
Congratulations on your overnight stand.
Contributed by Peter Cook to BBC Radio *Quote ... Unquote* (22 February 1976).

2 What should Herod Antipas (d. AD 40) have said to Salome when she asked for John the Baptist's head on a platter?
Sorry, dear, brains are off.

3 What would Henri de Toulouse-Lautrec, the diminutive French painter (1864–1901), have said to Mae West?
Why don't you come down and see me some time?

FARTING

1 John Aubrey (1626–97) in his *Brief Lives* records that the Earl of Oxford, Edward de Vere, making of his low obeisance to

**Queen Elizabeth, happened to let out a fart, at which he was
so abashed and ashamed that he went to travel, seven years.
On his return the Queen welcomed him home and said: 'My
lord, we have forgot the fart.'**

According to Sophia Hardy Wilson, writing in the *Independent* Magazine (3 July
1993), 'there is a similar story in the *Arabian Nights*, but in this case the
traveller returns and meets a child and asks him how old he is, to which the
child replies: "I was born in the year of the Great Fart".'

FEMINIST JOKES

1 **In a world without men, there will be no crime and a lot of
happy, fat women.**

Attributed to one Marion Smith, this saying was the cause of legal action in the
US in 1994 when a cartoonist wished to sue a TV programme for lifting the
caption from one of her works. The programme was *Living Single*, a Fox
comedy series, first aired in August 1993. Presumably the cartoonist was Nicole
Hollander whose line 'Can you imagine a world without men? No crime and
lots of happy, fat women' had been anthologized and quoted before 1993.

2 **A woman without a man is like a fish without a bicycle.**

Mrs C. Raikes of Moseley, Birmingham contributed this to BBC Radio *Quote ...
Unquote* (1977), writing: 'I felt you had to share in this pearl of wisdom I found
yesterday on a lavatory wall in Birmingham University. Written in German, it
translates as . . .' Indeed, the chances are that the saying may have originated
in West Germany where it is known in the form, *'Eine Frau ohne Mann ist wie
ein Fisch ohne Velo!'* It has become one of the best known of feminist slogans.

Compare, however, what Arthur Bloch in *Murphy's Law . . .* (also 1977) calls'
'Vique's Law': 'A man without religion is like a fish without a bicycle.' On 8
January 1979, Arthur Marsall contributed the interesting variant: 'A woman
without a man is like a moose without a hatrack.' In Haan & Hammerstrom
Graffiti in the Big Ten (1981) is 'Behind every successful man is a fish with a
bicycle.'

3 **Men who put women on pedestals rarely knock them off.**

Graffito, quoted in Rachel Bartlett (ed.), *Off the Wall* (1982). Compare 'Men
put women on pedestals so they can look up their skirts' — graffito quoted in
Rennie Ellis & Ian Turner, *Australian Graffiti Revisited* (1979). And Woody Allen:
'It was partially my fault we got divorced. I had a tendency to place my wife
under a pedestal' — quoted in Bob Chieger, *Was It Good For You Too?* (1983).

4 **Mummy, mummy, what's an orgasm?
I dunno. Ask your father.**

Graffito, quoted in Rachel Bartlett (ed.), *Off the Wall* (1982). The following are
also from this source:

5 Jesus was a typical man – they always say they'll come back but you never see them again.

6 Equality is making him sleep in the wet patch.

7 How did you find yourself this morning?
   I just rolled back the sheets and there I was.

8 Look, Cinderella, maybe you should skip the ball and go to the consciousness-raising group instead.

9 Some day my prince will come, however I'll have nothing to do with it.

10 Why are girls called birds? Because they pick up worms.

11 All relationships are give and take. You give, he takes.

12 When all that is stiff is his socks, take the money and run.

13 **DISARM ALL RAPISTS**
    – it's not their arms I'm worried about.
    Included in Reisner & Wechsler, *Encyclopedia of Graffiti* (1974).

See also under DUMB MEN JOKES; LIGHT-BULB JOKES 7; WOMEN 1, 4.

FEUDALISM
1 Feudalism: it's your count that votes.
   In *Graffiti 4* (1982).

FEZ
1 An Egyptian met another Egyptian and said: 'I don't remember your name but your fez is familiar.'

FICTION
1 The author of this novel and all the characters mentioned in it are completely fictitious. There is no such city as Manchester.
   Prefatory note to *Shabby Tiger* (1934) by Howard Spring, British novelist (1889–1965).

FIRST WORLD WAR

1 **Archduke Franz Ferdinand found alive. First World War a mistake.**

Graffito contributed to BBC Radio *Quote ... Unquote* (29 January 1979) by John Butcher who said he saw it in the British Museum. Compare what Alan Clark, the British politician, wrote in his published *Diaries* (entry for 28 June 1983): 'I often think of that prize-winning spoof headline in the *New York Daily News* in 1920: "Archduke found alive, World War a Mistake".'

FLIRTS

1 **Flirt: a woman who thinks it's every man for herself.**

2 *To Bernard Shaw, after an empty flirtation:* **You had no right to write the preface if you were not going to write the book.**

Edith Nesbit, British writer (1858–1924).

FLOGGING

1 **I like sadism, necrophilia and bestiality. Am I flogging a dead horse?**

Included in *Graffiti Lives OK* (1979). The addition 'No, just an old joke' was included in *Graffiti 4* (1982).

FLOWERS

1 **A man forgot to buy his wife her favourite anemones on her birthday. The shop only had bits of greenery left, which he duly purchased. The forgiving wife was not the slightest bit put out by the modest gift: 'With fronds like these,' she exclaimed, 'who needs anemones?'**

Told in John Crosbie, *Crosbie's Dictionary of Puns* (1977).

FOOD

1 **It is said that Hell is where the food is British and the police are French. And Heaven is the other way about.**

Lord Bethell, British Conservative peer, quoted in 1990.

Compare EUROPEANS 1, 2.

FOOLS

1 **A fool and his money are some party.**

2 **Fools' names and fools' faces are always found in public places.**

Written after a list of graffitoed names. Reported by Nancy Dannevik of Los Angeles in *Graffiti 4* (1982). Also recorded in Haan & Hammerstrom *Graffiti in the PAC Ten* (1981).

3 **Are you trying to make a fool out of me? No, I never interfere with nature.**

Compare 'When he said we were trying to make a fool of him, I could only murmur that the Creator had beat us to it' — Ilka Chase, American actress and author (1905–), quoted in *The Treasury of Humorous Quotations*, ed. by Evan Esar & Nicolas Bentley (1951).

4 **Kenneth Williams, the British comedian, was taking part in a Christmas radio show in which a group of comedians challenged the intelligent participants of the *Brain of Britain* show. Williams wailed out loud: 'I don't want to look like a fool.' The chairman, Robert Robinson, commented: 'Nature has already seen to that.'**

Told by Williams on BBC Radio *Quote ... Unquote* (12 June 1980).

FOOT-IN-MOUTH DISEASE

The phrase 'to put one's foot in it', meaning to make a gaffe, an awkward mistake, was established by the early 19th century. But what precisely is the 'it' into which one is putting the foot? In the 20th century, it became clear that it was one's mouth. 'Every time he opens his mouth at the Town Hall, he puts his foot in it, so they call him "the foot and mouth disease". Ha. Ha.' – J.B. Priestley, When We Are Married *(1938). '"Dentopedology" is the science of opening your mouth and putting your foot in it. I've been practising it for years' – Prince Philip, quoted in Prochnow and Prochnow,* A Treasury of Humorous Quotations *(1969). I prefer to call it foot-in-mouth disease.*

1 **A former headmaster of Llandovery College said the following in a prayer during morning assembly many years ago: 'Bless us in our intercourse, be it for business or pleasure . . .'**

Contributed to *Foot in Mouth* (1982) by John Jenkins, Llandovery.

2 **'My mother was notoriously bad at remembering names. One year at a seaside boarding house, Father suggested she should memorize some everyday word which rhymed with the name she wanted to remember. For a lady whose name was**

Crummock, Father suggested "stomach". Next day, as this dignified lady entered the dining room, Mother paused a moment for thought and then chirped happily: "Good morning, Mrs Kelly!"'

Contributed to the same collection by Sylvia Torkington, Stockport.

3 'As a young girl I was introduced by a friend at a party to a formidable (to me – terrifying) uncle of his. Proud at least to have remembered his name I said ingratiatingly, "How do you do, Mr Todd." A moment's awful silence ensued. Then my friend said: "Actually, it's Sweeney".'

Contributed to the same collection by Kathleen Newell, Chigwell.

FOREIGN OFFICE

1 A man was standing at the top of Whitehall asking a policeman for directions. 'Can you tell me which side the Foreign Office is on?'

   Replied the policeman, 'Ours, I should hope.'

FREE —— JOKES

In the 1970s particularly, a number of campaigning slogans written up as graffiti were of the 'Free ——' or 'Free the —— (+ number)' variety. This led to additional scrawls and to the invention of other numerical groups whose freedom was being demanded.

1 **FREE WALES**
  – with every five gallons.

A Welsh nationalist slogan from next to a filling station. Contributed to BBC Radio Quote ... *Unquote* (19 April 1978) by Neil Kinnock MP from his (then) Bedwelty constituency.

2 **FREE WALES**
  – who from? What for?

Included in *Graffiti Lives OK* (1979).

3 **FREE WALES**
  – from the Welsh.

From Newport, included in *Graffiti 3* (1981).

4 **FREE GEORGE DAVIS**
  – with every packet of cornflakes/gallon of petrol.

Included in *Graffiti Lives OK* (1979). In 1975, George Davis was given a seventeen-year prison sentence for taking part in a robbery and for wounding with intent to avoid arrest. Those who believed in his innocence wrote 'Free George Davis now' and 'George Davis is innocent, OK' all over the East End of London. The campaign was taken up elsewhere and in May 1976 Davis was released from prison but not pardoned. In July 1978 he was sentenced to fifteen years' gaol for his part in a subsequent bank robbery.

5 **Free collective bargaining – he's innocent.**
Graffito from Oxford, contributed to BBC Radio *Quote ... Unquote* (14 August 1980) by Chris Robinson.

6 **Free the Beethoven 9.**
Spotted by A.R. Burrett in 1983 at a pub used by musicians of the Amsterdam Concertgebouw.

7 **Free the Grecian 2000.**

8 **Free the Heinz 57.**
Contributed to BBC Radio *Quote ... Unquote* (5 February 1979) by Phil Abel of London N10, who saw it at Alexandra Palace.

9 **Free the Indianapolis 500.**
Contributed to the same edition by Rev Ian Cooper of Sunbury-on-Thames.

10 **Free the Intercity 125.**
Graffito from near Paddington station, contributed to BBC Radio *Quote ... Unquote* (14 August 1980) by Roger Price of London SE17.

11 **Free the Renault Five now.**
Reported from Ireland (June 1990).

12 **Free the UB40.**

13 **FREE ASTRID PROLL**
– no thank you, I've got two already.
On Granada TV *Cabbages and Kings* (18 November 1979). Proll, a suspected German Baader-Meinhof terrorist, was arrested in London in September 1978.

14 **FREE WOMEN!**
– where?!
Slogan and graffitoed addition, contributed by Rachael Heyhoe Flint to Granada TV *Cabbages and Kings* (15 July 1979). Also contributed as seen in Edinburgh to BBC Radio *Quote ... Unquote* (7 August 1980) by Charles Milne of Glenrothes, Fife.

FREEDOM
1 *Escaped prisoner:* **'I'm free, I'm free!'**
   Little boy: **'That's nothing, I'm four.'**

FRENCH, THE
1 **If the French won't buy our lamb, we won't use their letters.**
   Written on the back of a British motorway juggernaut during the 'Lamb War',
   1980. Included in *Graffiti 3* (1981).

2 **How ghastly the British were to France. Look what they did to
   Joan of Arc. When they were asked why they had burned
   Joan of Arc, they replied: 'We were cold.'**
   Contributed by Arthur Marshall to BBC Radio *Quote ... Unquote* (29 January 1979).

FREUDIAN SLIPS
*This sort of thing occurs when, by seeming to make a mere verbal error,
we give away our real intentions – as when a host offering to take a female
guest's coat, says: 'Can I take your clothes off?'*

1 **I recall a delightful moment in 1973 when watching a court-
   room scene in a show called** *Is Your Doctor Really Necessary?*
   **at the Theatre Royal, Stratford East, London. The judge was
   addressing three leggy ladies who were the cause of much
   distraction in the court. But the actor playing the judge
   stumbled over his lines and declared roundly (corpsing the cast
   in the process), 'Stop clittering up the court!'**

FRIENDS
1 **There is no spectacle more agreeable than to observe an old
   friend fall from a roof-top.**
   Sometimes it is a 'neighbour': 'Even a virtuous and high-minded man may
   experience a little pleasure when he sees his neighbour falling from a roof.'
   The earliest citation to hand dates only from 1970. One suspects that, like so
   many other 'Confucian' sayings, it has nothing whatever to do with the Chinese
   philosopher who, nevertheless, undoubtedly did exist and who did say a number
   of wise things (some through his followers). Even when not prefaced by
   'Confucius, he say . . .' there is a tendency – particularly in the US – to ascribe
   any wry saying to him. With regard to this one, similar thoughts have occurred
   to others: 'Philosophy may teach us to bear with equanimity the misfortunes of
   our neighbours' – Oscar Wilde, *The English Renaissance of Art* (1882); 'I am
   convinced that we have a degree of delight, and that no small one, in the real

misfortunes and pains of others' — Edmund Burke, *On the Sublime and Beautiful* (1756); and, especially, as David Cottis of London SW15 and others have pointed out: 'In the misfortune of our best friends, we find something that is not displeasing to us [*Dans l'adversité de nos meilleurs amis, nous trouvons toujours quelque chose qui ne nous déplaît pas*]' — Duc de la Rochefoucauld (1665).

FROGS

1 **Q. What is red and green and goes 500 miles per hour? A. A frog in a blender.**
In Haan & Hammerstrom Graffiti in the *Big Ten* (1981).

2 **Q. What's green and goes red at the flick of a switch? A. Kermit in a liquidizer.**
Told by Daniel Waring, Plymouth (1986).

3 **You have to kiss an awful lot of frogs before you find a prince.**
Graffito contributed to BBC Radio *Quote ... Unquote* (5 June 1979) by Prue Philip of Sheffield.

FROZEN

1 **MANY ARE COLD, BUT FEW ARE FROZEN.**
T-shirt available in the US, 1982. Included in Reisner & Wechsler, *Encyclopedia of Graffiti* (1974).

See also ESKIMOS 1.

FUNERALS

1 *On the large number of mourners at film producer Harry Cohn's funeral:* **'Same old story: you give 'em what they want and they'll fill the theatre.'**
George Jessell, American entertainer (1898–1981) — quoted in L. Hellman, *Scoundrel Time* (1976). Has also been attributed to Red Skelton. An unattributed version appears in Oscar Levant, *The Unimportance of Being Oscar* (1968).

2 **There is nothing like a morning funeral for sharpening the appetite for lunch.**
Arthur Marshall, *Life's Rich Pageant* (1984).

3 **One old man greeted another with the words, 'Hello, George, I thought you were dead.' The other old man replied firmly,**

'No, I'm not dead.' So the first old man said, 'If you're not dead, whose funeral did I go to in February?'

Contributed by Donald Beman of London SW1 to BBC Radio *Quote ... Unquote* (20 July 1985).

F-WORD, THE

1 **Q. Why do people write 'F*** the Pope' on toilet walls?**
   A. Because they can't be bothered to write 'F* the Moderator of the General Assembly of the Church of Scotland.'**

Contributed by Stewart Gellatly of Edinburgh to *Graffiti 3* (1981).

2 **Fighting for peace is like f****** for virginity.**

From Covent Garden in 1978, included in *Graffiti Lives OK* (1979).

FURS

1 **The first wearer of your fur coat died in it.**

Slogan at an anti-seal-hunting rally, reported by Joan Bakewell on BBC Radio *Quote ... Unquote* (5 April 1978).

2 **I'VE GOT WHAT EVERY WOMAN WANTS.**
   – oh, I suppose you're in the fur coat business.

In *Graffiti 4* (1982).

G...

GAYS *See HOMOSEXUALS.*

GENERALIZATIONS

1 **All good generalizations are false, including this one.**

GENES

1 **I have nothing to declare but my genes.**

Included in *Graffiti 2* (1980).

2 **Nuclear waste fades your genes.**
Photographed by Chris Furby included in Graffiti 3 (1981).

3 **Q. How can you tell the sex of a chromosome?**
A. By taking down its genes.
From Oxford, included in *Graffiti 2* (1980).

GENITALS

1 **Genitals prefer blondes.**
From New York City, included in Reisner & Wechsler, *Encyclopedia of Graffiti* (1974).

2 *Written below light switch in lavatory:* **'A light to lighten the genitals.'**
From Oxford, included in *Graffiti Lives OK* (1979).

See ALITALIA 2.

GENTLEMEN

1 **A gentleman knows how to play the accordion, but doesn't.**
Attributed to Al Cohn, the American saxophonist (1925–88).

2 **GENTLEMEN LIFT THE SEAT**
– not you Momma, sit down.
Included in *Graffiti Lives OK* (1979). The injunction that used to be found in lavatories ('that marvellously unpunctuated motto', as Jonathan Miller said in *Beyond the Fringe*, 1961, 'or perhaps it's a loyal toast?!') coupled with what you saw written underneath when you complied (a catchphrase from Ben Lyon, the American entertainer).

GEOGRAPHY

A special category of SCHOOLBOY HOWLERS from the geography classroom. The HOWLERS here were collected by Mr D.F. of the University of Manchester School of Education (December 1990), though several of them are quite widely known.

1 **The benefit of longitude and latitude is that when a man is drowning he can call out what latitude and longtitude he is, and we can find him.**

2 **A virgin forest is a forest in which the hand of man has never set foot.**

3 The only signs of life in the tundra are a few stunted corpses.

4 Tundras are the treeless forests of South America.

5 **Q.** Name six animals peculiar to Arctic regions.
A. Three bears and three seals.

6 The cold at the North Pole is so great that the towns there are not inhabited.

7 Zanzibar is noted for its monkeys. The British Governor lives there.

8 The people of Japan ride about in jigsaws.

9 The climate of Bombay is such that its inhabitants have to live elsewhere.

10 People go about Venice in gorgonzolas.

11 Floods from the Mississippi may be prevented by putting big dames in the river.

GOD

1 Not only is there no God, but try getting a plumber on weekends.

Woody Allen, 'My Philosophy', *Getting Even* (1975).

2 To the lexicographer, God is simply the word that comes next to go-cart.

Samuel Butler, English writer (1835–1902), quoted in *The Treasury of Humorous Quotations*, ed. by Evan Esar & Nicolas Bentley (1951).

3 GOD IS ALIVE. SPEAK TO HIM.
– it's cheaper after six.

From Sydney Opera House, reported by John Richard Dadson of Loughton, Essex (1983).

4 When God made man she was only testing.

Graffito in North Kensington. Contributed to BBC Radio *Quote ... Unquote* (26 April 1978) and photographed by Brian Sutton of London W11.

5 When God made man she was having one of her off days.

From Covent Garden, in *Graffiti 4* (1982).

6 **WHEN GOD MADE MAN SHE WAS ONLY JOKING**
– and woman was the punchline.
From Birmingham, contributed by S.D. Wain of Aldridge to *Graffiti 4* (1982).

7 **God may be dead, but 50,000 social workers have risen to take his place.**
In Haan & Hammerstrom *Graffiti in the Big Ten* (1981).

8 **God is good, E & OE.**
From Kano, Nigeria, in *Graffiti 4* (1982). (E & OE is the trade term for 'Errors and Omissions Excepted.)

9 **The country vicar was congratulating a man from the village who had created a wonderful garden out of a rubbish tip: 'Ah, it's wonderful what God can do in a garden with a little help.' To which the gardener replied: 'But you should have seen it when 'E had it to 'Imself.'**
Story told by Bernard Miles, and recounted by his daughter Sally on BBC Radio *Quote ... Unquote* (27 October 1984). Surely it must have been a *Punch* cartoon caption once upon a time?

10 **Sudden prayers make God jump.**
Contributed by Barry Cryer to BBC Radio *Quote ... Unquote* (8 January 1979), but said to have appeared in the *Sunday Times* (July 1977).

11 **Q. What is the difference between God and Professor ——?**
A. God is here but everywhere. Professor —— is everywhere but here.
From the University of East Anglia, included in *Graffiti 3* (1981).

12 **God is dead – Nietzsche.**
Nietzsche is dead – God.
Included in *Graffiti Lives OK* (1979), but also in Reisner & Wechsler, *Encyclopedia of Graffiti* (1974).

13 **God was a woman – until she changed her mind.**
Included in *Graffiti Lives OK* (1979).

14 **GOD WILL PROVIDE**
– only God knows if there is a god.
– God knows if there is a god.
From Birmingham, included in *Graffiti 3* (1981).

15 **God made animals great and small, some that slither and some that crawl, and Rochester police employ them all.**
At Strood, included in *Graffiti 2* (1980). Compare BRITISH RAIL 11.

16 **'Mum, does God use our bathroom?'**
'No, why on earth should he do that?'
'Because Dad was standing outside the door this morning, asking "My God, are you still in there?"'
Included in *Babes and Sucklings* (1983).

17 **Q. What is the difference between God and Santa Claus?**
A. There is a Santa Claus.
Included in Reisner & Wechsler, *Encyclopedia of Graffiti* (1974).

18 **IN SIX DAYS THE LORD MADE HEAVEN AND EARTH, THE SEA AND ALL THAT IN THEM IS**
– he was self-employed.
Added to church poster, Essex, included in *Graffiti 3* (1981).

19 **God is not dead – he just couldn't find a place to park.**
Included in *Graffiti Lives OK* (1979), previously in Reisner & Wechsler, *Encyclopedia of Graffiti* (1974).

20 **God is not dead, but alive and well and working on a much less ambitious project.**
Graffito from Muswell Hill contributed by Maureen Lipman to Granada TV *Cabbages and Kings* (22 July 1979).

21 **God is not dead – merely out to lunch.**
Contributed by Philip H. Turner to *Graffiti 2* (1980).

22 **GOD IS BLACK**
– yes, she is.
Included in *Graffiti 2* (1980). Compare 'J'ai vu Dieu – il etait noir. Il etait femme' – from Paris (1978)

23 **GOD IS DEAD**
– Oh no I'm not!
The rejoinder was written in large Gothic letters. Contributed to BBC Radio *Quote ... Unquote* (3 May 1978) by Spike Milligan.

24 **PREPARE TO MEET THY GOD**
– evening dress optional.
Slogan and graffitoed addition on bridge over the A1. Described on Granada TV *Cabbages and Kings* (15 July 1979).

25 **The trouble with God is he thinks he's Peter Hall.**
Contributed by Ian McKellen to BBC Radio *Quote ... Unquote* (19 June 1979).
Compare the joke related by George Orwell in a footnote to a 'London Letter'
to the *Partisan Review* (17 April 1944): 'Stories are told of Eisenhower [and]
Montgomery interchangeably. For example: Three doctors who had just died
arrived at the gates of Heaven. The first two, a physician and a surgeon, were
refused admittance. The third described himself as a psychiatrist. "Come in!"
said St Peter immediately. "We should like your professional advice. God has
been behaving in a very peculiar way lately. He thinks He's General
Eisenhower (or Montgomery)".'

GOD'S INTENTIONS
*'If God had intended us to —— he would have given us the ——' is a
format phrase presented as a reason for not doing something or to explain
why something is the way it is. As formats go, it has been going for a long
time.*

1 **'My [model flying machine] elicited a reproof from the
Headmaster, who happened to see it [c. 1893]. "Men," he
said, "were never meant to fly; otherwise God would have
given them wings." The argument was convincing, if not striking,
having been used previously, if I am not mistaken, by Mr
Chadband.'**
Lord Berners, *First Childhood* (1934). Well, sort of: in *Bleak House*, Chap. 19
(1853), Charles Dickens writes: '[Chadband] "Why can't we not fly, my friends?"
[Mr Snagsby] "No wings".'

2 **My mother says if God had intended men to smoke He'd have
put chimneys in their heads.**
From Act II of J.B. Priestley's play *When We Are Married* (1938). And from the
same source:

3 **Tell your mother from me that if God had intended men to
wear clothes He'd have put collar studs at back of their necks.**
Obviously linked to these: Michael Grosvenor Myer of Cambridge recalled
(1994): 'A friend of my far-off youth, informed by a friend-of-her-parents
busybody that 'if God had meant us to smoke he'd have put chimneys in our
heads', rejoined that 'had He intended us to wear clothes he'd have given us
fur.'

4 **If God had intended us to fly, he'd never have given us the
railways.**
Michael Flanders in the revue *At the Drop of Another Hat* (1963).

5 **If God had meant us to travel tourist class He would have made us narrower.**
Martha Zimmerman, American air hostess, quoted in the *Wall Street Journal* (1977).

6 **If God had not meant us to write on walls, he would never have given us the example.**
Included in *Graffiti 2* (1980).

7 **If God had intended Jewish women to exercise, he'd have put diamonds on the floor.**
Attributed to Joan Rivers.

8 **If God had intended them to be lifted and separated, he would have put one on each shoulder.**
Scarborough radio DJ Gregg Scott reminded me (1994) of what comedienne Victoria Wood once said of a slogan used to promote Playtex 'cross-your-heart' bras.

9 **I always said, if God had meant us to fly, he'd have given me guts.**
In the final chapter of David Lodge's novel, *Changing Places* (1975), 'Morris Zapp' comments thus, after a close air miss.

10 **If God had intended us to fly, He would have sent us tickets.**
Attributed to Mel Brooks by Frederic Raphael in 1994.

GOLDWYNISMS

As Samuel Goldwyn (1882–1974) himself once declared, 'Goldwynisms! Don't talk to me about Goldwynisms. Talk to Jesse Lasky!' But the Polish-born film mogul's life-long struggle with the English language deserves a place in a book like this. Some of the ones least likely to be genuine (they used to run competitions to invent them . . .):

1 **We can get all the Indians we need at the reservoir.**

2 **Too caustic? To hell with the cost, we'll make the picture anyway.**

3 **It's spreading like wildflowers!**

4 **Who wants to go out and see a bad movie when they can stay at home and see a bad one for free on TV?**

5 **We have all passed a lot of water since then.**

6 Going to call him William? What kind of a name is that? Every Tom, Dick and Harry's called William. Why don't you call him Bill?

7 Yes, my wife's hands are very beautiful. I'm going to have a bust made of them.

8 Why only *twelve* disciples? Go out and get thousands!

9 If you can't give me your word of honour, will you give me your promise?

10 I would be sticking my head in a moose.

11 I read part of the book all the way through.

12 You ought to take the bull between the teeth.

13 Anyone who goes to a psychiatrist needs to have his head examined.

14 I'll give you a definite maybe.

15 First, you have a good story, then a good treatment, and next a first-rate director. After that you hire a competent cast and even then you have only the mucus of a good picture.

16 This makes me so sore, it gets my dandruff up.

17 The A-bomb — that's dynamite!

18 Let's bring it up to date with some snappy 19th-century dialogue.

19 Tell me, how did you love the picture?

20 I don't remember where I got this new Picasso. In Paris, I think. Somewhere over there on the Left Wing.

21 That's my Toujours Lautrec.

22 You just don't realize what life is all about until you have found yourself lying on the brink of a great abscess.

23 This is written in blank werse.

24 I want you to be sure and see my *Hans Christian Anderson*. It's full of charmth and warmth.

See also CLICHÉS 2.

GOOD NEWS/BAD NEWS JOKES

I expect these first arose in the 1960s. They have a precise structure with the 'good news' often (though not invariably) being given first. Then the 'bad news' happily negates the 'good news'.

1   The German concentration camp commandant ordered his prisoners to gather round and stand before him. 'I hef zom good nooss and some bed nooss,' he barked. 'Fust, the good nooss. You are to leave this kemp! You vill be free! Half of you are to be sent to England and half of you are to be sent to ze United States. End now ze bed nooss! Ze top half of you is to be sent to England, ze bottom half is to be sent to the United States!'

Sorry about this. I think I heard it in the 1960s.

2   Bad weather forced a plane to keep on circling over the airfield. Finally, the pilot announced over the P.A. system: 'Ladies and gentlemen, I have some bad news and some good news. The bad news is that we are running out of fuel. The good news is that I am parachuting down to get help.'

Included in *The Best of 606 Aggie Jokes* (1988).

3   Doctor to patient: 'I've got some good news and some bad news. The bad news is that we've got to amputate both your legs. The good news is that the guy in the next bed wants to buy your slippers.'

Told by Lenny Henry in *Lenny Henry Live* at the Hackney Empire, reported in the *Independent* (25 January 1989), but old even then.

4   Moses was sent by the Israelites to the top of Mount Sinai to negotiate with God over the Commandments. He came down exhausted after ten days with a list of 310 Commandments. The Israelites angrily sent him back to negotiate a better deal. Three more days passed before a gaunt Moses reappeared: 'I have some good news and some bad news,' he said. 'The good news is I've got the list down to ten. The bad news is that adultery is still in.'

Retold in the *Financial Times* (2 April 1992).

5   There was a 'good news, bad news' joke about a starving army in the desert. The bad news was that there was only

camel dung to eat. The good news was that there was plenty
of it.

Told in *Today* (23 June 1992).

6 A bishop called all the clergymen in his diocese together. 'I've
got some good news and I've got some bad news,' he told
them. 'The good news is I spoke to God the other day and
everything's OK. The bad news is She called me from Salt
Lake City.'

7 Commenting on the leadership style of President Clinton, a
journalist put it this way: the good news is that America finally
has a feminine leader. The bad news is that she's a man.

In the *Guardian* (18 March 1993).

8 The death of a political leader *can* be kept quiet. The
amazingly protracted demise of General Franco led to a nice
joke which told of someone asking Prince Juan Carlos of Spain,
the heir-in-waiting, whether he wanted the good news or the
bad news. 'Tell me the good news,' he said. 'Franco ' dead,'
came the reply. 'What's the bad news?' asked Juan Carlos.
'You will have to tell him.'

Told in Jerrold M. Post & Robert S. Robins, *When Illness Strikes the Leader*
(1993).

9 The bad news is I left my electric toothbrush running all night.
The good news is the bathroom is now absolutely spotless.

···

GOODNESS

1 When I'm good, I'm very, very good. But when I'm bad, I'm
better.

Mae West, in the film *I'm No Angel* (US, 1933).

2 *Replying to the exclamation 'Goodness, what beautiful
diamonds'*: 'Goodness had nothing to do with it, dearie.'

Mae West, in the film *Night After Night* (US, 1932) — script by Vincent Laurence
from the novel by Louis Bromfield.

···

GOVERNMENT

1 Don't vote. The Government will get in.

From Oxford, included in *Graffiti Lives OK* (1979).

2 **These days govt is a four-letter word.**
From San Francisco, included in Reisner & Wechsler, *Encyclopedia of Graffiti* (1974).

See also ELECTIONS.

GRANDPARENTS

1 **The old woman had been going on a bit, so when she asked, 'Have I ever told you about my lovely grandchildren?', one of the listeners replied, 'No – and I may say how truly grateful we are that you haven't?'**

GRAFFITI

1 **When the British 1870 Education Act became law, extending the benefits of teaching to more and more young people, an MP commented that, 'the chief effect will be that graffiti will be more numerous, better written . . . and lower down.'**
According to A.J. Wood of Pitsford, Northampton. Contributed to BBC Radio *Quote ... Unquote* (24 May 1978).

2 **Graffiti is for people who can't write books.**
In Haan & Hammerstrom *Graffiti in the Big Ten* (1981).

3 **Carved on blackboard supplied for graffiti in pub: 'Where's the bloody chalk then?'**
From Barnet, included in *Graffiti 2* (1980).

4 **Graffiti is the curse of the cleaning classes.**
From Leeds, in *Graffiti 4* (1982).

5 **I hate graffiti. I hate all Italian food.**
Contributed to BBC Radio *Quote ... Unquote* (19 April 1978) by M.R. Turner of Guernsey.

6 **The views expressed on this wall are not necessarily those of Aberystwyth Urban District Council.**
Included in *Graffiti 2* (1980).

7 **This door will shortly appear in paperback.**
Graffito inscribed at the bottom of a marvellous collection of international graffiti in a public lavatory opposite the Royal Shakespeare Theatre in

Stratford-upon-Avon. Contributed to BBC Radio *Quote ... Unquote* (10 May 1978) by Christine Daniels (then aged 15) of Cleethorpes, South Humberside.

8 **Say no to London's third aerosol.**
Graffito contributed by Alan Coren to Granada TV *Cabbages and Kings* (18 November 1979).

GRASS
1 **Grass is nature's way of saying, 'High'!**
From Radcliffe Station, Manchester, included in *Graffiti 2* (1980).

2 **If you can remember the Sixties, you weren't there.**

GRAVES
1 **The grass is always greener on the other fellow's grave.**
Graffito said to come from a cemetery in Lewisham. Contributed by Spike Milligan to BBC Radio *Quote ... Unquote* (12 April 1978).

GRAVESTONES *See EPITAPHS.*

GREAT MAN JOKES
The expression to the effect that 'behind every great (or successful) man is a great woman' has given rise to any number of joke variations. Working backwards:

1 **As usual there's a great woman behind every idiot.**
John Lennon, quoted in 1979.

2 **Behind every successful man you'll find a woman who has nothing to wear.**
L. Grant Glickman, quoted 1977, or James Stewart, quoted 1979.

3 **We in the industry know that behind every successful screenwriter stands a woman. And behind her stands his wife.**
Groucho Marx, quoted in 1977.

4 **The road to success is filled with women pushing their husbands along.**
Lord Thomas R. Dewar, quoted in 1967.

5 **And behind every man who is a *failure* there's a woman, too!**
John Ruge, cartoon caption, *Playboy* (March 1967).

6 **Behind every successful man stands a surprised mother-in-law.**
Hubert Humphrey, in a speech, 1964. Attributed to Brooks Hays in the
form 'Back of every achievement is a proud wife and a surprised
mother-in-law' in Herbert V. Prochnow Snr & Jnr, *A Treasury of Humorous
Quotations* (1969).

7 **Every great man has a woman behind him . . . And every
great woman has some man or other in front of her, tripping
her up.**
In *Love All*, a little-known play by Dorothy L. Sayers which opened at the Torch
Theatre, Knightsbridge, London on 9 April 1940 and closed before the end of
the month.

8 **Behind every great woman is a man telling her she's ignoring
him.**
Included in Nan Tucket, *The Dumb Men Joke Book* (Volume II, 1994). Just for
contrast.

See also FEMINIST JOKES 2.

GREETINGS
1 **Every time Mr Macmillan comes back from abroad Mr Butler
goes to the airport and grips him warmly by the throat.**
Said by Harold Wilson, obviously before 1963 when Harold Macmillan
resigned as British Prime Minister. In the 1964 Broadway version of *Beyond
the Fringe*, the Duke of Edinburgh was given the similar line, 'I was very
well received [in Kenya, at independence]. Mr Kenyatta himself came to
the airport to greet me and shook me warmly by the throat as I got off the
plane.'

GRILS
1 **I LOVE GRILS**
  – You mean girls, stupid!
  – What about us grils?
Contributed to BBC Radio *Quote ... Unquote* (21 June 1978) by Richard Boston.
A version is included in Reisner & Wechsler, *Encyclopedia of Graffiti* (1974).

GROCERS

1 It was most unfortunate when the grocer's assistant fell backwards into the bacon slicer. You see, everyone got a little behind with their order.
Current by the 1920s?

GUERRILLAS

1 **Q.** What do you call a 6'6" Angolan guerrilla with a sub-machine-gun and six hand grenades?
A. Sir!
Included in *Graffiti 3* (1981).

GYNAECOLOGIST

1 Did you hear about the gynaecologist who papered the hall through the letterbox?
From a pub near Charing Cross hospital. Observed by Neil Kinnock (1982).

2 **Gynaecologists, look up a friend today.**
Quoted in Bruce Ridley (ed.), *Wall Flowers: A Collection of Australian Graffiti* (1981).

GREEN ISSUES

1 KEEP AUSTRALIA GREEN
– have sex with a frog.
From Sydney, Australia, included in *Graffiti 3* (1981).

HALEY, BILL
American musician and bandleader (1926–81).

1 **Q.** How did Bill Haley die?
A. He fell off the mantelpiece while trying to rock around the clock.
From Hertford, Herts. (1981).

HALITOSIS
1 **Halitosis is better than no breath at all.**
Included in *Graffiti 2* (1980).

2 **Oh! that halitosis. It's so thick – a greyhound couldn't jump it.**
Sir Cecil Beaton on the halitosis of Professor Tancred Borenius, quoted in
Hugo Vickers, *Cecil Beaton* (1985).

HANDS
1 **No hand signals – the driver of this vehicle is a convicted Arab
shoplifter.**
Car sticker included in *Graffiti 2* (1980).

2 **No hand signals. They're busy.**
Car sticker included in *Graffiti 5* (1986).

3 **The future of Scotland is in your hands.**
Male lavatorial graffito included in *Graffiti Lives OK* (1979). This joke
dates back to the days when 'Your future is in your hands' was used as a
slogan for the British Conservative Party in the 1950 General Election.
The Conservatives were returned to power under Winston Churchill the
following year. Churchill himself had used the idea in an address to
Canadian troops aboard RMS *Queen Elizabeth* in January 1946: 'Our future
is in our hands. Our lives are what we choose to make of them.' The
slogan led to the inevitable lavatorial joke, as in Keith Waterhouse,
Billy Liar (1959): '"No writing mucky words on the walls!" he called. I did
not reply. Stamp began quoting, "*Gentlemen, you have the future of England
in your hands*".'

HECKLERS
1 **A young Conservative politician was being given a hard time
at a rowdy public meeting. At one point in his speech,
exasperated by all the interruptions, he exclaimed, 'I can
hardly hear myself speak.'**
    A voice from the crowd cried, 'You're not missing much'
Recounted by Ian Hislop on BBC Radio *Quote ... Unquote* (27 July 1985).

HELL *See EUROPEANS.*

HENRY VIII, KING
English sovereign (1491–1547).

1 A London Transport poster showed Henry VIII buying a ticket
and saying, 'A return to the Tower [of London], please.'
Underneath, someone had added: 'And a single for the wife.'
Graffito contributed to BBC Radio Quote ... Unquote (7 June 1978) by J.H.
Langton of Grimsby.

See also HISTORY 6, 7, 11.

HERNIA
1 Join the Hernia Society — it needs your support.
Graffito contributed by Rachael Heyhoe Flint to Granada TV *Cabbages and
Kings* (6 June 1979).

HERPES
1 **Q. What is the difference between herpes and true love?
A. Herpes lasts forever.**
From New York City, included in *Graffiti 5* (1986).

2 I'VE GOT HERMES
– surely you mean *herpes*?
– NO, I'M THE CARRIER.
Included in *Graffiti 5* (1986).

HESITATION
1 He who hesitates has lost the parking spot.
From Australia, in *Graffiti 4* (1982).

HITLER, ADOLF
German Nazi leader (1889–1945).

1 The jazz musician Bobby Hackett was noted for never having a
bad word to say about anybody. He said of Hitler, 'Well, he
was the best in the field.'
Told in *Jazz Anecdotes* (ed. Bill Crow, 1991).

HISTORY

A special category of SCHOOLBOY HOWLERS from the history classroom.

1 **After Queen Elizabeth had got safely across the puddle on which Raleigh had put his cloak, she said: 'I am afraid I have soiled your coat.' Raleigh replied in French, 'Mon Dieu et mon droit' which means 'My God, you're right!'**
Related on BBC Radio Quote ... Unquote (8 February 1976). Not surprisingly, something of the sort is also to be found in Sellar and Yeatman, *1066 and All That*, Chap. XVII (1930): 'Blondin eventually found [King Richard I] by singing the memorable song . . . called "O Richard et mon Droit" ("Are you right, there, Richard?")'

2 **The Romans did not conquer Whales because they did not understand what the welsh were saying.**
Included in *Foot in Mouth* (1982).

3 **The Black Hole of Calcutta was when two hundred English soldiers were locked up in a tiny room with a little widow with a very small hole . . . and in the morning most of them were dead!**
Same source, as also the following:

4 **And Sir Francis Drake said: 'Let the Armada wait. My bowels can't.'**

5 **Queen Elizabeth knitted Sir Walter Raleigh on the deck.**

6 **Henry VIII always had difficulty getting Catherine of Aragon pregnant.**

7 **Henry VIII's wives — Chattering of Aragon, Amber Lin, Jane Saymore, Ann of Cloves, Catherine Purr.**

8 **The Pope was inflammable.**

9 **Viking ships could sail up rivers because they had hoars.**

10 **Suffragettes were things the Germans shot under water to kill the British in the First World War.**

11 **After his divorce from Catherine of Aragon, Henry VIII married Anne Boleyn, and Archbishop Cranmer consummated the marriage.**
Included in *Say No More!* (1987).

12 **Queen Elizabeth I never had any peace of mind because Mary Queen of Scots was always hoovering in the background.**
Told by Jilly Cooper by 1984.

13 **Pompeii was destroyed by an overflow of saliva from the Vatican.**
Contributed to BBC Radio *Quote ... Unquote* (15 December 1981) by Mr K.F. Banner of Crowborough.

14 **It is important to study history in order that we may learn all about our descendants.**
This and the rest of the howlers in this section were collected by Mr D.F. of the University of Manchester School of Education (December 1990):

15 **In Sparta, all boys who were not able to walk were killed when born.**

16 **Alexander the Great entered Troy disguised as a wooden horse.**

17 **Julius Caesar was murdered by the Ides of March. As he was dying he looked up and said: 'You two brutes!'**

18 **Write all you know about Nero . . .
The less said about Nero the better.**

19 **Nero was a cruel emperor of Rome. He was a great artist, but was so cruel he killed himself to keep from being killed.**

20 **The Romans didn't like the early Christians because they wouldn't go to gladiola fights or burn insects before the Emperor's statue.**

21 **William Tell shot an arrow through an apple while standing on his son's head.**

22 **The Edict of Nantes was a law passed by Louis XIV forbidding all births, marriages and deaths in France for a period of one year.**

23 **The French Revolution was caused by overcharging taxies.**

24 **Give King Alfred's views on modern life had he been alive today.
If Alfred had survived to the present day he would be such an exceedingly old man that his views on any subject would be quite worthless.**

25 In the Middle Ages, the monks were very good men. They went into peoples' houses and helped everyone, doing every man's work. About this time, the population of England increased threefold.

26 About this time King Henry went mad and bore a son.

27 Mary, Queen of Scots, was playing golf with her husband when news was brought to her of the birth of her son and heir.

28 Queen Elizabeth was a very wise, good queen and so she never married.

29 Drake was playing bowls when he was told the Invisible Armada was in sight.

30 The Long Parliament said that no persons were to be beheaded without their consent.

31 Queen Victoria was the only queen who sat on a thorn for 63 years.

32 The Natchez Indians rose up and massaged all the French at Fort Rosalie.

33 General Braddock was killed in the French and Indian war. He had three horses shot under him and a forth went through his clothes.

34 Hardships suffered by the southerners after the Civil War: the wives of the aristocrats and of the gentle birth patiently made their husbands' trousers out of their own.

HOLLYWOOD

1 Hollywood is a place where people from Iowa mistake themselves for [movie] stars.

Attributed to Fred Allen, US comedian (1894–1956), in Maurice Zolotow, *No People Like Show People* (1951).

2 Strip the phoney tinsel off Hollywood and you'll find the real tinsel underneath.

Attributed to Oscar Levant, US pianist and actor (1906–72), in the early 1940s. In Flexner, *Listening to America* (1982).

3 Working for Warner Bros is like f****** a porcupine; it's a hundred pricks against one.

Wilson Mizner, quoted in David Niven, *Bring on the Empty Horses* (1975).

4 **[Hollywood is] a trip through a sewer in a glass-bottomed boat.**
Attributed to Wilson Mizner by Alva Johnston, *The Legenday Mizners* (1953).

HOME
1 **Home is where the television is.**
From Covent Garden, London, in *Graffiti 4* (1982).

2 **Home is where you hang your head.**
Attributed to Groucho Marx, on Granada TV *Cabbages and Kings* (15 July 1979).

HOMOSEXUALS
1 **MY MOTHER MADE ME A HOMOSEXUAL**
– if I got her the wool, would she make me one?
One of the most well-known graffiti exchanges – at least on the British side of the Atlantic. It was included in Reisner & Wechsler, *Encyclopedia of Graffiti* (1974). 'How many balls do you think it would take?' is an alternative addition reported by Michael Easther of Hamilton, New Zealand (1987).

2 **Young man, well hung, with beautiful body is willing to do anything. P.S. If you see this, Bill, don't bother to call, it's only me. Tony.**
From New York City, included in Reisner & Wechsler, *Encyclopedia of Graffiti* (1974).

3 **First the bad news. While you were away, a gang of gays broke in and redecorated your apartment.**
Told by Robin Williams on HBO-TV *Catch a Rising Star Tenth Anniversary* (1982) – quoted in Bob Chieger, *Was It Good For You Too?* (1983). However, I believe that in the musical *Chorus Line* (1975) this had already appeared in the form, 'Did you hear about the gay burglar? He used to break into people's houses when they were away and rearrange the furniture . . .'

4 **A gay is someone who likes his vice versa.**
In *Graffiti 4* (1982).

5 **Be gay now and avoid the Bum's rush.**
From Sydney, Australia, in *Graffiti 4* (1982).

See also LESBIANS.

HONEYMOONS

1 Announcer David Bellan was introducing a programme called
Starsound on BBC Radio 2 and said, apropos a request: 'I
hope you're listening, Bernard, as your wife tells me that
"Calamity Jane" will bring back memories of your honeymoon.'
Contributed to BBC Radio *Quote ... Unquote* (19 April 1978).

HOSPITALS

1 After two days in hospital, I took a turn for the nurse.
Rodney Dangerfield, American comedian (1921–), quoted in Bob Chieger, *Was
It Good For You Too?* (1983).

HOT DOGS

1 The noblest of all dogs is the hot-dog; it feeds the hand that
bites it.
Laurence J. Peter, one of his own sayings included in his *Quotations for Our Time*
(1977).

HOT PANTS

1 Those hot pants of hers were so damned tight, I could hardly
breathe.
Attributed to Benny Hill, British comedian (1924–92).

HOUSE OF LORDS, THE

1 The cure for admiring the House of Lords is to go and look at it.
'A severe though not unfriendly critic of our institutions' quoted by Walter
Bagehot, English political writer (1826–77), in *The English Constitution* (1867).

HOWE, SIR GEOFFREY

*British Conservative politician (1926–), later Lord Howe, who famously
turned on his former leader, Margaret Thatcher, after she had treated him
badly, and – in a speech – began the process which led to her fall from
power.*

1 When Margaret Thatcher sacked Howe from the position of
Foreign Secretary in her Government, she planned to replace
him with John Major. 'I am very sorry, Geoffrey,' she told him,
'but I've decided to put John Major in the Foreign Office.' 'Oh,

that's all right,' replied Howe, 'I'm sure he'll be a great help to me.'

Told in the *Observer* (16 October 1994).

HUMMING BIRDS

1 **Humming birds have forgotten the words.**

Quoted in Bruce Ridley (ed.), *Wall Flowers: A Collection of Australian Graffiti* (1981).

HUMPTY DUMPTY

1 **Humpty Dumpty sat on a wall**
Humpty Dumpty had a great fall
All the king's horses and all the king's men
Had scrambled eggs for the next four weeks.

From Hertford, Herts, included in *Graffiti 4* (1982).

2 **HUMPTY DUMPTY WAS PUSHED – by the CIA.**

Graffito contributed by Joan Bakewell to Granada *TV Cabbages and Kings* (12 August 1979). And to BBC Radio *Quote ... Unquote* (26 June 1980) by Sue Shearman of Leytonstone.

3 **Q. Why couldn't Humpty Dumpty be put together again?**
A. Because he wasn't all he was cracked up to be.

HYPOCHONDRIA

1 **Hypochondria is the one disease I haven't got.**

From BBC Radio *The Burkiss Way* (14 February 1978), written by David Renwick and Andrew Marshall.

IBSEN, HENRIK
Norwegian dramatist (1828–1906)

1 **W. Somerset Maugham said of Ibsen: 'In every play a**
stranger comes into the room, opens a window to let in fresh

air and everyone dies of pneumonia.'
Untraced.

ICE-BREAKING

1 Candy
Is dandy
But liquor
Is quicker.

Ogden Nash, US poet (1902–71) – 'Reflection on Ice-Breaking' from *Hard Lines* (1931).

IDENTITY CRISIS

1 I'm going through an identity crisis. Signed: Gerald, Geraldine and George III.

Quoted in Bruce Ridley (ed.), *Wall Flowers: A Collection of Australian Graffiti* (1981).

IDIOMS

1 *Overheard in a café near to Victoria Station in London:* 'A foreign gentleman, well-versed in the English use of euphemisms, asked a harassed waitress for "the cloakroom". She replied: "We 'aven't got one, you'll 'ave to use the 'atstand."'

Contributed by Mrs P.S. of Eastbourne to *Eavesdroppings* (1981).

INCEST

1 Let's keep incest in the family.

From California, included in *Graffiti 2* (1980), also a bumper sticker.

2 Call it incest – but I want my mommy.

Included in Reisner & Wechsler, *Encyclopedia of Graffiti* (1974).

3 Incest – a game the whole family can play.

Included in *Graffiti 3* (1981). Or 'New from Waddingtons, Incest – a game for all the family.' But on 14 November 1959, Rupert Hart-Davis was already writing: 'I'm also told that the latest popular game is called Incest – all the family can join in!' (*The Lyttelton Hart-Davis Letters*, 1982).

INCONTINENCE
1 HARWICH FOR THE CONTINENT
— Frinton for the incontinent.
Sign on Colchester station with addition — one of the most famous of graffiti.
Related by Arthur Marshall on BBC Radio Quote ... Unquote (5 April 1978).

INDECISION
1 I used to be indecisive — but now I'm not so sure.
Contributed by Brian Johnston to BBC Radio Quote ... Unquote (21 August
1979). But compare from Christopher Hampton's play The Philanthropist
(1970): 'Philip (bewildered): I'm sorry. (Pause.) I suppose I am indecisive.
Pause.) My trouble is, I'm a man of no convictions. (Longish pause.) At least, I
think I am.'

INFERIORITY COMPLEXES
1 I ought to have an inferiority complex but I haven't.
From the University of Sheffield, included in Graffiti 5 (1986). An early
version: 'My inferiority complexes aren't as good as yours', included in Graffiti
2 (1980).

INFLATION
1 Having a little inflation is like being a little pregnant.
Attributed to Leon Henderson, US economist (1895–1986).

INITIALS
And what they really stand for . . .
1 BBC (British Broadcasting Corporation)
Bring Back Comedy; Boring But Clean.

2 CIE (Córas Iompair Éireann, Irish bus and rail system until
1987):
'Cycling Is Easier', 'Crash Into Everything'.

3 CNN (Cable News Netowrk)
Chicken Noodle News
By 1991.

4 IBA (Independent Broadcasting Authority)
Interrupted By Adverts.

5 IBM (International Business Machines)
   I've Been Moved; Intercourse Better than Masturbation.

6 MBE (Member of the Order of the British Empire)
   My Bum's Everybody's.

7 NASA (National Aeronautics and Space Administration)
   Needs Another Seven Astronauts.

8 WIMPEY (construction firm)
   We Import More Paddies Every Year.

9 YMCA (Young Men's Christian Association)
   Yesterday's Muck Cooked Again.

INSULTS

1 Recovery with aplomb, overheard at a party in Vancouver:
   One man said: 'All the students at Simon Fraser are either
   football players or old bags.' The other replied: 'My wife goes
   to Simon Fraser!' And the first saved himself by saying, 'Oh,
   really? What position does she play?'
   Contributed by Mr H. Tucker of York to BBC Radio Quote ... Unquote (26 May
   1982). In The Best of 606 Aggie Jokes (1988), this reappears with the initial line,
   'football players or fast women'.

INSURANCE

1 Bo Peep did it for the insurance.
   Included in Graffiti 2 (1980).

INSURANCE CLAIMS

*The ludicrous massacring of the language engaged in by people filling out
insurance claims has been celebrated in many places, not least by the
comedian Jasper Carrott on his* A Pain In the Arm *record album. The
following list of examples was compiled by Tommy Sexton of Saltney
Ferry, near Chester (and contributed to Channel 4* Countdown *in
February 1988). He says they are actual reports taken from the files of
an insurance company offices in Hereford. And who are we to doubt it?
The difficulty these people have in expressing themselves is all too
plausible:*

1 The telephone pole was approaching, I was attempting to swerve out of the way when I struck the front end.

2 An invisible car came from nowhere, struck my car and vanished.

3 I collided with a stationary truck coming the other way.

4 Coming home I drove into the wrong house and collided with a tree I don't have.

5 The other car collided with mine without giving warning of its intention.

6 I thought my window was down, but I found out it was up when I put my head through it.

7 A truck backed through my windshield into my wife's face.

8 The guy was all over the road. I had to swerve a number of times before I hit him.

9 I pulled away from the side of the road, glanced at my mother-in-law and headed over the embankment.

10 In an attempt to kill a fly, I drove into a telegraph pole.

11 I had been shopping for plants all day and was on my way home. As I reached an intersection a hedge sprung up, obscuring my vision, and I did not see the other car.

12 I had been driving for forty years when I fell asleep at the wheel and had an accident.

13 I was on my way to the doctor's with rear end trouble when my universal joint gave way, causing me to have an accident.

14 As I approached the intersection, a sign suddenly appeared in a place where no stop sign had ever appeared before. I was unable to stop in time to avoid the accident.

15 To avoid hitting the bumper in front, I struck the pedestrian.

16 My car was legally parked as it backed into the other vehicle.

17 I told the police that I was not injured but, on removing my hat, found that I had a fractured skull.

18 I was sure the old fellow would never make it to the other side of the road when I struck him.

19 The pedestrian had no idea which way to run, so I ran over him.

20 I saw a slow-moving, sad-faced old gentleman as he bounced off the roof of my car.

21 The indirect cause of the accident was a little guy in a small car with a big mouth.

22 I was thrown from my car as it left the road. I was later found in a ditch by some stray cows.

INVISIBLE MAN
1 'Excuse me, sir, the Invisible Man is waiting outside.'
   'Tell him I can't see him.'

IRAN
1 NO ALCOHOL IN IRAN, BUT YOU CAN GET STONED ANY TIME
   — and the Ayatollah Khomeini will shake you warmly by the stump.
   Included in *Graffiti 3* (1981).

2 Important notice: will all travellers visiting Iran please visit the British Embassy immediately on arrival
   — And then go next door to the psychiatrist.
   Notice and addition, London airport, 1980 — included in *Graffiti 2* (1980).

See also AYATOLLAH KHOMEINI.

IRISH JOKES
As I hope I make clear in the Introduction, I do not consider Irish jokes to be racist or unfair, but merely another version of the minority/stupidity joke that crops up in so many nations around the world. Nor do I believe that the resurgence of the conflict between the British and the Irish Republicans since 1969 has had a great deal to do with the wave of Irish jokes that was obvious by the mid-1970s (the first Official Irish Joke

Book *was published in 1979). British jokes about the Irish had long predated this. A few jokes from a rather daunting amount of material:*

1 **Cleanliness is next to Godliness — only in an Irish dictionary.**
Contributed by James Burke to BBC Radio Quote ... Unquote (5 February 1979),

2 **Cunnilingus is an Irish airline.**
Included in *Graffiti Lives OK* (1979).

3 **What did the Irishman call his pet zebra?**
Spot.

4 **Our Catholic priest is not too bright. He thinks VAT 69 is the Pope's telephone number.**
Current by the 1950s.

5 **The motorist drove into an Irish garage and asked the mechanic if he would check that the indicator lights were working. So the mechanic stood at the rear while the motorist turned the indicator switch on. 'Yes, they are. No, they're not. Yes, they are. No, they're not . . . .'**
Also included in *The Best of 606 Aggie Jokes* (1988).

6 **It takes 51 Irishmen to write on a wall. One to hold the pen and the other fifty to move the wall.**
Graffito contributed to BBC Radio Quote ... Unquote (5 June 1980) by Richard Hathway who saw it at Bristol University.

7 **The Irish wear two contraceptives to be sure, to be sure.**
Included in *Graffiti 5* (1986).

8 **THE IRISH ARE BASTARDS**
— yes, they've got English fathers.
Reported from Eastbourne by Allan Robinson of Polegate, Sussex, included in *Graffiti 3* (1981).

9 **Definition of an Irish cocktail: a pint of Guinness with a potato in it.**
Contributed to an HTV programme *All Kinds of Everything* (7 May 1981).

10 **The Irish don't know what they want and won't be happy until they get it.**
Included in *Graffiti 5* (1986).

11 **Stop press – Irish boat people reach Vietnam.**
From Hertford, Herts. (1981), in *Graffiti 4* (1982).

12 **Give Vietnam back to the Irish.**
Graffito on railway bridge near Harrow. Contributed to BBC Radio *Quote* ...
Unquote (19 June 1980) by Mrs Julie Shepherd of Rickmansworth.

13 **KEEP THE BOAT PEOPLE OUT**
– sink the Irish ferry.
Slogan and graffitoed addition. Contributed to BBC Radio *Quote* ... *Unquote* (25
December 1979) by A.S. Lloyd of Frampton Cotterell, Bristol.

14 **What's an Irish contraceptive like? Hand me that ball of wool**
and I'll knit you one.
Included in *Graffiti 5* (1986).

15 **Did you hear about the Irish bookworm that was found dead**
in a pile of bricks.
Told by Caroline Lewis, Plymouth (1986).

16 *Notice in Irish hotel:* **'Please do not lock the door as we have**
lost the key.'
Included in *Foot in Mouth* (1982).

17 **Did you hear about the Irishman who burnt both his ears?**
How did that happen?
Well, he was doing the ironing and the telephone rang.
But you said he burnt both his ears.
Yes. As soon as he put the phone down, it rang again.

18 **Why is an Irishman like China?**
Plenty paddy fields.
An Irish joke told to Lord (Gerry) Fitt by a Chinese man in London and
recounted by him on BBC Radio *Quote* ... *Unquote* (3 August 1985).

19 **An Englishman, a Scotsman and an Irishman were all working**
on the same building site together and they always stopped at
the same time to eat their packed lunches. One day the
Englishman opened up his Tupperware container and
screamed, 'Oh no, not ham sandwiches again, if I have ham
sandwiches again I'm seriously going to kill myself.' The Scot
investigated his lunchbox and screamed in anguish, 'Och noo –

salmon sandwiches again. If the wife does me these one more time, a'm a gaunty kill masel.' The Irishmen then opened his lunchbox and exclaimed in disgust, 'Bejayzus, if I have cheese once more, I tell you, I'm going to kill myself.'

Next day, lunchtime came round again. The Englishman opened his sandwiches only to find ham again. With a despairing cry of 'Ham sandwiches, I can't bear them any more,' he ran along the girder and flung himself off, falling five floors to his death. The Scot then opened his lunch, found salmon sandwiches, emitted a strangled 'Och nooooo, salmon again, ah cannae bear it na more,' and in turn flung himself to his death. Finally, the Irishman then opened his lunch, and, faced with the grim prospect of Irish Cheddar sandwiches yet again, leapt to his death from the girder.

At the funeral for all three men, held a week later, the three widows are weeping and wailing together. The English wife said, 'I don't understand, I thought he liked ham.' The Scot's widow was similarly baffled and sobbed, 'I don't understand it either. Jock would have said something if he really didn't like salmon.' Finally, the Irish wife sniffed forlornly, 'I just don't understand Paddy's behaviour at all – he always made his own sandwiches.'

JEANS *See under ENDS.*

JEHOVAH'S WITNESSES

1 Answering the door to two people who introduced themselves by saying 'Good morning, we're Jehovah's Witnesses', the white-bearded man replied, 'Good, I'm Jehovah. How are we doing?'

Contributed by Rachel Dufton of South Wonston, Winchester to BBC Radio *Quote ... Unquote* (21 August 1980). She said the man with the white beard might have been the author T.H. White.

JESUS CHRIST

1 JESUS LIVES
– does this mean we won't get an Easter holiday then?
Slogan and addition from Bristol, included in *Graffiti 3* (1981).

2 **Jesus said to them: 'Who do you say that I am?' They replied: 'You are the eschatological manifestation of the ground of our being, the kerygma of which we find the ultimate meaning in our interpersonal relationships.' And Jesus said: 'What?'**
From St John's University, New York, included in *Graffiti Lives OK* (1979).

3 **Jesus Christ is alive and well and signing copies of the Bible at Foyles.**
Included in *Graffiti 2* (1980). Compare: 'God is not dead! He is alive and autographing Bibles at Brentano's' – in Reisner & Wechsler, *Encyclopedia of Graffiti* (1974).

4 **WHAT WOULD YOU DO IF CHRIST CAME TO LIVERPOOL? – move St John to inside left.**
Graffito addition to a notice outside a church in Liverpool, contributed by Norrie Hearn of High Ham, near Langport, in Somerset to BBC Radio *Quote ... Unquote* (1 January 1979). Said to have appeared 'some years ago' even then. Ian St John played for Liverpool football club from 1961 to 1971.

5 **JESUS SAVES – with the Woolwich.**
Slogan and addition spotted on a bridge in Wandsworth by Richard Clarke of Maidstone, contributed to BBC Radio *Quote ... Unquote* (1978). Not exactly a new sort of joke even then. In Reisner & Wechsler, *Encyclopedia of Graffiti* (1974), 'Jesus saves, Moses invests, but only Buddhas pays dividends' is said to have been found 'during World War II'.

JEWISH JOKES

That is to say jokes told (mostly) by the Jews about themselves:

1 **I'm not really a Jew; just Jew-ish, not the whole hog, you know.**
Jonathan Miller in 'Real Class' in the revue *Beyond the Fringe* (1961).

2 **When they circumcised Herbert Samuel they threw away the wrong bit.**
Attributed to the British Prime Minister, David Lloyd George (1863–1945), by John Grigg in the *Listener* (7 September 1978). Samuel was a prominent Jewish Liberal politician around the time of the First World War.

3 **The same question was posed to three men of God – 'When does life begin?' The Roman Catholic priest replied: 'At the moment of conception.' On the other hand, the Anglican clergyman said it was: 'When the child is born.' As for the Rabbi: 'Ah, well,' he said, 'life begins when the children are married, the dog has died and the mortgage has been paid off.'**

Told by Raymond Harris at the Savage Club, London, November 1994.

4 **Beware of the Jewish Mafia – Kosher Nostra?**

Contributed by Alfred Stone of Dagenham to *Graffiti 4* (1982).

5 **A crucifix? Oy vey, have you got the wrong vampire!**

6 **And then there was the Spanish Catholic girl called Carmen Gonzales who married a Jew called Hymie Cohen. There was absolutely no problem with the two religions. Hymie was most insistent that his wife should still follow the faith she was born into. The only condition he laid down was that she would accompany him to the synagogue on the Sabbath. Hence, her weekends were very busy – in fact from Friday night to Sunday lunchtime she really didn't know whether she was Carmen or Cohen.**

Current by the late 1950s.

7 **The man had been eating at the same restaurant in New York City for twenty years and always ordered chicken soup. But this time, when the waiter brought it, the man called him back.**

'Waiter, will you please taste this soup,' he said.

The waiter threw up his hands. 'Taste the soup? You come here for twenty years, you always have the chicken soup, and now for the first time you ask me to taste the soup first!'

'Waiter,' said the man, 'please taste the soup.'

'What's wrong with you? It's an insult for you to ask me to taste the soup. How could there be anything wrong with it?'

'Taste the soup!'

'All right, all right. You insist, so I taste the soup. Now, where's the spoon?'

'Aha!' said the man.

A version of this story appears in Leo Rosten, *The Joys of Yiddish* (1968).

JOKES

1 As the years rolled by, the prisoners in the top security prison soon exhausted their supply of jokes. In fact, so familiar had the jokes become that they had taken to referring to them by numbers — to save them the bother of telling the stories (many of them of a shaggy dog nature).

One day, desperate for amusement, one of the old lags said he wanted to tell a joke.

'OK, let's hear it,' said his cell-mate.

'"26" . . .'

The response was negative. Not a laugh, not even a smile.

'I'll try another one then. "17" . . .'

Still no response.

'It's a good joke, that number 17,' said the prisoner to whom the joke had been told, 'but, like they say, it's the way you tell 'em . . . .'

JUDGES

1 **I wanted to be a Judge, but they found out my Mum and Dad are married.**

Graffito in cell under court, contributed to BBC Radio *Quote ... Unquote* (14 August 1979) by John Leslie of East Molesey. This cropped up again in the *Financial Times* (17 July 1985): 'In the largest of the cells beneath the court in the Strand a graffito still exists which runs, "I was going to be the Lord Chief Justice until they discovered my mother was married".'

2 *Judge:* **'Have you ever been up before me?'**
Defendant: **'I don't know, your honour — what time do you get up?'**

An ancient vaudeville joke given a new lease of life when Dewey 'Pigmeat' Markham, a black vaudeville veteran, was brought back to take part in a series of blackout sketches on CBS TV's *Rowan and Martin's Laugh-In* in the 1960s. Performed on CBS TV *Rowan and Martin's Laugh-In* and included on the record album *Laugh-In '69* (1969). The build-up was the chant, 'Here comes de judge!' In July 1968, Pigmeat and an American vocalist called Shorty Long both had records of a song called 'Here Come(s) the Judge' in the US and UK charts. These contained similar groan-worthy lines:

3 *Judge:* **'Ten dollars or thirty days?'**
Defendant: **'Well, judge, I'll take the ten dollars.'**

Performed on CBS TV *Rowan and Martin's Laugh-In* and included on the record album *Laugh-In '69* (1969).

4 *The Nudist.* Judge Pigmeat had to decide on the case of a young man who stood accused of parading up and down the streets with no pants on. 'Are you married?' 'Yes, your honour,' replied the accused. 'How long have you been married?' 'Three years, your honour.' 'And how many children do you have?' 'I have nine children. After we'd been married one year my wife presented me with twins. Then a year later, it was triplets. Just now she has given birth to quads.'

'Case dismissed,' ruled Judge Pigmeat. 'There's is no case to answer. This man is clearly not a nudist. I mean, this man hasn't ever had *time* to put his pants on!'

From 'The Trial', the B-side of the 'Here Comes the Judge' record single (1968).

5 Back in the early 1960s, two British High Court judges were comparing notes.

'How much do you give these wretched homosexual johnnies?' asked one.

'Oh, half a crown a time, usually,' replied the other.

6 *F.E. Smith:* 'He was drunk as a judge.'
Judge: 'The expression as I have always understood it is "sober as a judge". Perhaps you mean "as drunk as a lord"?'
F.E. Smith: 'Yes, my lord.'

Smith (1st Earl of Birkenhead) was placed in this famous exchange by Bryan Magee in BBC Radio *Quote ... Unquote* (26 April 1994).

7 *Judge:* 'Are you trying to show contempt for this court?'
Witness: 'No, yer 'onour, I'm trying to hide it.'

JURIES
1 'M'lud, we find the defendant not guilty — but we would love to hear all the evidence again.'

Alleged remark by the jury foreman at the trial of Cynthia Payne whose colourful activities running a suburban brothel entertained the nation in February 1987. She was acquitted on a charge of controlling prostitutes in the famous 'sex for luncheon vouchers' case. Alas, when I referred to this joke in the *Sunday Times* later that year, I received a stern rebuke from one of the female members of the jury. In fact, I think it was probably the caption to a newspaper cartoon.

JUST FANCY THAT

1 'Lorry driver John Hey Mellor was found guilty of carless driving and was fined £150 with £51.30 costs.'
Yorkshire Evening Post, by 1982.

2 'Three people were taken to hospital yesterday after a 12ft hole opened up under them in the Quick Turnover Fruiterers in Gillingham High Street, Kent.'
Sunday Express, by 1982.

3 'Due to injury, the part of an Executioner will be played by Malcolm Ransom.'
Programme change from the Manchester Royal Exchange Theatre, by 1982.

4 'It happened soon after the last war when many civilians were still wearing Utility Clothing. My husband had to change trains at Basingstoke and went into the Tea Room for a cup of tea. A couple entered. The man was wearing an almost identical hat and coat and carried a very similar week-end case to my husband's. They sat at the next table. The man opened his newspaper and the woman went to the tea counter. A few minutes later the woman put the tray of tea and biscuits on the table and whispered into my husband's ear: "Shan't be long, darling. I'm just going to the doings".'
Contributed by Hilda F. Read of Barking to *Foot in Mouth* (1982).

5 'During a disagreeable discussion on dogs, my mother-in-law made the following observation: "Well, I think some dogs ought to be compulsorily castrated. They shouldn't be allowed to increase willy-nilly".'
Contributed by Mr P. Brantley of Harlington to the same book.

6 'Sex queen Fiona Richmond had promised to auction her knickers to raise cash for the children, but she had to let them down on the day.'
The Mercury (Leicester?), by 1982.

7 'Full-length undertakers coat, left shoulder slightly worn, £6.'
Advertisement in the *Chester Observer*, by 1982.

8 'WINDSOR CINEMA. *Endless Love.* Cancelled due to technical problems.'
Advertisement in the *South Wales Evening News*, 1982.

9 'Blizzards, snow drifts and icy roads have wrecked the county
   council highways budget and plunged Surrey into chaos. Taken
   by surprise by one of the most severe winters of the century,
   finance chiefs are gritting their teeth.'
   Surrey Advertiser, by 1982

JUSTICE

1 Justice must not only be seen to be done but has to be seen to
   be believed.
   Attributed by Peter Cook to 'Beachcomber', J.B. Morton, the British humorist
   (1893–1979), on BBC *Radio Quote ... Unquote* (5 June 1980).

KAMIKAZE PILOTS

1 Did you hear about the Kamikaze pilot who went on 1200
   missions?
   Included in *The Best of 606 Aggie Jokes* (1988). The same joke formed the basis
   of a prolonged sketch on BBC Radio *The Burkiss Way* (Series 2, Programme 12,
   1977).

KARMA

1 SORRY, BUT MY KARMA JUST RAN OVER YOUR DOGMA.
   Slogan on T-shirt available in the US, 1982.

KENNEDY, EDWARD
American Democratic politician (1932–).

1 **Q.** Senator Kennedy, what would you do to straighten out the
      economy?
   A. Let's drive off that bridge when we come to it.
   In Haan & Hammerstrom Graffiti in the *Southwest Conference* (1981).

2 **A blonde in every pond.**
Reagan for President, Kennedy for Chauffeur.
Re-elect Carter, Free Joan Kennedy.
Button slogans in 1980, when Edward Kennedy attempted to win the Democratic presidential nomination.

3 **After Kennedy had been photographed indulging in some sexual shenanigans on board a yacht off the Florida coast, someone asked him in the Senate what his position was on 'offshore drilling'.**

See also STICKERS 3.

KERRY JOKES
As IRISH JOKES are to the British, so Kerry jokes are to the Irish themselves. The denizens of County Kerry are the minority within the Irish nation singled out for abuse. The strand was established by 1987:

1 **Q. How do you tell which is the bride at a Kerry wedding?**
A. She's the one wearing white gumboots.

2 **Did you hear about the Kerryman who won the Nobel Prize for Agriculture? He was out standing in his field.**

3 **And then there's the one about the Kerry wife who said she had been rinsing the ice cubes a moment ago and now couldn't find them.**
Recalled in the *Independent* (12 May 1993).

KHOMEINI *See AYATOLLAH KHOMEINI.*

KILROY
1 **Alas, poor Yorlik, I knew him backwards.**
Graffito from Leicester, described on Granada TV *Cabbages and Kings* (18 November 1979).

KIDS
1 **Be nice to your kids. They'll choose your nursing home.**

KISSES

1 **High heels were invented by a woman who had been kissed on the forehead.**
Christopher Morley, American writer and editor (1890–1957), quoted in *The Treasury of Humorous Quotations*, ed. by Evan Esar & Nicolas Bentley (1951).

2 **Whoever called it necking was a poor judge of anatomy.**
Groucho Marx, 1970 – quoted in Bob Chieger, *Was It Good For You Too?* (1983).

3 **Two people kissing always look like fish.**
Andy Warhol, *From A to B and Back Again* (1975) – quoted in Bob Chieger, *Was It Good For You Too?* (1983).

4 **When women kiss, it always reminds me of prize-fighters shaking hands.**
H.L. Mencken, *Chrestomathy* (1949).

KNICKERS

1 **Why can't a woman with a wooden leg give change for a pound note?**
Because she's only got half a knicker!
Supposedly an old music-hall groaner revived by Spike Milligan in his script for BBC Radio *The Last Goon Show At All* (5 October 1972) – though it had been used in the original *Goon Show* in the 1950s.

KNOCK-KNOCK JOKES

'Knock, knock' was a catchphrase said to have been used in the UK by the British music-hall comedian Wee Georgie Wood (1895–1979). He used it, for example, in a radio programme in 1936. This, however, was possibly an imported American device to warn that a dubious joke was coming up. From Variety *(19 August 1936): 'Manager Russell Bovim of Loew's Broad, Columbus, cashed in handsomely on the "Knock Knock" craze now sweeping the country.'*

Better known is the 'knock-knock' joke – the name given to a type of (usually punning) joke popular especially in the UK and US from the 1950/60s and popularized by CBS TV's Rowan and Martin's Laugh-In *(1969–73):*

1 **Knock, knock!**
Who's there?
Sam and Janet.

Sam and Janet who?
'Sam and Janet evening . . .'

2 **Knock, knock!**
Who's there?
Owl.
Owl who?
Owl you know unless you open the door.

3 **Knock, knock!**
Who's there?
Richard Milhous.
Richard Milhouse who?
Ah . . . how quickly people forget!
Printed in *Radio Times* (19–25 October 1974) – Richard M. Nixon had been
ousted from the US presidency the previous August.

4 **Knock, knock!**
Who's there?
E.T.
E.T. who?
E.T. come, E.T. go.
From British school kids, quoted by Caroline St John-Brooks in *New Society*
(2 June 1983).

5 **Knock knock!**
Who's there?
Your underwear.
Your underwear who?
Your underwear the yellow went when you brush your teeth
with Pepsodent.
Quoted in the *Washington Post* (5 December 1993).

6 **Knock, knock!**
Who's there?
O.J.
O.J. who?
You're on the jury!
Reported from the US in August 1994 when the black football player and movie
star O.J. Simpson was charged with murdering his ex-wife and a waiter. Given
his fame, there were doubts as to whether a sufficiently unbiassed jury could be
called.

7 **Knock, knock!**
   Who's there?
   Adolph.
   Adolph who?
   Adolph ball hit me in de mowf. Dat's why I dawk this way.
   Included in John S. Crosbie, *Crosbie's Dictionary of Puns* (1977).

8 **Knock, knock!**
   Who's there?
   Mayonnaise.
   Mayonnaise who?
   Mayonnaise have seen the glory of the coming of the Lord!

9 **Knock knock.**
   Who's there?
   Tijuana.
   Tijuana who?
   Tijuana punch in the nose?
   Performed on CBS TV *Rowan and Martin's Laugh-In* and included on the record
   album *Laugh-In '69* (1969).

10 **Knock, knock!**
    Who's there?
    Ammonia.
    Ammonia who?
    Ammonia little girl and I can't reach the doorbell.

11 **Knock, knock!**
    Who's there?
    Dishwasher.
    Dishwasher who?
    Dishwasher the way I spoke before I had false teeth.

12 **Knock, knock!**
    Who's there?
    Euripedes.
    Euripedes who?
    Euripedes trousers, you buy me another pair.

13 **Knock, knock!**
    Who's there?
    Nicholas.
    Nicholas who?
    Nicholas girls shouldn't climb trees.

14 **Knock, knock!**
Who's there?
Dr Livingstone.
Dr Livingstone who?
Dr Livingstone I. Presume.

'Dr Livingstone I. Presume' was a character joke by 1973 when he appeared in BBC Radio *The Betty Witherspoon Show*.

15 **Knock, knock!**
Who's there?
Yvonne.
Yvonne who?
Yvonne to be alone.

16 **Knock, knock!**
Who's there?
Astronaut.
Astronaut who?
Astronaut what your country can do for you but what you can do for your country.

KOALA BEARS

1 **Q. What kind of shoe does a koala wear?**
A. Gum boots.

Told by Daniel Waring, Plymouth (1986).

KURDS

1 **One of my most treasured moments from the wireless comes from about 1980 and was when a foreign correspondent was referring to the Kurdish autonomy movement in Iran and Iraq. He said, 'There is a danger of civil war if the Kurds don't get their way.'**

Contributed to BBC Radio *Quote ... Unquote* (28 August 1980) by Mr E.E. Harding of Bromley, Kent. This only goes to confirm one theory about the roots of humour, that people don't make up jokes, the jokes are there in the English language waiting to be let out. As I noted in *The Guinness Book of Humorous Anecdotes*, Ronald Pearsall in his survey of Victorian humour, *Collapse of Stout Party* (1975) relates that this joke was alive and well 'a hundred years ago . . . In New College common room, Walter Thursby, don and explorer, related how he had scaled Mount Ararat. The snow was not so bad as expected, he explained, but because of marauding tribes a guard of Kurdish soldiers had been provided. Later Arthur Riding went up to him and commented: "I understand you took some Curds with you to show the whey."' In addition, *Punch* had the punning headline 'Kurds and their ways' on 12 February 1881 (Vol. LXXX).

LADA JOKES

Jokes about the supposed inadequacies of the cheap, plain, Russian-made motor car, the Lada, were already common in Britain by 1987. One explanation for the popularity of the jokes was that they helped cover the embarrassment of those who had paid too much for other types of motor car! In Russia itself, the cars had been extremely popular since the early 1970s. Even today, in the UK, people continue to buy them and the importers laugh off the jokes, saying they have helped establish the brand.

For variety's sake, the names of the Skoda and the Yugo may be inserted in these jokes:

1 **How do you double the price of a Lada? Fill up the petrol tank.**
Reported in *Today* (9 October 1989).

2 **Q. What is worse than owning a Lada?**
A. Owning two Ladas.

3 **Q. What do you call a Lada with two Rottweilers in the back seat?**
A. A very nice car.
Reported in *The Times* (2 August 1991).

4 **Q. What do you call an open-topped Lada?**
A. A skip.
Reported in *The Times* (27 September 1991).

5 **Q. What's the difference between a Lada and an Essex girl?**
A. No Russian wants to get his hands on a Lada.
Reported in *Today* (25 November 1991).

6 There is the story of the Muscovite who beggars himself for fifteen years in order to save up for a Lada. The day comes when he has enough money and he dashes off to the showrooms. The salesman beams. 'Congratulations, comrade, your car will be here in ten years' time.' 'Great!' replies the customer. 'Will that be morning or afternoon?'

Reported in the *Guardian* (1 February 1992).

7 Why does a Lada have heated rear windscreens? To keep your hands warm when you push it.

Reported in *The Times* (30 October 1992).

8 Last laugh. In Russian, the word 'lada' means 'beloved'.

Reported in *The Times* (30 November 1991).

LAPEL BADGE JOKES *See under STICKERS.*

LAST PERSON

1 Would the last person to leave the country please switch off the lights.

Included in *Graffiti 2* (1980). On 9 April 1992, this line suffered a revival when on the day of the British General Election, the *Sun* newspaper's front page headline was: 'IF KINNOCK WINS TODAY WILL THE LAST PERSON IN BRITAIN PLEASE TURN OUT THE LIGHTS.'

LAVATORIES

1 VENI, VIDI, VIVI.

Graffito reported from Bexley, in Granada TV *Cabbages and Kings* (11 August 1979).

LAW, THE

1 If you like laws and sausages, you should never watch either one being made.

Widely-attributed to Otto von Bismarck (1815–98), the German statesman, but unverified. Also has been attributed to the French revolutionary statesman Honoré Gabriel de Riqueti [Comte de Mirabeau, 1749–91]. He is supposed to have said, 'Laws are like sausages; you should never watch them being made.'

See also under JUDGES and LAWYERS.

LAWS, JOKE

1 **When your cat has fallen asleep on your lap and looks utterly content and adorable you will suddenly have to go to the bathroom.**

'Rule of Feline Frustration' included in Arthur Bloch, *Murphy's Law and Other Reasons Why Things Go Wrong* (1977).

2 **The amount of flak received on any subject is inversely proportional to the subject's true value.**

'Potter's Law', also included in the above.

3 **When all else fails, read the instructions.**

'Cahn's Axiom', quoted by Paul Dickson in *Playboy* (April 1978).

4 **A falling body always rolls to the most inaccessible place.**

Theodore M. Bernstein, in *The Careful Writer* (1967).

5 **Gnomes always draw curtains where there are views.**

Ada Louise Huxtable, in the *New York Times* (16 November 1975).

6 **The possibility of a young man meeting a desirable and receptive young female increases by pyramidal progression when he is already in the company of (1) a date, (2) his wife, (3) a better-looking and richer male friend.**

Ronald Beifield, quoted by Allan L. Otten, in the *Wall Street Journal* (2 February 1975).

7 **A shortcut is the longest distance between two points.**

Charles Issawi, in the *Columbia Forum* (Summer, 1970).

8 **(1) When in charge, ponder.**
(2) When in trouble, delegate.
(3) When in doubt, mumble.

James Boren, quoted in *Time* Magazine (23 November 1970).

9 **Did you ever notice how much faster wood burns when you personally cut and chop it yourself?**

Quoted on CBS TV *Apple's Way* (12 January 1975).

10 **As soon as you replace a lost object, you will find it.**

David Brinkley, quoted by Ann Landers, in the *Poughkeepsie Journal* (26 March 1978).

11 **At bank, post office or supermarket, there is one universal law
which you ignore at your own peril: the shortest line moves the
slowest.**
Bill Vaughan, quoted in *Reader's Digest* (July 1977).

12 **The longer one saves something before throwing it away, the
sooner it will be needed after it is thrown away.**
James J. Caulfield (March 1968), quoted in Harold Faber, *The Book of Laws* (1979).

13 **If it works well, they'll stop making it.**
Jane Otten and Russell Baker, quoted by Alan L. Otten, in the *Wall Street
Journal* (26 February 1976).

14 **Whatever happens in government could have happened
differently, and it usually would have been better if it had.**
Charles Frankel, *High on Foggy Bottom* (1970).

15 **The more underdeveloped the country, the more
overdeveloped the women.**
John Kenneth Galbraith, quoted in *Time* Magazine (17 October 1969).

16 **Anyone who says he isn't going to resign four times, definitely
will.**
John Kenneth Galbraith, quoted in *Time* Magazine (7 November 1973).

17 **News expands to fill the time and space allocated to its
coverage.**
William Safire, in the *New York Times* (6 September 1973).

18 **When the weight of the paperwork equals the weight of the
plane, the plane will fly.**
Donald Douglas, quoted by Alan L. Otten in the *Wall Street Journal* (26 February
1976).

19 **Seven-eighths of everything can't be seen.**
'The Iceberg Theorem', quoted in the *Daily Mail* (10 March 1979).

20 **It is impossible to make anything foolproof because fools are
so ingenious.**

21 **The place you are trying to get to is always on the extreme
edge of the page on the street-map.**
Contributed to BBC Radio *Quote ... Unquote* (1986?) by Violet Rutter of London
NW6.

22 **When ripping an article from a newspaper, the tear is always into and never away from the required article.**
Contributed to the same programme by Alan Fraser of Stockport.

23 **When all else fails — and the instructions are missing — kick it.**
Contributed to the same programme, rather alarmingly, by an anonymous donor in the Department of Anaesthetics at Harrow hospital.

24 **Acceptable invitations only arrive when you can't accept them.**

25 **If you buy a record for the A side, in time you will find that you are only able to tolerate the B side.**

26 **When your car or central heating is due for servicing — and nothing is positively wrong with it — the servicing will result in the machine *having* to be serviced again within the month.**

27 **No matter how you have searched, there will always be one teaspoon left at the bottom of the washing-up water.**
A law promulgated by Irene Thomas (1920–) in her book *The Bandsman's Daughter* (1979).

LAWRENCE OF ARABIA
1 **'Florence of Arabia' — the feminist version.**

2 **Q. Who rides a camel and carries a lamp?**
A. Florence of Arabia.

LAWYERS
1 **Q. What do you call 1000 lawyers at the bottom of the sea?**
A. A start.
Told in *Harpers & Queen* (January 1995).

2 **Q. What's the difference between a lawyer and a sperm?**
A. A sperm has a one in a million chance of turning into a human being.

3 **Q. What's the difference between a lawyer and a haddock?**
A. One's cold and slimy, the other's a fish.

4 **How many lawyers does it take to change a light bulb?**
Six. One to hold the bulb, and five to turn the man round.
Also told about Irishmen. Alluded to in a *Guardian* leading article (8 February 1994).

5 **How many lawyers does it take to change a light bulb?**
How many can you afford?
Quoted in the *Financial Times* (27 May 1994).

LEAKS

1 **Do you know what happened when Noah's Ark sprang a leak?**
Well, first of all, a little dog plugged the hole with his nose. As the hole widened, Noah's wife was obliged to substitute her elbow. Finally, Noah himself wedged his bottom into the fissure. Which is why — the story goes on — dogs have cold noses, women have cold elbows and Father spreads his coat-tails when he stands with his back to the fire.
Told to me by Philip Purser (January 1994). Antony Jay, with all the benefits of his classical education, subsequently pointed out that this story also, or originally, was one of Stanley Holloway's famous recitations. Written by Marriott Edgar, 'The 'Ole in the Ark' (1937) explains how Noah plugged a leak in his vessel with various parts of the anatomy, including a bloodhound's. It concludes:

> And that is how Noah got 'em all safe ashore,
> But ever since then, strange to tell,
> Them as helped save the Ark has all carried a mark,
> Aye, and all their descendants as well.
>
> That's why dog has a cold nose, and ladies cold elbows
> — You'll also find if you enquire
> That that's why a man takes his coat-tails in hand
> And stands with his back to the fire.

LECTURES

1 **Definition of a lecture: a means of transferring information from the notes of the lecturer to the notes of the student without passing through the minds of either.**
From the University of Warwick, included in *Graffiti 2* (1980).

LEGS

1 **In a survey carried out to see what men liked about women's legs: 27% of men said they preferred women with fat legs**

and 15% said they preferred women with thin legs. The remaining 58% said they preferred something in between.

From Reading, included in *Graffiti 2* (1980).

LEMMINGS

1 **100,000 lemmings can't be wrong.**

From Balliol, Oxford, included in *Graffiti Lives OK* (1979).

LENNON, JOHN

British popular singer and songwriter (1940–80).

1 **JOHN LENNON LIVES**
– no wonder I can't get the bloody probate signed. Yoko Ono.

Slogan and addition from Leeds (1981), contributed by Robert McWatt to *Graffiti 5* (1986).

LEOPARDS

1 **Q. Why do leopards have a spotted coat?**
A. Because stripes make them look fat.

Told by Caroline Lewis, Plymouth (1986)

LESBIANS

1 **Do lesbians enjoy a little bit of how's your mother?**

From Hamilton, New Zealand (1983), contributed by W.M.G. to *Graffiti 5* (1986).

2 **Many years ago I chased a woman for almost two years, only to discover her tastes were exactly like mine: we were both crazy about girls.**

Groucho Marx, in *The Groucho Letters* (1967) (from one dated 28 March 1955).

LETTER BOMBS

1 **A letter bomb is a post mortem.**

Quoted in Bruce Ridley (ed.), *Wall Flowers: A Collection of Australian Graffiti* (1981).

LIBERALS

1 **A liberal is a conservative who has been arrested.**

In two places in *The Bonfire of the Vanities* (1987), Tom Wolfe quotes this, but is clearly referring to an established saying. On the other hand, in the Fall 1993 issue of the American *Policy Review*, James Q. Wilson is credited with the observation: 'There aren't any liberals left in New York. They've all been mugged.' The original definition may well have been, 'A conservative is a liberal who's been mugged by reality.'

LIFE

1 **Life is just a bowl of toenails.**
Graffito on the wall of an Oxford college. Contributed to BBC Radio *Quote ... Unquote* (31 May 1978) by John Colman of Chesham, Buckinghamshire.

2 **This is not a dress rehearsal, this is real life.**
From the Eight-O Club, Dallas, Texas, included in *Graffiti 3* (1981).

3 **THE FIRST THREE MINUTES OF LIFE CAN BE THE MOST DANGEROUS
– the last three minutes are pretty dodgy too.**
Hospital notice and addition, included in *Graffiti 2* (1980).

4 **Life is like a sewer. What you get out of it depends on what you put in.**
Tom Lehrer, US songwriter and entertainer (1928–) on the record album, *An Evening Wasted with Tom Lehrer* (1953).

5 **The living are just the dead on holiday.**
Attributed to Maurice Maeterlinck, Belgian poet and playwright (1862–1949), but unverified. In a 1980 episode of BBC TV's *Dr Who* ('Destiny of the Daleks'), scripted by Terry Nation, occurred the line: 'Who was it that said the living are the dead on holiday?'

6 *At a Halloween party where people were ducking for apples:* **There, but for a typographical error, is the story of my life.**
Dorothy Parker, quoted in John Keats, *You Might As Well Live* (1970).

7 **Take me or leave me. Or as most people do: both.**
Attributed to Dorothy Parker.

8 **No good worry worry anything. By'm by, we all asame – Nothing!**
Australian aborigine saying.

9 **Life is what happens to us while we are making other plans.**
Quoted in the lyrics of Lennon's song 'Beautiful Boy' (included on his 'Double

Fantasy' album, 1980), but not his. In Barbara Rowe's *The Book of Quotes* (1979), she ascribes the 'Life is . . .' saying to Betty Talmadge, divorced wife of Senator Herman Talmadge, in the form 'Life is what happens to you when you're making other plans.' Dr Laurence Peter in *Quotations for Our Time* (1977) gives the line to 'Thomas La Mance', who remains untraced.

LIFTS/ELEVATORS
1 **LIFT UNDER REPAIR. USE OTHER LIFT.**
– this Otis regrets it is unable to lift today.
Graffito on notice, contributed to BBC Radio *Quote ... Unquote* (16 February 1982) by Malcolm Watson of Sutton-on-the-Forest, York.

2 **IN CASE OF FIRE DO NOT ATTEMPT TO USE THE LIFTS**
– try a fire extinguisher.
Graffito on notice in lift, University College, Cardiff. Contributed by Tim Duncan of Barry to *Graffiti 3* (1981).

LIGHT-BULB JOKES
Light-bulb jokes are a popular way of describing notable traits of minorities and groups of people. They almost certainly originated in the US in the 1970s.

1 **How many Californians does it take to change a light bulb?**
Eight. One to turn the bulb and seven to share the experience.
This is the first example that I have been able to find – in Haan & Hammerstrom *Graffiti in the Big Ten* (1981).

2 **How many San Francisco straights does it take to screw in a**
light bulb?
Both of them.
Told by the American comedian Kerry Hosler in 1982 – quoted in Bob Chieger, *Was It Good For You Too?* (1983).

3 **How many Virginia politicians does it take to change a light**
bulb?
One to change the bulb and the other two to reminisce about
how great the old light bulb was.
Told in the *Washington Post* (15 January 1986). This one reemerged in Australia in a different form as recounted in *The Times* (London) (13 January 1990): 'How many Country and Western stars does it take to change a light bulb?' 'Ten. One to change it and nine to sing about what a good ol' bulb it was.'

4 **How many Harvard medical students does it take to change a light bulb?**
One, to stand there and hold it while the world revolves around him.
Told by Perri Klass in her book about Harvard Medical School, *A Not Entirely Benign Procedure* (1987).

5 **How many Aggies does it take to change a light bulb?**
Three. One to put the bulb in the socket and two to turn the ladder.
Included in *The Best of 606 Aggie Jokes* (1988).

6 **How many Chicago economists does it take to change a light bulb?**
None. The market will see to it.
Or 'market forces will see to it' — *Financial Times* (1 September 1989).

7 **How many feminists does it take to change a light bulb?**
That's not funny!
The Times (20 January 1990).

8 **How many MI5 officers does it take to change a light bulb?**
None. We prefer to leave you in the dark.
Alluded to in *The Times* (10 February 1990).

9 **How many members of the Militant Tendency does it take to change a light bulb?**
It's no use trying to change it. You've got to smash it.
Financial Times (2 July 1990).

10 **How many Tories does it take to change a light bulb?**
500. One to change the bulb, and 499 to give a standing ovation.
Told in the *Independent* (11 December 1990).

11 **How many Russians does it take to change a light bulb?**
What light bulb?
Same source. This reemerged in the *Washington Post* (5 December 1993) as: 'How many New Crimea cab drivers does it take to change a light bulb?' 'Vair ees light bulb, pliss?' (In this context, 'New Crimea' was an invented name for the state of Washington DC.)

12 **How many Japanese does it take to change a light bulb?**
Four. One to change the bulb, one to wave the red flag and

blow the whistle, one to redirect the traffic while the operation
is in progress, and one to bow afterwards and apologize for
keeping the customer waiting.

The Independent (11 February 1991).

13   **How many social workers does it take to change a light
     bulb?
     None. They form a support group called Coping with Darkness.**

Quoted in the *Observer* (14 April 1991), from an American source.

14   **How many *Punch* editors does it take to change a light bulb?
     All 13. One to change the bulb, and the other 12 to say how
     much better the old one was.**

Quoted, as told by David Thomas, the last *Punch* editor, in the *Sunday Times* (21
July 1991).

15   **How many Soviet generals does it take to change a light bulb?
     Two. One to take the new one out and the other to put the old
     one back in.**

Quoted in the *Independent* (21 August 1991).

16   **How many British Chancellors does it take to change a light
     bulb?
     None. You see, there is probably nothing really wrong with the
     bulb. It's purely a cyclical problem which will correct itself.
     Look, I think I can already see a faint flicker . . .**

Quoted in the *Daily Telegraph* (18 November 1991), from a Credit Lyonnais
capital markets group circular.

17   **How many politically correct people does it take to change a
     light bulb?
     Are you sure 'light bulb' isn't a derogatory term?**

Alluded to in *The Times* (21 December 1991).

18   **How many surrealist painters does it take to change a light
     bulb?
     The fish!**

Quoted in the *Daily Telegraph* (15 May 1992).

19   **How many Poles does it take to change a light bulb?
     Just because it is broken, there's no reason to change it.**

Told in *Today* (6 July 1992)

20 **How many Treasury ministers does it take to change a light bulb?
None. Government policy is that the light is working and getting brighter all the time.**
Quoted in the *Guardian* (21 October 1992).

21 **How many Scottish Office civil servants does it take to change a light bulb?
None. Twelve of them write a report 'The New Darkness Explained: A guide for Businessmen.'**
Quoted in the *Sunday Times* (13 December 1992).

22 **How many actors does it take to change a light bulb?
Twelve. One to take out the bulb and the other eleven to say, 'You were wonderful, darling!'**
Heard by me at about this time in 1992 and evolving to the following in the *Independent on Sunday* (23 May 1993): 'How many hairdressers does it take to change a light bulb? Two — one to change the light bulb, and one to stand back and say: "Fabulous, Gary!"' Compare no. 28 below.

23 **How many actors does it take to change a light bulb?
Ten. One to do it and the rest to say: 'That should be me up there.'**

24 **How many public relations executives does it take to screw in a light bulb?
We'll look into that and get right back to you with an answer.**
Told to me by Charles G. Francis of New York (1992). Variations include 'How many publicity officers . . . ? Give me a fax number and I'll get back to you on that one.' 'How many PR men . . . ? None that I am aware of, but that's a personal view.'

25 **How many car mechanics does it take to change a light bulb?
Six. One to scratch his head, one to say 'We can't touch it till Tuesday', and four to add up the bill.**
Told in *Today* (30 September 1993).

26 **How many therapists does it take to change a light bulb?
None. The light bulb must really want to change itself.**
Same source.

27 **How many doctors does it take to change a light bulb?
Two. One to do the job and another to give a second opinion.**

28 **How many hairdressers does it take to change a light bulb?**
    Three. One to do the job and two to say how nice it looks.

29 **How many Jewish mothers does it take to change a light bulb?**
    None – 'Don't worry about me, I'll just sit here in the dark. No
    one ever calls. No one ever phones . . .'
    Quoted in the *Observer* (21 November 1993).

30 **How many Brazilian footballers does it take to change a light**
    bulb?
    One. And a panel of experts to describe It as art.
    Quoted in the *Guardian* (8 July 1994).

31 **How many MPs does it take to change a light bulb?**
    Two. One to screw it in and the other to screw it up.
    Quoted as told by a Tory MP, the *Guardian* (4 November 1994).

32 **How many yuppies does it take to screw in a light bulb?**
    None. Yuppies only screw in a jacuzzi.

33 **How many sociologists does it take to change a light bulb?**
    It isn't the light bulb that needs changing. It's the system.

34 **How many pagans does it take to change a light bulb?**
    None. They live in eternal darkness.

35 **Why does it take two women with premenstrual tension to**
    change a light bulb?
    It just does. All right?

    See also under BLONDE JOKES and LAWYERS.

LIMBO DANCERS

1 **Beware limbo dancers.**
   Graffito written along the bottom of a lavatory cubicle door. Contributed to
   BBC Radio *Quote ... Unquote* (19 April 1978) by Roy Hudd.

2 **Beware Irish limbo dancers.**
   Graffito written along the *top* of a lavatory cubicle door. Contributed to BBC
   Radio *Quote ... Unquote* (29 May 1980) by Harold Urmson of Morecambe.

3 **Limbo dancers are under-achievers.**
   Quoted in Bruce Ridley (ed.), *Wall Flowers: A Collection of Australian Graffiti*
   (1981).

LIMERICKS

1 **There once was a young man called Stencil**
   Whose prick was as sharp as a pencil.
   He punctured an actress,
   Two sheets and a mattress,
   And dented the bedroom utensil.
   I think I first heard this and the following one in the early 1980s. They do not
   appear in G. Legman's magisterial survey *The Limerick* (two volumes, 1964,
   1969).

2 **A tired old fairy from Rome**
   Took a leprechaun back to his home.
   As he entered the elf
   He said to himself
   I'd be much better off in a gnome.

3 **Nymphomaniacal Alice**
   Used a dynamite stick for a phallus.
   They found her vagina
   In North Carolina
   And her ass-hole in Buckingham Palace.
   Legman dates this one '1942–1951'

4 **On the chest of a barmaid in Sale**
   Were tattooed the prices of ale,
   And on her behind,
   For the sake of the blind,
   Was the same information in Braille.
   Legman has a version of this about a 'harlot from Yale', dated 1941.

5 **There was a young man from Calcutta**
   Who had the most terrible stutta.
   He said, 'Pass the h-ham
   And the j-j-j-jam,
   And the b-b-b-b-b-b-butta.'

6 **There was a young lady of Tottenham,**
   Who'd no manners or else she'd forgotten 'em.

At tea at the vicar's
She tore off her knickers,
Because, she explained, she felt 'ot in 'em.

Legman finds a source for this in 1903.

7 There was a young girl of Madras
Who had the most beautiful ass.
But not as you'd think
Firm, round and pink,
But grey, with long ears, and eats grass.

Legman finds a source for this in 1940.

8 There was a young lady of Exeter
So pretty that men craned their nexetter.
One was even so brave
As to take out and wave
The distinguishing mark of his sexetter.

Legman finds this '1927–1941'.

9 There was a young man in Florence
To whom all art was abhorrence.
So he got slightly tipsy
Went to the Uffizi
And peed on the paintings in torrents.

Said to have been seen at the Uffizi, included in *Graffiti 2* (1980). Legman finds two limericks from 1941-2 which both make use of the Florence/abhorrence/ torrents rhyme but on different themes.

See also BESTIALITY 3.

LITTER
1 KEEP THIS BUS TIDY
– throw your tickets out of the window.

Notice and graffitoed addition, contributed by Martin Jarvis to Granada TV *Cabbages and Kings* (5 August 1979).

LITTLE OLD LADIES
1 All the big women die young, that's why we're left with little old ladies.

Graffito in Paris. Contributed to BBC Radio *Quote ... Unquote* (8 December 1981) by John B. Walton of Portbury, Bristol.

LOBOTOMY

1 **I'd rather have a full bottle in front of me than a full frontal lobotomy.**

Graffito from Leicester University, contributed to BBC Radio Quote ... Unquote (19 February 1979) by Bob Baker.

LOS ANGELES

1 **Q. What's the difference between L.A. and yoghurt?**
A. A yoghurt is a live culture.

Included in Graffiti 5 (1986).

LOVE

1 **Make love not war – see driver for details.**

Graffito/car sticker contributed by Graeme Garden to Granada TV Cabbages and Kings (22 July 1979). 'Make love, not war' was a 'peacenik' and 'flower power' slogan of the mid-1960s. It was not just applied to the Vietnam War but was used to express the attitude of a whole generation of protest. It was written up (in English) at the University of Nanterre during the French student revolution of 1968. Coinage has been attributed to 'G. Legman', a sexologist with the Kinsey Institute, though this is also the name of the editor of The Limerick (1964/9).

2 **Make love not war – I'm married, I do both.**

Contributed by Barbara Kelly to Granada TV Cabbages and Kings (5 August 1979).

3 **Until I discovered women I thought love was a pain up the arse.**

From Hatfield Polytechnic, included in Graffiti 2 (1980).

4 **When people say, 'You're breaking my heart,' they do in fact usually mean that you're breaking their genitals.**

Jeffrey Bernard, British journalist (1932–) in the Spectator (31 May 1986).

5 **Love – the delightful interval between meeting a beautiful girl and discovering that she looks like a haddock.**

John Barrymore, quoted in Bob Chieger, Was It Good For You Too? (1983).

6 **Love is not the dying moan of a distant violin – it is the triumphant twang of a bedspring.**

Attributed to S.J. Perelman, American writer (1904–79).

7 **Nothing is better for the spirit or body than a love affair. It elevates the thoughts and flattens stomachs.**
Barbara Howar, *Laughing All the Way* (1973).

LOVELACE, LINDA
American porn movie star, notably in Deep Throat *(1972).*

1 **Linda Lovelace's mother went down on the Titanic.**
Contributed by John Delzotto, Five Dock, New South Wales and Karen Ward, Killara, NSW, to *Graffiti 4* (1982).

2 **Linda Lovelace has gone down in my estimation.**
Included in *Graffiti 5* (1986).

LUNATICS
1 **A visitor was walking round a lunatic asylum when it was having an open day. When he came across an inmate holding a fishing rod over a flower bed, he did not wish to seem to laugh at him and so asked, 'How many have you caught today?' Replied the inmate: 'I'd say you were about Number Six.'**
I think I read this is a students' rag week magazine in the late 1950s.

2 **A visitor inquired as to what was the problem with a certain patient in a mental institution. 'Ah,' came the reply, 'he thinks he is a poached egg and spends his days seeking a suitable piece of toast upon which to sit.'**
I remember this from my childhood in the 1950s. Now I find that it occurs in *Punch* (Vol. 122, p. 135) in 1902.

MALAPROPISMS
These verbal blunders are named after the wonderful character 'Mrs Malaprop' in Sheridan's play The Rivals *(1775) who had an unerring – if not inspired – instinct for choosing the wrong word – 'headstrong as an*

allegory on the banks of the Nile', 'the very pineapple of politeness', and so on. Shakespeare and Smollett had seized upon this quite common human failing before him but it was Sheridan who named the complaint, employing the French phrase mal à propos, *meaning 'inopportunely, inappropriately'. From the following, you will be left in no doubt that Mrs Malaprop is still alive and well wherever English is spoken:*

1 **Overheard from a conversation between two women: 'She's got trouble with her eye. Doctor says it's a misplaced rectum.'**
Contributed to BBC Radio Quote ... Unquote (29 January 1979) by Mrs Eileen Woodward of Halstead, Essex.

2 **'Scottish Chamber Orchestra: Simon Rattle conducts a bizarre juxtaposition: [Beethoven's] "Erotica" and Weill's *Seven Deadly Sins*".'**
From *The Times* (date unknown).

3 **'Of her son, taking his finals before embarking on an international job, a cousin of mine said: "Of course, if he does well in them, the world is his lobster."'**
Contributed to BBC Radio Quote ... Unquote (21 August 1980) by A.M.D. Carrier, London SW7.

4 **'She also said about her daughter-in-law who was in hospital about to have a Caesarian baby: "Nothing to worry about. With a father who's a top surgeon, she's bound to get R.I.P. treatment."'**
From the same source.

5 **'Oh, I do like my bidet! You don't have to have any blankets on the bed.'**
Contributed to BBC Radio Quote ... Unquote (12 February 1979) by Huw Pudner of Craig Cefn Parc, Swansea.

6 **And then there was the old lady who was rather puzzled by that line from the Beatles' song, 'The girl with colitis goes by ...'.**
OK, if you don't get it, she meant 'the girl with kaleidoscope eyes' from 'Lucy in the Sky with Diamonds' from the *Sgt Pepper* album (1967). Quoted in *Babes and Sucklings* (1983).

7 **'I can't hear a thing. I'll have to go to the archaeologist about my ears.'**
Well, it was one old woman speaking to another. Contributed to BBC Radio Quote ... Unquote (17 August 1985) by Miss Elizabeth Scott of Halifax, West Yorkshire.

8 'While holidaying in a small village in Scotland I was speaking to an elderly inhabitant who had had a day out in Edinburgh. At one point she said: "I wanted to cross the road, but I dinna ken how to work the Presbyterian Crossing."'

Contributed by Helen Kerr Green of Market Drayton to *Foot in Mouth* (1982).

9 *Of a certain book, Mr Stewart West of Cleethorpes heard someone say in a bookshop:* **'I heard it sterilized on** *Woman's Hour* . . . '

Contributed to BBC Radio *Quote ... Unquote* (23 February 1982).

10 *During a performance of* **Fidelio** *at Leeds:* **'Darling, I never knew Fellatio could be such fun!'**

Contributed to *Say No More* (1987).

11 *Overheard in a bookshop:* **'Do you have a copy of** *Dining Out in Paris and London* **by George Orwell?'**

Contributed to BBC Radio *Quote ... Unquote* (24 August 1985) by John Bell of Guildford.

12 'Two mothers chatting about a recently held fancy dress party. One asked: "And did your little daughter enjoy herself?" The other replied: "Oh, yes, she looked very sweet. We dressed her up in one of those Japanese commodes."'

Contributed to BBC Radio *Quote ... Unquote* (9 March 1982) by Pam Fox of Worplesdon.

13 'A lady who used to come to help with the housework was talking to my sister about her son's forthcoming marriage: "His employers have been very good to him. As he had no holiday time left they have granted him passionate leave for his honeymoon".'

Contributed by Mrs E.F. Holmes of Holland on Sea to *Foot in Mouth* (1982).

14 'A local Mrs Malaprop spoke endlessly of her husband who suffered a lot with his "slipped dick". She had been on holiday in a Caraway Van, the only complaint being that there was only one Emanuel Saucepan provided.'

Contributed by Gerald V. Hall of Bath, similarly.

15 'I was in the company of an elderly lady recently and there was some argument as to the whereabouts of her airman son at the end of the last war. Finally, to settle the matter, she

said: "Well, I know he was home on leave in May 1945 as we gave him a V.D. party."'
Contributed by Kathleen Richardson of Uxbridge, similarly.

16 'I went to see an old lady and asked how she was: "Oh dear, I've 'ad an 'orrid shock," she said. "My neighbour next door went to one of them parties last night and fell down dead with a trombonist".'
Contributed by Helen Wiggs of Wimborne, similarly.

17 'My dear old mother and I were discussing a friend who had just left his wife for a newer model. She said: "I think it's disgusting. Where would he be without her? Do you remember when he was doing that PhD? She used to do all his typing — and she used to sit up all night helping him with his faeces.'
Contributed to BBC Radio Quote ... Unquote (12 January 1982) by Bill Duffield of Banbury.

18 'I collected my Grandmother (aged 78) from a Christmas party where everyone had supplied a dish. She got in the car and announced that her tummy was giving her jip. When asked why, she replied: "Well, dear, I had chicken in Harpic."'
Contributed to BBC Radio Quote ... Unquote (17 July 1980) by Gillian Parker of Moulton, near Newmarket.

19 'My elderly aunt told me she had been to see the play "Arsenal and Old Lace."'
Contributed to BBC Radio Quote ... Unquote (29 May 1980) by Mrs A. Alexander, Newcastle-upon-Tyne.

20 'Two Winchester boys have run away to join the British Legion.'
A BBC Radio 2 newsreader allegedly said this, according to David Simpkins of Pulborough, Sussex (BBC Radio Quote ... Unquote, 4 September 1979).

21 *What the woman said to her friend as they were passing the Women's Hospital:* 'That's where I had my ex-directory . . .'
Contributed to BBC Radio Quote ... Unquote (29 September 1984) by Mrs E.M. Carberry of Fallowfield, Manchester.

22 'A crony at work told me a friend of his was up before the bench: "For living on the immortal earnings of his wife . . .".'
Contributed by John Taylor to *Foot in Mouth* (1982).

23 *First Female Relative:* 'When I was on holiday in Spain, I nearly got stung by those huge jellyfish.' *Second Female Relative:* 'You mean the Portuguese Menopause?'

Contributed to BBC Radio Quote ... Unquote (31 July 1980) by R.N.W. Ellis of Llangammach Wells.

24 *An ITN reporter announced excitedly:* 'Mr Thorpe insisted that he hadn't known Andrew Newton before he went to goal, hadn't seen him while he was in goal, and had no contact with him since being released from goal.'

After a press conference given by Jeremy Thorpe. Recalled on BBC Radio Quote ... Unquote (24 December 1977).

25 'Ample, rosy-faced lady with bulging shopping bags on bus: "Yerse, she took up wiv one of them new-fangled religions. You know, the Seven Day Adventuresses".'

Contributed by Constance Darg of Tonbridge, similarly.

26 'The event was a nativity play and the Angel Gabriel announced his presence to the Virgin Mary with the words: "Hail! Thou that art highly-flavoured . . .".'

Contributed by Angela Hoyle of Halifax, similarly.

27 'At a Labour committee meeting in the Midlands, the Chairman, in his opening remarks, was heard to say: "Brothers, as you all know, certain allegations have been made against me. I will reply to these at the next meeting after I have confronted the alligators."'

Contributed to BBC Radio Quote ... Unquote (26 January 1982) by Leslie Thomas.

28 'My mother was having a cataract operation and the lady in the next bed told her that she was suffering from a "Detached retinue".'

Contributed to BBC Radio Quote ... Unquote (26 June 1979) by Jane Baker of Thame.

29 **From the programme for a production of Verdi's** *Un Ballo in Maschera* **at the Palace Theatre, Manchester:**

'SYNOPSIS
ACT ONE
A small pizza in Venice . . .'

Contributed by Paul Hindle of Prestwich to Granada TV *Cabbages and Kings* (15 July 1979).

30 'Received directly, face-to-face, in conversation with a friend some years ago: "Ah, poor soul, she's got something eternal, you know. She's got a cyst on her aviary."'
Contributed to BBC Radio *Quote ... Unquote* (31 July 1979) by Dorothy Mair of Brighton

31 'One of our WRVS members asked an old lady if there was anything she wanted. She replied: "Yes, I'd like a long-sleeved Cardinal to keep me warm".'
Contributed to BBC Radio *Quote ... Unquote* (9 March 1982) by Mrs J.M. Thomassen of Bexhill-on-Sea.

32 'When I was working in a canteen, one of the staff said: "You know why we are rushed off our feet? Because they keep giving them those luncheon vultures."'
Contributed to BBC Radio *Quote ... Unquote* (15 December 1981) by Mrs J. Grist of Hampton, Middlesex.

33 'My mother rang me up in a great state of excitement and said, "Darling, isn't it wonderful, Virginia Woolf has won Wimbledon?"'
Contributed by Jilly Cooper to BBC Radio *Quote ... Unquote* (29 May 1980).

34 'My husband won't be here today. He's gone to the solicitor's to add a *cul-de-sac* to his will.'
Contributed to BBC Radio *Quote ... Unquote* (8 September 1984) by Mr W.J. Rowell of Kettering, Northamptonshire.

35 On the subject of childbirth, Mrs Malaprop is reassuring: 'You'll be all right. My friend's daughter had a Cesarewitch, and she was fine.'
Contributed to BBC Radio *Quote ... Unquote* (6 December 1986) by Peggy Frost of Hatch End, Middlesex.

36 'Did you know Doris had died?' 'Oh, no! Mind you, she had sugar beet for years, didn't she?'

37 'She has a pepsi ulcer, poor dear . . .'

38 *Evidence of hanky-panky between her daughter and the boy-friend was adduced by one Liverpudlian. Said she:* 'It was there for all to see . . . a used conservative on the mantel-piece.'
Told by Beryl Bainbridge on BBC Radio *Quote ... Unquote* (29 September 1984).

39 *Two passing ladies were discussing the hats they would wear at a forthcoming wedding. Said one:* 'No, my dear, I think you'll look best in a **pillar-box**.'

40 *In the doctor's surgery:* 'Have you been keeping all right?' 'Oh, I've been so busy, I've been working like a **Trojan horse**!'

41 'Mother was recounting how the Vietnamese Boat People still tended to stick together in their adoptive countries: "You know, they all live in a **gâteau**."'
Contributed to BBC Radio *Quote ... Unquote* (1 September 1984) by Mary Phillips of Sutton, Surrey.

42 'Father had a nasty carbuncle on his back. His housekeeper telephoned the daughter with the dire news: "Your poor father's been taken away in great pain. He has a **bungalow** on his back . . .".'
Contributed to BBC Radio *Quote ... Unquote* (1 September 1984) by Mrs Hazel Noble of Mill Hill, London.

43 Laura Corrigan was an American who set up as a society hostess in London. When she bought a house in Grosvenor Street, she referred to it as: 'My little *ventre-à-terre*.'

44 'All the food is polluted now with **monoglutium sodomite**.'

45 'He promised he could fix the roof, and he seemed quite *bona fido*.'

46 *A proud mother was explaining why she liked to dine at her daughter's:* 'She is such a good cook. She's a **condom blue**, you know.'

47 *Observing a painting done by a friend:* 'Oh, very **birazze**!'

48 'I regard myself as one of the last **Bastilles** of the British Empire'.

49 'No, they didn't have any family. He was **impudent**, you see.'

50 'My husband has made a right good job of our bathroom, I can tell you. He's painted it in white and **Mongolia**.'

∎∎

51 *A very old man was pleased to have been invited to attend his neighbour's wedding. He said proudly*: 'I'm going to the church and to the conception afterwards.'
Contributed to BBC Radio Quote ... Unquote (14 September 1985) by Marjorie Davies of Porthcawl.

52 'We've recently bought a beautiful three-piece suite in stimulated leather.'

53 'Of course, we'll be quite comfortable, he's on a granulated pension.'
Contributed to BBC Radio Quote ... Unquote (29 December 1980) by Mr A.V. Dunmall of Sidcup.

54 'There's nothing I like more on an evening like this than a long cool John Thomas.'

55 'I told him a hundred times it was no use, but it was like duck's water off his back.'

56 'His mother told him always to masturbate thirty-two times before swallowing.'

57 'He's in considerable pain because of his swollen tentacles.'

58 'My niece is going to apply for a divorce because her marriage has never been consumed.'

59 'He had to get his biceps right down my throat.'

60 'And they bought gifts – Gold, Frankenstein and Myrrh.'

61 'I simply cannot stand the new vicar – he fornicates all over you.'

62 'Does your headmaster believe in capital punishment in the classroom?'

63 'I think he's bitten off a bit of a white elephant there.'

64 'I've got this blouse with Border Anglesey around the neck.'

65 'She was walking down the aisle carrying the most beautiful bunch of Friesians.'

66 **'And so we switched on the emotion heater and went to bed.'**
Contributed to BBC Radio *Quote ... Unquote* (7 August 1980) by Owen Ascroft of Hove.

67 **'He's wonderful for his age, you know. He has all his facilities.'**

68 **'I often walk through the students' compost.'**

69 **'Well, the ball's in your frying pan now.'**

70 **'Don't fly off at a tangerine, lad.'**

71 **'Well, my favourite saint is the one who looked after all the birds and the animals. What was his name? – Francis of Onassis . . . .'**
Contributed to BBC Radio *Quote ... Unquote* (19 June 1979) by David Bennett of Hitchin.

72 **'I met a woman whose husband was in hospital and asked how he was. She replied: "Not good. They gave him a post mortem yesterday."'**
Contributed to BBC Radio *Quote ... Unquote* (29 December 1981) by Joan Hewitt of Maryport, Cumbria.

MANAGEMENT
1 **'Do you know why our boss has been given the nickname "Thrombosis"?'**
  'No, why?'
  'Well, I had to look it up and in the medical dictionary it said "Thrombosis" was a bloody clot that buggered up the system.'
Current by the 1960s.

MANCHESTER
1 **What's the best thing to come out of Manchester? The M62.**
Compare 'The shortest way out of Manchester is notoriously a bottle of Gordon's gin' – William Bolitho, British writer (1890–1930), from 'Caliogstro and Seraphina' in *Twelve Against the Gods* (1930). However, *The Times* (21 June 1921) was writing: 'Certainly if drink, in the proverbial saying, has proved on occasion "the shortest way out of Manchester . . .".'

MANKIND

1 It is difficult to love mankind unless one has a reasonable private income and when one has a reasonable private income one has better things to do than loving mankind.

Hugh Kingsmill, British writer (1889-1949), quoted in Richard Ingrams, God's Apology (1977).

MANNERS

1 On the Continent people have good food, in England people have good table manners.

George Mikes, How To Be An Alien (1946).

MANURE

1 A: What are you going to do with that manure?
B: I'm going to put it on my rhubarb.
A: That's funny. We put custard on ours.

MARRIAGE

1 'Heard in the sermon at a marriage – the priest holy, innocent and slightly dotty, said: "Sometimes in a marriage, the couple have been known to get on top of each other . . .".'

Contributed by the Revd. B. Paul Gilroy of Ewloe to Foot in Mouth (1982).

2 Marriage isn't a word but a sentence.

Included in Graffiti 5 (1986).

3 The only really happy people are married women and single men.

Attributed to H.L. Mencken.

4 Marriage is a wonderful institution – but who wants to live in an institution?

Included in Graffiti 2 (1980). Compare 'Marriage is a great institution, but I'm not ready for an institution yet', a line attributed to Mae West.

5 'My mother said it was simple to keep a man – you must be a maid in the living room, a cook in the kitchen and a whore in the bedroom. I said I'd hire the other two and take care of the bedroom bit.'

Jerry Hall, American model (1956–), attributed remark by 1985.

6 **It begins when you sink into his arms and ends with your arms in his sink.**
From Cambridge, included in *Graffiti 2* (1980).

7 **'My wife and I were setting off on our honeymoon late in the evening, and an aged relative, on hearing that we had quite a distance to travel, inquired: "Are you going all the way tonight?"'**
Contributed to BBC Radio *Quote ... Unquote* (1 December 1981) by Matthew Cochrane of Maghull, Merseyside.

8 **Even if we take matrimony at its lowest, even if we regard it as a sort of friendship recognized by the police ...**
Robert Louis Stevenson, *Virginibus Puerisque* (1881).

9 **'On our tenth wedding anniversary my wife sent me a card saying, "Thank you for seven wonderful years."'**
Told about his ex-wife by David Hamilton on BBC Radio *Where Were You In '62?* (10 May 1983).

10 **WHAT DO YOU HAVE IN COMMON WITH YOUR HUSBAND? – we were both married on the same day.**
Advertisement for women's magazine article and addition, included in *Graffiti 2* (1980).

11 **I'm not going to make the same mistake once.**
Warren Beatty, US film actor (1937–), quoted in Bob Chieger, *Was It Good For You Too?* (1983).

MARX, KARL
German political theorist (1818–83).

1 *Je suis Marxiste – tendance Groucho.*
From Paris in May 1968, included in *Graffiti Lives OK* (1979).

MARX, CHICO
American film comedian (1886–1961).

1 **There are three things that my brother Chico is always on: a phone, a horse or a broad.**
Attributed to Groucho Marx.

MASOCHISM

1 **Sadism and masochism mean never having to say you're sorry.**
Graffito, quoted in Rachel Bartlett (ed.), *Off the Wall* (1982).

MASTURBATION

1 *Woman:* **You are the greatest lover I have ever known.**
Allen: **Well, I practise a lot when I'm on my own.**
Woody Allen, *Love and Death* (1975).

2 **Don't knock masturbation, it's sex with someone I love.**
Woody Allen, *Annie Hall* (1977).

3 **Masturbation is the thinking man's television.**
Christopher Hampton, British playwright (1946–) in *The Philanthropist* (1970).

4 **I'll come and make love to you at five o'clock. If I'm late, start without me.**
Tallulah Bankhead, quoted in Ted Morgan, *Somerset Maugham* (1980).

5 **You know what I like about masturbation? You don't have to talk afterwards.**
Milos Forman (1980) – quoted in Bob Chieger, *Was It Good For You Too?* (1983).

6 **The good thing about masturbation is that you don't have to dress up for it.**
Truman Capote, quoted in Bob Chieger, *Was It Good For You Too?* (1983).

7 **I just fell in love with my hand.**
From Wisconsin, in Haan & Hammerstrom *Graffiti in the Big Ten* (1981). Earlier from Vietnam (dated 1971) with the addition 'Don't you wish you were ambidextrous' in Reisner & Wechsler, *Encyclopedia of Graffiti* (1974).

8 **Masturbation is the art of coming unscrewed.**
In Haan & Hammerstrom *Graffiti in the Southwest Conference* (1981).

MEANNESS

1 **'Staying at a seaside boarding house where the portions were rather small, a woman was offered honey in a pot not much bigger than a thimble. Said she, sweetly, to the landlady: "Ah, I see you keep a bee . . .".'**
Contributed to BBC Radio *Quote ... Unquote* (20 July 1985) by Reg Capstic of Tebay in Cumbria.

2 *In reply to robber demanding 'Your money or your life!':*
I'm thinking it over.
Jack Benny, US comedian (1894–1974), his basic joke from the 1930s onwards.

MEDIOCRITY
1 **Only the mediocre are always at their best.**
Graffito from the Hyde Park Underpass, London, contributed to BBC Radio
Quote ... Unquote (29 May 1980) by Mark Elsen of Southport. Among those
credited with originating this remark are Jean Giraudoux, Max Beerbohm and
W. Somerset Maugham (the latter specifically referring to writers). Of these,
the Beerbohm appears in S.N. Behrman's Conversations with Max (1960) in the
form: 'Only mediocrity can be trusted to be always at its best.' The Maugham
appears in Quotations for Speakers and Writers (1969). The Giraudoux appears
without source in Robert Byrne's The 637 Best Things Anybody Ever Said (1982).

MEEKNESS
1 **And the meek shall inherit the earth, if that's all right with the
rest of you.**
Graffito on a wall in Sunderland. Contributed to BBC Radio Quote ... Unquote
(24 May 1978) by Mr B. Skelton of Boldon, Tyne and Wear.

2 **The meek shall inherit the earth, but not its mineral rights.**
Included in Graffiti 3 (1981). Has also been attributed to J. Paul Getty, the
American oil tycoon (1892–1976).

MEMBERS
1 **When she saw the sign 'Members Only', she thought of him.**
Spike Milligan, Puckoon (1963).

MEN
1 **Men are those creatures with two legs and eight hands.**
Jayne Mansfield, US film actress (1932–67), attributed.

2 **Give a man a free hand and he'll try to put it all over you.**
Mae West in the film Klondike Annie (1936).

3 **No innocent man buys a gun and no happy man writes his
memoirs.**
Raymond Duff Payne, quoted in Garrison Keillor, Lake Wobegon Days (1986).

MENU MISTAKES

Misprints and mistranslations observed in restaurant menus found as far afield as Ely, Athens, Venice, Funchal, Torremolinos, Rome, Paris, Barcelona and in the Caledonian Road, London – not to mention in Japan, Kenya, Jamaica, Crete, Libya, and the United States.

1 **All cocktails are served with a cherry and a small wooden prick.**

2 **Half-fresh grapefruit.**

3 **Satiated calamary**

4 **Potage of soup.**
Contributed by Professor John Taylor to BBC Radio Quote ... Unquote (24 July 1979).

5 **Hen soup.**

6 **Foul soup.**

7 **Shrotted pimps.**
Contributed to BBC Radio Quote ... Unquote (15 January 1979) by Sian Lancaster of Balcombe Forest, Sussex, from a restaurant where she herself once worked.

8 **Gratinated nuddles.**

9 **Shrimps in spit.**
A hotel in Rome offered prawns grilled on a skewer with these words. Contributed to BBC Radio Quote ... Unquote (14 June 1978) by Mrs. V. Womerseley from Bath.

10 **Hard egg with sauce mayonnaise.**

11 **Frightened eggs.**

12 **Roll Map.**

13 **Bowel tomato surprise.**
Audrey and Richard Ryder of Faringdon clasped their stomachs when they read this in a taverna in Crete. Contributed to BBC Radio Quote ... Unquote (24 May 1978).

14 **Dreaded veal cutlet.**

15 **Larks in the spit.**

16 **Spited rooster.**

17 **Battered codpieces.**

18 *Sole Bone Femme* **(Fish Landlady Style)**

19 **Drowned squid.**
Spotted in a canal-side restaurant in Venice by David Jackson of Eastbourne.
Contributed to BBC Radio *Quote ... Unquote* (24 May 1978).

20 **God whipped in cream.**
From Paris. Contributed by Ursula Smith of Evreux to BBC Radio *Quote ...
Unquote* (22 June 1977).

21 **Bacon and Germs.**
From Funchal. Contributed by Kingsley Amis to BBC Radio *Quote ... Unquote*
(7 June 1978).

22 **Yellow Lasagne – Tuesday. Green Lasagne – Wednesday.**

23 **Utmost of chicken.**
Chicken supreme!

24 **Tasteful chicken in paperbag.**
Contributed to BBC Radio *Quote ... Unquote* (24 July 1980) by Sara Squires –
who saw it in a London Chinese restaurant.

25 **Potatoes in shirt.**

26 **English Teak and Kidney.**
Contributed to BBC Radio *Quote ... Unquote* (24 July 1980) by Mrs Mary Button
of Herne Bay.

27 **Porn shops.**
In a taverna in Crete, Mrs M.A. Liddell of London SW1 found, disappointingly,
that this only meant 'pork chops'. Contributed to BBC Radio *Quote ... Unquote*
(24 May 1978).

28 **Veal Gordon Blue.**

29 **Raped carrots.**
From Paris. Contributed by Ursula Smith of Evreux to BBC Radio *Quote ...
Unquote* (22 June 1977).

30 **Sweet smalls pie.**
From a restaurant in Barcelona, contributed by Peter Hebert of London NW8
to Granada TV *Cabbages and Kings* (12 August 1979).

31 *Assiette Anglaise* **(Dishy Englishwoman).**
Contributed by Ann Leslie to BBC Radio *Quote ... Unquote* (15 January 1979),
from a Parisian *menu touristique*.

32 **Jam Trat.**

33 **Tarts of the house at pleasure.**

34 **La Spume du Chef (with ice).**

35 **Sherry Trifle and Randy Snaps.**
Contributed to BBC Radio Quote ... Unquote (24 July 1980) by Mrs V. Elleson of Durham.

36 **Café au lit.**

37 **Garlic Coffee.**
Contributed by Professor John Taylor to BBC Radio Quote ... Unquote (24 July 1979).

38 **'I am not very keen on all this German food,' said the diner. 'It's just one greasy sausage after another.'**
'I'm so sorry you do not like our food,' replied the German host, 'but, cheer up, the *würst* is yet to come . . . .'
Contributed to BBC Radio Quote ... Unquote (1 June 1977) by Polly Toynbee.

MICKEY MOUSE
1 **One Christmas, a rich man's kid asked if he could have a Mickey Mouse outfit. So his father bought him an advertising agency.**
Told variously about similar institutions in the 1980s.

MISSION IMPOSSIBLE
1 **Mission impossible — Maidenhead revisited.**
Contributed by L.R. Ekblom of Woodford Green to *Graffiti 5* (1986).

MICE
1 **It is difficult to explain to white mice that black cats are lucky.**
Graffito in Covent Garden, London. Contributed to BBC Radio Quote ... Unquote (5 January 1982) by Clyde Stevens of London SW6.

MILITARY INTELLIGENCE
1 **Military Intelligence is a contradiction in terms.**
Said to come from a Ministry of Defence building in London (where it remained briefly), included in *Graffiti Lives OK* (1979). Attributed to Groucho Marx by A. Spiegelman and B. Schneider, *Whole Grains*.

MILK
1 **The famous screen actress was advised by her physician that she should bathe daily in milk to help her with a skin condition**

she had. 'Pasteurised?' she asked. 'No,' replied the physician,
'only up to your tits.'

Current by the late 1950s.

MILLIPEDES

1 **Q. Why don't millipedes play football?**
**A. Because by the time they've tied on their football boots,
the game's over . . . .**

Told by Caroline Lewis, Plymouth (1986).

MINDS

1 **Both parachutes and minds work best when they are open.**

MINKS

1 **How do girls get minks? The same way minks get minks.**

Contributed by Joan Bakewell to BBC Radio *Quote ... Unquote* (26 June 1979).

MISPRINTS

1 **In the mid-1970s, the Notting Hill Carnival in London often
ended in clashes between revellers and the police. One year,
the *Daily Star* rushed to tell its readers that towards the end of
the Late Summer Bank Holiday scuffles had broken out in the
crowd. Unfortunately, it got one letter wrong and told its
presumably somewhat bemused readership that 'towards the
end of the day *souffles* broke out in the crowd.'**

Well, that's how I tell it, but the actual text of the (undated) article is, in fact:
'Sid Scott made his début at a reggae concert . . . and stopped a riot. As
"souffles" broke out in the huge crowd, he told the fans: "This is nothing to do
with you or the police. It's just an unfortunate incident".'

2 **'*Armand Hammer's* opinions of Prince Charles came in a
telephone interview from Los Angeles with the Sunday Times. "In
my opinion he will make a great king. He is a young man wise
beyond his ears . . . ."'**

By 1987.

3 **'Brigadier Bollsover, the bottle-scarred veteran, died at his
home last week, aged 85.'**

A famous misprint, but did it ever appear in this or any other form? In Nat J.

Ferber, *I Found Out* (1939) it is related that once on the New York *American* the term 'battle-scared hero' was hastily corrected in a later edition and came out reading 'bottle-scarred hero'.

4 *Reporting on the vote about Sunday opening of pubs in Wales, a newspaper stated:* **'At the Llandrindod Wells headquarters of the Seven Day Opening council a special election room was set up, complete with swigometer.'**

By 1984.

5 *A newspaper published the following correction:* **'In an article by Ian Craig in Thursday's paper it should have been reported that Dave Eager made a deft speech to the Tory Conference in Brighton.'**

By 1987.

6 *From the radio listings in the* **Daily Telegraph: '11.00 Frank Muir Goes Into Pubic Transport.'**

Contributed by Richard Banyard of Bristol to Granada TV *Cabbages and Kings* (23 May 1979).

MISTRESSES

1 **When you marry your mistress, you create a job vacancy.**

Sir James Goldsmith, British industrialist (1933–), attributed.

2 **When the Spanish wife discovered that her husband was keeping a mistress, all hell broke loose. But – as he patiently explained to her – he had to have a mistress because his main competitor in business did. The wife was appeased and the situation continued.**

Then, shortly afterwards, husband and wife were at the opera and he pointed out his main competitor who was sitting with his mistress a few rows away. 'And,' he added, 'if you look two rows in front of us – that woman with the tiara – that's my one.'

'Well dear,' exclaimed the wife, 'I think ours is the better looking of the two.'

A version of this story was given in the *Observer* (16 December 1994).

MONOPOLIES

1 **How come there's only one Monopolies Commission?**

In *Graffiti 4* (1982).

MOORE, DUDLEY
British musician and actor (1935–).

1 **Dudley Moore is a phallic thimble.**
Graffito, quoted in Rachel Bartlett (ed.), *Off the Wall* (1982).

MOTHERS
1 **'Sometimes when I look at my children I say to myself, "Lillian, you should have stayed a virgin."'**
Lillian Carter, American mother of President Carter (1898–1983), made this remark in 1980, specifically with regard to her son, Billy.

2 **Q. What's old and wrinkled and hangs out your trousers? A. Your mother.**
Graffito from Railway Square, Sydney, Australia. Contributed by Tim Denes of Mosman, NSW, to *Graffiti 5* (1986).

3 **A new mother soon becomes a chief cook and bottom washer.**

4 **There's no accounting for tastes, as the woman said when somebody told her her son was wanted by the police.**
Franklin Pierce Adams, American humorist (1881–1960), quoted in *The Treasury of Humorous Quotations*, ed. by Evan Esar & Nicolas Bentley (1951).

5 **My wife is the kind of girl who'll not go anywhere without her mother, and her mother will go anywhere.**
John Barrymore, American actor (1882–1942).

MOTHERS-IN-LAW
1 **Peter remained on friendly terms with Christ notwithstanding Christ's having healed his mother-in-law.**
Samuel Butler, English writer (1835–1902), quoted in *The Treasury of Humorous Quotations*, ed. by Evan Esar & Nicolas Bentley (1951).

2 **My mother-in-law broke up my marriage. One day my wife came home early and found us in bed together.**
Attributed to Lenny Bruce, American satirist (1923–66).

See also CHRISTMAS 4; FAMILIES 2.

MOTIVATIONAL SPEAKERS

1 The speaker was very anxious to find a way of bringing home to his audience how really important dynamism and enthusiasm were in making a success of one's working life. Then, just as he was entering the lecture theatre, he noticed the word 'PUSH' written up on the door. This seemed to him the perfect slogan to draw to his audience's attention.

And so, as he reached the climax of his speech, the speaker said, 'And if there is one word which encapsulates the secret of how to get on business, then that word is the one which is written right there on the door to this hall.'

The audience, to a man, swung its eyes to the door where — in clearly-defined letters — it saw what the speaker decreed was the secret of advancement in business. It was the one word, 'PULL'.

In the days before the term 'motivational speaking' had been invented, I heard this story told in a 'careers lecture' at school, around 1960.

MOTOR CARS

1 When a man buys a motor car, he doesn't always know what he is letting himself in for.

A most useful quotation — from Jaroslav Hasek's *The Good Soldier Svejk* (1923). Svejk's charwoman tells him of the assassination of Franz Ferdinand — the event that triggered off the First World War — as the Archduke drove through Sarajevo in a motor car. Svejk deduces the above from this occurrence. Hasek's humour is oblique at the best of times (some would say imperceptible) and another translator renders this passage much more meekly, thus: 'Yes, of course, a gentleman like him can afford it, but he never imagines that a drive like that might finish up badly.'

MUSIC

1 Live music is an anachronism, and now is the winter of our discothèque.

Remark made by the British writer and broadcaster, Benny Green (1927–), by 1976.

2 If music be the food of love, how about a bite of your maracas?

Quoted in Bruce Ridley (ed.), *Wall Flowers: A Collection of Australian Graffiti* (1981).

MYTHS

1 **What is a myth?**
A female moth, of course.
A Christmas cracker joke, yeah verily. Recounted in the *Sunday Telegraph* (20 December 1987).

2 **What's a myth?**
A lady with a lisp but no husband.

NAPOLEON

1 **Napoleon wore his sleeve on his heart.**
Included in *Grattiti 5* (1986).

See also SAILORS 1.

NATIONAL COMPARISONS

1 **An Englishman is never happy unless he is miserable. A Scotsman is never at home except when he is abroad. An Irishman is never at peace unless he is fighting.**
Said to date from the 19th century.

See also EUROPEANS.

NECROPHILIA

1 **Necrophilia means never having to say you're sorry.**
In *Graffiti 4* (1982).

2 **Incest is relatively boring.**
Necrophilia is dead boring.
Graffito written up in a private place in Maidenhead library. Contributed to BBC Radio *Quote ... Unquote* (31 May 1978) by N.B. Bryson.

See also FLOGGING.

NERVOUS BREAKDOWNS

1 Nervous breakdowns are hereditary — we get them from our children.

Included in *Graffiti* 2 (1980).

NEUROTICS

1 Neurotics build castles in the air. Psychotics live in them. Psychiatrists charge the rent.

From Birmingham University, included in *Graffiti* 2 (1980). Sometimes 'Psychotics smash the windows' is inserted.

NEVERTHELESS

1 A university lecturer was giving a lecture on the subtleties of the English language. 'Take the word "nevertheless",' he said. Consider how many other words and expressions have a similar meaning — "however", "notwithstanding that", "moreover", "in any case" — there is a multitude of them. But "nevertheless" has a subtlety of meaning all its own and sometimes it is the only word that will do. I will give you an example. There was a ceilidh in the Highlands of Scotland where the next performance was being announced by the Fear an Tighe. "We shall now have a song from Miss Jeannie Macleod," he said. "She's a wee whore," came a voice from the back. "Never-the-less, she will now sing . . .".'

Told to me by Donald Adaway of Thurso, Caithness, in October 1994. He said he first heard it 'thirty years ago'. Compare ACTORS AND ACTING 3.

NEWS ITEMS

Most famously in BBC TV's The Two Ronnies, *the announcing of cod news items has become a staple of broadcast comedy in recent years. The form of words and the condensed nature of the information serves to heighten the punch.*

1 Scotland Yard is now fairly certain that the Royal Albert Hall has been stolen. They have issued a description of a man they would like to interview in connection with the robbery. He was last seen boarding a number 74 bus carrying a large brown paper parcel.

Known by 1958.

2 **Prince Philip flew into London airport last night. It is hoped to have it rebuilt by the end of the week.**
Known by 1958.

NEWSPAPER HEADLINES

1 **BOOK LACK IN ONGAR.**
Private Eye headline on a librarians' strike in Essex. By 1979.

2 **PLAN TO BAN ROOFTOP PARKING.**
From the Derby *Evening Telegraph*, contributed by Paul Whitaker of Chaddesden, Derby, to Granada TV *Cabbages and Kings* (15 July 1979).

3 **INCEST MORE COMMON THAN THOUGHT IN U.S.**
British newspaper, by 1979.

4 **NEW SCREWING METHOD CUTS FATIGUE AND INCREASES PRODUCTIVITY.**
Mechanical Engineering, by 1982.

5 **THEY'RE OFF, HAROLD TELLS QUEEN.**
By 1976.

6 **JOINT BODY PLAN FOR CEMETERY.**
Hereford Times, by 1982.

7 **BODY IN GARDEN WAS A PLANT, SAYS WIFE.**
From the *South China Morning Post*, contributed to BBC Radio *Quote … Unquote* (5 February 1979) by S/Sgt G.A. Tapping. When he was serving in Hong Kong, he said, Malcolm X was arrested in the United States and his garden dug up by the police. They found a body there and this headline resulted from their interview with his wife.

8 **MACARTHUR FLIES BACK TO FRONT.**
Said to date from 1950/51 when MacArthur was in confrontation with President Truman in Washington. Contributed to BBC Radio *Quote … Unquote* (21 June 1978) by Richard Boston.

9 **ICELANDIC FISH TALKS – NOT LIKELY**
Grimsby Evening Telegraph, by 1979.

10 **YOUTH HIT BY TRAIN RUSHED TO TWO HOSPITALS.**
Harrow Observer. Contributed to BBC Radio *Quote … Unquote* (19 June 1980) by Margaret Brand.

11 **WALK-OUT BY 150 CRIPPLES TOP HOSPITAL.**
Yorkshire Post, by 1979.

12 **SARDINE LIVING IN OSAKA MINI-HOTEL.**
The Times, by 1982.

13 **LUCKY VICTIM WAS STABBED THREE TIMES.**
Hackney Gazette, by 1982.

14 **PATIENTS CUT TO EASE CROWDING.**
Bristol Evening Post, by 1982.

15 **DEFENDER'S BROKEN LEG HITS HAVERHILL.**
Cambridge Evening News, by 1982.

16 **OUSTED RSPCA MAN SAYS HE WAS A SCAPEGOAT.**
The Times, by 1984.

17 **FATHER OF 7 SHOT DEAD. MISTAKEN FOR RABBIT.**
New York newspaper.

NEW YORK

1 New York . . . is not Mecca. It just smells like it.
Neil Simon, California Suite (1976) .

NICKNAMES

1 Because so many Welsh people share the same surname —
Jones, Evans — a tradition has grown up of distinguishing
between the various ones by applying a nickname. So, 'Jones
the Post' was invented to distinguish him from 'Jones the Milk',
as well as a whole range of slyly affectionate epithets such as
'Hallelujah Evans' to mark out a man who sang loudly in
chapel. Then there was a window-cleaner called Davis in South
Wales who was distinguished by the nickname 'Chamois Davis
Jnr'.

Vernon Noble and I included this last in our book A Who's Who of Nicknames
(1985) believing that it was an actual example. On the other hand, I now know
that Les Dawson referred to the same nickname in BBC TV's The Dawson Watch
(Christmas 1980), so perhaps it is no more than a joke.

NIXON, RICHARD M.

US Republican President (1913–94).

1 NIXON IS THE FIRST PRESIDENT TO HAVE AN ASS-HOLE FOR
VICE-PRESIDENT.
– no, Eisenhower was.

From the University of Michigan, 1970 – included in Reisner & Wechsler,
Encyclopedia of Graffiti (1974). (Nixon was Eisenhower's Vice-President 1953–61.)

NOISE

1 An American tourist was standing on the green sward facing
Canterbury Cathedral while the great bells rang out across the
town. A benevolent old clergyman, seeing the visitor, went up
to him and tried to engage him in conversation.

'I take it, sir, that you are a stranger,' he began.

The tourist, cupping his hand to his ear, said, 'Hey?'

The clergyman raised his voice. 'I assume, sir, that you are
not a resident of these parts?'

'Eh?' said the American.

The clergyman pressed on with renewed effort. 'If you are
newly come to this place it must seem to you, even as it does
to those who dwell in these cloistered and holy precincts, that
the music of our glorious bells comes floating down to one
almost like the voice of the Almighty Himself, seeking through
the medium of their old brazen throats to communicate the
message of peace on earth, goodwill to all men, to us His
children here below.'

'What?' inquired the visitor.

'Er – what I meant to say,' said the clergyman, 'was that one
must carry away from here, after hearing our chimes, the
conviction in his soul that really he has been in communication
with Deity itself – that the voices of the angels have cried out
to him. Er – is it not so, my friend?'

The American shook his head. 'I'm sorry,' he said. 'I can't
make out a word you are saying because of these goddam
bloody bells!'

I remember hearing a version of this story in the 1950s. This one is based on Irvin
S. Cobb's even longer effort in *A Laugh a Day Keeps the Doctor Away* (1921).

2 *Angry neighbour*: 'Didn't you hear me banging on your ceiling
last night?'
Hungover neighbour: 'Oh, that's all right. We had a party last
night and were making lots of noise ourselves.'

NORTHERN IRELAND

1 ULSTER SAYS NO
   – but the man from Del Monte says Yes.

A wall in Fermanagh 'has long born this graffito', according to *The Times* (14 August 1986), but then a wag added: 'And he's a real orange man'. This is the bringing together of two slogans, one political, the other commercial. 'Ulster Says No' came to be the main Loyalist slogan following the Anglo-Irish 'Hillsborough' agreement of 1985 which seemed to encourage 'cross-border' cooperation between Britain and the Republic of Ireland. 'De man from Del Monte he say "yes"' was a line from a TV commercial about that time which suggested that Del Monte Fresh Fruit was not shipped until it had been subjected to rigorous selection procedures. Del Monte was then the largest distributor of fresh pineapples and the third largest distributor of bananas in the world.

2 Join the RUC and come home to a real fire.

Graffito observed by F. Vaughan, Belfast, in 1986. Following the Anglo-Irish agreement a number of the homes of RUC officers had been burned.

Compare WALES AND THE WELSH 1.

3 A staunch Ulster Protestant die-hard lay dying of an incurable disease. He gathered all his like-minded Orange friends about his bed and then proceeded to thunder at them some catastrophically bad news. 'Brothers!' he bellowed, 'I have to tell yuh that, preparing as I yum to me-at my may-ker, I have decayded to embrayuss the Roman Catholic church!'
   When they had picked themselves up off the floor, his friends demanded to know what had made him decide to take this appalling step.
   'Well-uh,' he replied, 'it seemed to me to be incontestubble, that I'd rather one of them died than one of us!'

Told by Richard Milbank (November 1994).

4 At a revivalist meeting in Northern Ireland, the Revd Dr Ian Paisley was holding forth on an eschatological theme, 'And when the day of judgement comes, there will be a great wailing and gnashing of teeth . . .', when he was interrupted by a little old lady at the front, who said, 'This is all very well, but what about those poor old folks like me that don't have any teeth?'
   Paisley thundered back, 'Teeth will be provided!'

See also POPES 5.

NOSE

1 **If your nose runs and your feet smell, you must be upside down.**
From Hertford, Herts, in *Graffiti 4* (1982).

NOSTALGIA

1 **Whatever did we do before we discovered nostalgia?**
Included in *Graffiti 2* (1980).

2 **NOSTALGIA IS ALL RIGHT, BUT IT'S NOT WHAT IT USED TO BE.
– but, don't worry, it will be one day.**
Contributed to BBC Radio *Quote ... Unquote* (7 June 1978) by Benny Green.
Nostalgia Isn't What It Used To Be was the title of Simone Signoret's 1978
autobiography and said to have been taken by her from a graffito. As
'Nostalgia ain't what it used to be', the remark has also been attributed to the
US novelist Peter de Vries.

NOTHING

1 **NOTHING ACTS FASTER THAN ANADIN
– then take nothing.**
Comment on advertisement, included in *Graffiti 2* (1980).

2 **NOTHING BEATS THE GREAT SMELL OF BRUT
– then why not use nothing?**
Ditto, in *Graffiti 3* (1981).

NOTICES AND SIGNS

1 **You are requested to take advantage of the chambermaid.**
From a Tokyo hotel room, c 1970, reported by Bruce M. Adkins of Gif-sur-
Yvette, France (1979).

2 *On a road sign stating 'Iver 1' was added the word 'big', hence
giving the message: 'Iver big 1'.*
Included in *Graffiti Lives OK* (1979).

3 **If you notice this notice you will notice that this notice is not
worth noticing. So don't notice it.**
From the University of Sydney, contributed by J.C.B. to *Graffiti 5* (1986).

4 **Convent of the Sisters of Charity.
NO PARKING. NO TURNING.**
In *Foot in Mouth* (1982).

5 **CONVENIENCES. CYCLISTS DISMOUNT.**
Notice in Southgate, London, by 1982.

6 **'I spent 1942–46 in Egypt. We used to go for a drink (lemonade) in the garden of the Summer Palace Hotel in Alexandria and we always giggled at the following notice in the garden: "CONSUMATION EST OBLIGATOIRE."'**
Contributed by Dorothy Heigham of Aldershot (1994).

7 **LESSON CHANGE TIME. If there is a fire alarm at this time, the whole school will immediately evacuate and assemble on the field.**
By 1982.

8 **ANYONE WANTING A MISTRESS DURING THE NIGHT SHOULD RING THE BELL.**
Notice observed in a British girls' school dormitory, when used as an army billet during the Second World War – and inordinately famous.

9 **STROKE PATIENTS. DON'T FEEL ALONE.**
Notice in doctor's waiting room, Colchester, by 1982.

10 **The Sisters, so called, of Mercy solicit tender alms. They harbour all kinds of diseases and have no respect for religion.**
An unusual warning notice near Milan cathedral (was it?), said to have been observed by Mark Twain, but untraced.

11 **Beware of pickpockets and especially of strangers offering to remove a stain from the clothing.**
Notice in the men's lavatory at the Royal Academy in London. Contributed to BBC Radio *Quote ... Unquote* (16 July 1983) by Martin Battersby of London SW10.

12 **LADIES UNACCOMPANIED ARE RESPECTFULLY REQUESTED TO USE TABLES FOR THEIR REFRESHMENTS AND NOT TO STAND AT THE BAR AND OBLIGE.**
Sign from a pub recorded by James Agate, *Ego 3* (1938).

13 **PLEASE SMOKE. THANK YOU FOR NOT JOGGING.**
Notice in New York City taxi, by 1987.

14 **ARE YOU LONELY?**
WHY NOT JOIN THE WEDNESDAY CLUB?
MEETING HERE AT 7.30
EVERY TUESDAY.

Contributed to BBC Radio Quote ... Unquote (6 October 1984) by Mr C.I.
Davies of Wrexham who spotted it outside a church in Ruabon, North Wales.

15 **SHOP ASSISTANT REQUIRED. NO OBJECTION TO SEX.**

Situation vacant advertisement, Looe, Cornwall. Before 1984.

16 **DOESN'T ANYONE OR ANYTHING WORK ROUND HERE?**
– Yes, I do. I put up the Out of Order signs.

Graffito and addition contributed to BBC Radio Quote ... Unquote (31 July 1979)
by H.T. Peplow of Dudley, who saw them on a Post Office stamp machine
beneath an 'Out of Order' sign.

Compare RADIO ARMENIA JOKES 2.

17 **NO SPITTING ON THURSDAYS.**

Alleged sign in Hollywood studio.

18 **IF YOU ENJOY GOOD FOOD, EAT AT OUR OTHER BRANCHES.**

Outside an Indian restaurant.

19 **LAST FILLING STATION BEFORE THE NEXT ONE.**

Outside garage on A565, near Southport.

20 **OUT FOR LUNCH. IF NOT BACK BY FOUR O'CLOCK, OUT**
FOR TEA ALSO.

On door of antique shop, Moretonhampstead, Devon

NUDISTS

1 **Nudists are people who wear one-button suits.**

Included in Reisner & Wechsler, *Encyclopedia of Graffiti* (1974).

2 **As four Aggies were going down the road they came to a**
high, solid brick wall. Wondering what was behind it, three of
the Aggies boosted the fourth so he could look over it.
'Looks like a nudist camp,' he exclaimed.
'Men or women?' his companions wanted to know.
'Can't tell,' he answered. 'They don't have any clothes on.'

Included in *The Best of 606 Aggie Jokes* (1988).

3 An Aggie went hunting and, when he was deep into a forest, he came upon a nude girl. 'Are you game?' he asked. 'Yes,' was her reply. So he shot her.

In the above book also.

NUNS

1 Feel superior – become a nun!

When I was at Oxford in the mid-1960s I remember seeing advertisements for telephonists (or perhaps for some job in the army) and the headline was something like, 'Be superior. Become an office supervisor'. This line followed inevitably.

2 The Mother Superior was asking the girls at a convent school what careers they were thinking of pursuing. One girl rather alarmed her by announcing that, when she left school, she was going to be a prostitute.

'A *prostitute!*' exclaimed the Mother Superior, 'Am I hearing right?'

'Yes, a prostitute,' said the girl.

'Oh, that's all right,' said the Mother Superior, 'for a horrible moment I thought you said *Protestant!*'

NURSERY RHYMES

1 Little Miss Muffet
Sat on her tuffet,
So nobody could get at it.
There came a big spider,
Who sat down beside her –
But he couldn't get at it either.

I wrote this in about 1966.

2 The Grand Old Duchess of York,
She *had* ten thousand men.
She'd march them up to the top of the hill,
Then say, 'Go on, do it again!'

Ditto.

3 Mary had a little lamb,
Its feet were made of lard.
And every time she took it out
It slipped back half a yard.

By about 1950.

4 **Mary had a little lamb.
The doctor was surprised.**

5 **Jack and Jill went up the hill
To fetch a pail of water.
Jill came down with half a crown
But not for fetching water.**

Included in *Why Was He Born So Beautiful and Other Rugby Songs* (1967).

NYMPHOMANIACS

1 **Definition of a nymphomaniac — a girl who trips you up and is under you before you hit the floor.**

From Warwick University, included in *Graffiti 2* (1980).

OBSCENE

1 **Save money on obscene phone calls — reverse the charges.**

Quoted in Bruce Ridley (ed.), *Wall Flowers: A Collection of Australian Graffiti* (1981).

2 **Women should be obscene and not heard.**

Included in Reisner & Wechsler, *Encyclopedia of Graffiti* (1974). Compare: 'Augustus John, then barely twenty-one, dined [with Oscar Wilde, but] found it difficult to say much in the presence of "the Master", remembering Wilde's quip that "little boys should be obscene and not heard"' — from H. Montgomery Hyde, *Oscar Wilde* (1976).

OEDIPUS

1 **COME HOME OEDIPUS, ALL IS FORGIVEN. MUM.
— over my dead body. Dad.**

Graffito from Sussex University library. Contributed to BBC Radio *Quote ... Unquote* (17 May 1978) by A.M. Vinicombe of Hove.

OFFICE LIFE

1 The boss called one of his chaps into the office and said, 'Do you know, it hasn't escaped me that every time United's playing at home mid-week you ask permission to go and visit your grandmother who's seriously ill.'
'What an incredible coincidence,' exclaimed the employee. 'You don't think, by any chance, she's faking it?'

OLD —— NEVER DIE . . . .

A notable use of the saying 'Old soldiers never die, they simply fade away' was made by General Douglas MacArthur when, following his dismissal by President Truman, he was allowed to address Congress on 19 April 1951. He ended: 'I still remember the refrain of one of the most popular barrack ballads of that day [turn of the century], which proclaimed, most proudly, that "Old soldiers never die. They just fade away." And like the old soldier of that ballad. I now close my military career and just fade away . . . .'

The origins of the ballad he quoted in fact lie in a British Army parody of the gospel hymn 'Kind Words Can Never Die' which (never mind MacArthur's dating) came out of the First World War. J. Foley copyrighted a version of the parody in 1920. In the 1980s, especially, the format of the phrase was used to comment on any number of jobs and groups of people:

1 Old baggage handlers never die, they just lose their grip.

2 Old bakers never die, they just quit making dough.

3 Old burglars never die, they just steal away.

4 Old chemists never die, they just don't react any more.

5 Old dieters never die, they just waist away.

6 Old D.I.Y. types never die – they just get plastered.

7 Old fairies never die, they merely blow away.

8 Old firemen never die, they just go to blazes.

9 Old fishermen never die, they just smell that way.

10 Old florists never die, they make other arrangements.

11 Old gardeners never die, they just spade away.

12 Old genealogists never die, they just lose their census.

13 Old golfers never die, they just putter away.

14 Old golfers never die, they simply lose their balls.

15 Old grave diggers never die, they just spade away.

16 Old hippies never die. They just take a trip.

17 Old informers never die, they just get put out to grass.

18 Old insurance agents never die, it's against their policy.

19 Old judges never die, they just cease to try.

20 Old lawyers never die, they just lose their appeal.

21 Old lawyers never die, they just rest their cases.

22 Old lumberjacks never die, they just pine away.

23 Old plagiarists never die, they just steal away.

24 Old plumbers never die, they just go down the drain.

25 Old poets never die, they just ride off into the sonnet.

26 Old postmen never die, they just lose their zip.

27 Old procrastinators never die, they just put it off.

28 Old professors never die, they just lose their faculties.
Graffito from the University of Nottingham, contributed by Peter Barnes of
Milton Keynes to Granada TV *Cabbages and Kings* (6 June 1979).

29 Old psychologists never die, they're forever Jung.

30 Old refrigerators never die. They just lose their cool.

31 Old skiers never die, they just go downhill.

32 Old soldiers never die – just their privates . . ..

33 Old soldiers never die, young ones do.

34 Old statisticians never die, they just average out.

35 Old storekeepers never die, they just sale away.

36 Old teachers never die, they just lose their class.

37 Old truckers never die, they just retyre.

38 Old weight watchers never die – they just fade away.

39 Old welders never die, they just pass the torch.

ONASSIS, ARISTOTLE
Greek-born shipping tycoon (1906–75).

1 **Q. What did Jackie Kennedy feel on her wedding night?
A. Old age creeping all over her.**
Joke told at the time of their marriage in 1968. Compare, from *Ballou's Dollar Magazine*, Vol. 1 (US, 1855): '"Old age is coming on me rapidly," as the urchin said when he was stealing apples from an old man's garden, and saw the owner coming.'

OPERA
1 **Opera in English is, in the main, just about as sensible as baseball in Italian.**
H.L. Mencken, American writer and editor (1880–1956), quoted in Frank Muir, *The Frank Muir Book* (1976).

2 **Opera is when a guy gets stabbed in the back and instead of bleeding he sings.**
Ed Gardner, American broadcaster (1905–63) in the 1940s radio show *Duffy's Tavern*, quoted in Muir, as above.

3 **Bed is the poor man's opera.**
Said to be an Italian proverb and quoted by Aldous Huxley in *Heaven and Hell* (1956). Compare 'Sexuality is the lyricism of the masses' — Charles Baudelaire, French poet (1821–67), in *Journaux Intimes* (published 1887).

ORAL SEX
1 **Oral sex! All you ever do is talk about it.**
Quoted in Bruce Ridley (ed.), *Wall Flowers: A Collection of Australian Graffiti* (1981).

2 **Aural sex produces eargasms.**

3 **I regret to say that we of the FBI are powerless to act in cases of oral-genital intimacy, unless it has in some way obstructed interstate commerce.**
J. Edgar Hoover, FBI Director (1895–1972) — quoted in Bob Chieger, *Was It Good For You Too?* (1983).

See also BLONDE JOKES 19, CUNNILINGUS and LOVELACE, LINDA.

ORANGUTANS *See under AMBITION.*

ORGASM

1 I finally had an orgasm . . . and my doctor told me it was the *wrong* kind.
Woody Allen, screenplay for the film *Manhattan* (1979).

2 In the case of some women, orgasms take quite a bit of time. Before signing on with such a partner, make sure you are willing to lay aside, say, the month of June, with sandwiches having to be brought in.
Bruce Jay Friedman, 'Sex and the Lonely Guy' in *Esquire* (1977).

3 Since most men can't keep it up long enough to fulfill woman's God-given — and soon to be Constitutioned — right to orgasm, the vibrator can take over while the man takes a leak.
Gore Vidal, in *Rolling Stone* (1980) — quoted in Bob Chieger, *Was It Good For You Too?* (1983).

See also FEMINIST JOKES 4.

ORGIES

1 'You get a better class of person at orgies, because people have to keep in trim more. There is an awful lot of going round holding in your stomach, you know. Everybody is very polite to each other. The conversation isn't very good but you can't have everything.'
Gore Vidal, interviewed on London Weekend Television *Russell Harty Plus* (1972).

OVERHEARDS

1 A young artist saw an eminent critic and a noble lord standing in front of one of his paintings, so he crept nearer to hear what they were saying about it. The noble lord said to the critic: 'Of the two, I prefer washing up.'
I described this joke as 'traditional' in my *Eavesdroppings* (1981). It has since been pointed out to me that T.H. White discussed a comic story current just after the Second World War in *The Age of Scandal* (1950): 'It is said that there was some conference or other at Lambeth, thronged with Archbishops, Cardinals, Patriarchs, Moderators and so forth. The Archbishops of Canterbury and

York were seen to be in earnest consultation in one corner of the room. Were they discussing a reunion with Rome or a revision of the Prayer Book? Thrilled with the ecclesiastical possibilities of such a meeting, one of the stripling curates managed to edge himself within earshot of these princes of the Church. They were discussing whether it was worse to wash-up or dry-up.'

2 **Listening to a noisy piece of music at the Philharmonic Hall in Liverpool, Mr H.W. Simpson found himself having to give ear also to a snatch of neighbouring conversation during a sudden quiet patch. The woman in front of him was declaring in full spate: 'Well, we always fry ours in lard!'**
Contributed to BBC Radio *Quote ... Unquote* (8 January 1979). Mr Simpson was not alone. In fact, this rates as a 'traditional' eavesdropping, variously reported as having been gathered in a concert audience, church congregation or group of nuns. It appears to have been around since the nineteenth century.

3 ***During the First World War:* 'My husband has been wounded in the Dardanelles . . . and they cannot find his whereabouts.'**
Contributed to BBC Radio *Quote ... Unquote* (25 August 1984) by Mrs V. Lewis of Handsworth, Birmingham. Her mother overheard it in the First World War. However, in BBC TV, *The Dawson Watch* (Christmas 1980), Les Dawson spoke the line 'During the war, I was shot in the Dardanelles' — with similar implications.

4 **Alfred Deller, the celebrated counter-tenor was walking behind two women when he overheard one say to the other, ''Ow's Flo? 'Ow's 'er feet?' The second woman replied, 'Well, of course, they're not much use to 'er now. Not as *feet*, that is . . .'**
Contributed to BBC Radio *Quote ... Unquote* (5 June 1979) by Paul Fincham of Suffolk — who heard it from Paul Jennings who had it from Deller.

5 **Young American when he saw Manet's painting '*Le Déjeuner Sur L'herbe*', a picnic at which one of the participants, a woman, is without clothes: 'Yeah, you always forget something at picnics . . .'.**
Contributed to BBC Radio *Quote ... Unquote* (26 May 1982) by Miss M.H. Browne of London W14.

6 **'Hallo, Ada, have a good holiday?'**
'Yes, lovely.'
'Where did you go?'
'Majorca.'
'Majorca? Where's that?'
'Don't know — we flew.'

Contributed to BBC Radio *Quote ... Unquote* (5 February 1979) by Mr G.A. Higgins of Halberton, Tiverton, Devon — one of several reports of a similar conversation at that time. Another was: 'Did you go to Portugal for your holiday?' — 'I don't know, my husband bought the tickets.'

7 **Brenda says his big toenails go off like revolvers.**
Contributed to BBC Radio *Quote ... Unquote* (17 July 1980) by Miss V.M. Smith of Croydon.

8 *Overheard from one of two women sitting together on a Nottingham bus:* **'Oh, yes, I've felt ever so much better since they painted my back passage spring green . . .'.**
Contributed to BBC Radio *Quote ... Unquote* (26 May 1982) by Mrs D. Tunbridge of Yeovil.

OWL AND PUSSYCAT JOKES

1 *A worried-looking owl was saying to a suspicious-looking cat:* **'I won't tell a lie. There have been other pussycats.'**
From the *New Yorker*, recounted in the London *Evening Standard* (13 May 1994).

2 *A variant on the Foreign Legion joke: an owl wearing a kepi and carrying a rifle is telling the sergeant:* **'I joined up to try to forget a pussycat . . . '.**
Recounted in the same place.

PAINT
1 **Did you hear about the decorator who died after drinking a tin of Supa-Gloss paint? They do say he had a lovely finish.**

PANTIES
1 **During the filming of Alfred Hitchcock's *Lifeboat* (1944), the director of photography complained to him about a difficulty he was having with the star, Tallulah Bankhead: 'Because of**

the confines of the lifeboat, I have to have my camera down low and we're shooting up a lot. Well, er, Miss Bankhead doesn't wear any panties. She has nothing on underneath. What am I going to do? I can see everything, and it's there on the film.'

Hitchcock paused before replying, and then said: 'Well . . . I don't know whether this is a problem for wardrobe, make-up, or hairdressing.'

Told in *Cary Grant: A Portrait in his own Words and by those who Knew him Best* (1991).

PARANOIDS

1 **Who says I'm paranoid? And why do they want to know?**

From Sydney University, Australia. Contributed by Janette L. Beard, Caringbah, NSW to *Graffiti 5* (1986).

2 **I wouldn't be paranoid if people didn't pick on me.**

Included in *Graffiti Lives OK* (1979).

3 **Just because you're paranoid, it doesn't mean to say they're not out to get you.**

Graffito in Kardomah café, Nottingham. Contributed to BBC Radio *Quote ... Unquote* (3 July 1979) by Kay Wheat and Paul Brough. Reisner & Wechsler in *Encyclopedia of Graffiti* (1974) have 'Help! the paranoids are after me' from the American Library Association Bulletin, April 1969).

PARENTS

1 **Parents are the very last people who ought to be allowed to have children.**

Ted Bell, an English university administrator (1925–), had an unusual problem – the above remark had been fathered on him and he did not know whether he was entitled to claim paternity. In March 1977, as Senior Assistant Registrar in charge of undergraduate admissions at the University of Reading, he was speaking to a mixed group of people about the increasing complexity of the selection procedures and the variety of guidance available to prospective students. 'In this respect, being a parent of three children myself,' he noted (1992), 'I happened to say that in my view, "Parents are the very last people who ought to be allowed to have children". Reporters were present (I had invited them), the words appeared in the *Guardian*, and they were repeated in "Sayings of the Week" in the *Observer*. Later, in 1980, they appeared under my name in the second edition of *The Penguin Dictionary of Modern Quotations*.'

In truth, Bell was merely saying what oft had been thought but ne'er so pithily expressed. According to *The Treasury of Humorous Quotations* (1951),

Bernard Shaw (inevitably) was credited with making the same point in rather more words: 'There may be some doubt as to who are the best people to have charge of children, but there can be no doubt that parents are the worst.' In fact, that was a misattribution. In Shaw's *Everybody's Political What's What?*, Chap. XIX (1944), he quotes *William Morris* ('great among the greatest Victorians as poet, craftsman, and practical man of business, and one of the few who remained uncorrupted by Victorian false prosperity to the end'). Speaking 'as a parent and as a Communist', Morris had said: 'The question of who are the best people to take charge of children is a very difficult one; but it is quite certain that the parents are the very worst.'

In the form 'Parents are the last people on earth who ought to have children', the remark has also been attributed to Samuel Butler, the British writer (1835–1902). It is said to be in his *Notebooks* but this has not been verified.

2 *Teacher (answering the phone):* **'I see — little Johnnie can't come to school today because he's got a fever. To whom am I speaking, please?'**
Voice: **'This is my father.'**

3 **Avenge yourself. Live long enough to be a problem to your kids.**
A van spotted in the M18 near Rotherham had this graffito on its back. Included in *Graffiti 5* (1986).

See also KIDS.

PARKING
1 **After she's parked the car, it's normally just a short walk to the pavement.**
A similar line is to be found in Woody Allen's film *Annie Hall* (US, 1977).

PARROTS
1 **Q. Why are there no aspirins in the jungle?**
A. Because the parrots eat 'em all.
Told by Sascha Waring, Plymouth (1986).

PASSION WAGONS
1 **Don't laugh. It might be your daughter in here.**
Written in the dust on a passion wagon, included in *Graffiti 2* (1980). Compare: 'Don't laugh. Your girlfriend may be inside' — seen on an auto in Haight Ashbury in the 1960s and quoted in Derek Taylor, *It Was Twenty Years Ago Today* (1987).

PASSPORTS

1 **If you look like your passport photo, in all probability you need the holiday.**
Attributed to Earl Wilson, US journalist (1907–87).

PATIENCE

1 *Con la patciencia et la saliva l'elephante la metio a la formiga*
('With patience and saliva, the elephant screws the ant').
Quoted by Valerie Bornstein in *Proverbium Yearbook of International Proverb Scholarship* (8:1991). (I think the original language may have been Mexican Spanish: it does not appear to be regular Spanish or Italian.)

PATIENTS

1 *Doctor:* **'Now, Mrs Jones, bend the knee, please.'**
Mrs Jones: **'Which way, doctor?'**
Contributed to BBC Radio *Quote ... Unquote* (before 1981) by J.M. McKenzie of Peterborough.

PEACE

1 *In the wilds:* **It's so quiet up here you can hear a mouse get a hard-on.**
John Belushi in the film *Continental Divide* (1981), script by Lawrence Kasdan — quoted in Bob Chieger, *Was It Good For You Too?* (1983).

PEERS

1 **There was a battle over lavatory signs in Britain's House of Lords, following the introduction of women members in their own right in 1958. The lavatories were originally labelled 'LIFE PEERESSES ONLY'. But, as Lady Wootton pointed out, 'We are very passionate that we are not women peeresses; peeresses are the wives of peers.' Now the lavatories are marked 'PEERS' and 'WOMEN PEERS'.**

PELICANS

1 **Q. Why do pelicans carry fish in their beaks?**
A. Because their pockets are full already.
Told by Caroline Lewis of Plymouth (1986).

PENGUINS

1 **I make love like a penguin – once a year.**
Included in *Graffiti 5* (1986).

PEOPLE

1 **There are two kinds of people in the world – those who divide the world into two kinds of people and those who don't.**
From the University of Texas, in Haan & Hammerstrom *Graffiti in the Southwest Conference* (1981).

2 **There are two kinds of people entitled to refer to themselves as 'we'. One is an editor, the other is a fellow with a tape-worm.**
Attributed to Bill Nye.

3 **There are only two sorts of pedestrian in Paris – the quick and the dead.**
First told to me by my French teacher on my first visit to Paris in 1959. However, to Lord Dewar (1864–1930), a British industrialist, is credited the joke that there are 'only two classes of pedestrians in these days of reckless motor traffic – the quick, and the dead'. George Robey ascribed it to Dewar in *Looking Back on Life* (1933). A *Times* leader in April that same year merely ventured: 'The saying that there are two sorts of pedestrians, the quick and the dead, is well matured.'

PIANOS

1 **'A piano is a piano is a piano' – Gertrude Steinway.**

2 **A woman's like a piano – if she's not upright, she's grand.**
Included in Reisner & Wechsler, *Encyclopedia of Graffiti* (1974).

PILES

1 **'My husband is a Minister much prone to gaffes. When a guest at a wedding reception told him that Mr So-and-So was in hospital for an operation on his piles, my husband commented: "Poor man, he *has* had a rough passage this year."'**
Contributed by Mrs J. Evans of Bradford to *Foot in Mouth* (1982).

2 **President Carter was ordered to rest by a doctor for what was described as an aggravated problem with haemorrhoids. A White House spokesman said that Mr Carter was being**

attended by his personal physician, Rear Admiral William Lukash.
From a *Daily Telegraph* report, c. 1978.

PLACE NAMES
1 **'There is a village near Maidstone in Kent called Loose. I do not know if the notice board still carries the caption outside their headquarters, but years ago it stated that it housed the "Loose Women's Institute."'**
Contributed to Channel 4 *Countdown* (26 March 1990) by Audrey Thomas of London SE17. Presumably a similar fate has befallen the W.I. at Ugley, near Bishop's Stortford. As for Idle in West Yorkshire, perhaps there is a notice outside the working men's club there.

PLACES
1 **.... is a dreadful place. I spent a month there last night.**
Joke formula.

PLANS
1 **The best laid plans of mice and men are filed away** *somewhere* **. . . .**
Graffito from Whitehall, described on Granada TV *Cabbages and Kings* (18 November 1979).

POETIC LICENCE
Amendments to famous lines of poetry – or, rather, to the subsequent lines – that somehow enhance the meaning, or not:

1 **Ah, did you once see Shelley plain?**
And was he such a frightful pain . . . ?
With my apologies to Browning. Most of the following are 'deflating additions' as they were called in *New Statesman* competitions of yesteryear:

2 **When you are old and grey and full of sleep**
You haven't got to bother counting sheep.
W.B. Yeats done over by H.A.C. Evans.

3 **When lovely woman stoops to folly**
The evening can be awfully jolly.
Oliver Goldsmith done over by Mary Demetriadis.

4 **Yet once more, O ye Laurels, and once more,
I deliver the "Telegraph" under the door.**
John Milton altered by Edward Blishen.

5 **Full fathom five thy father lies,
His aqualung was the wrong size.**
Shakespeare seen to by June Mercer Langfield.

6 **Birds in their little nests agree
With Chinamen but not with me.**
Hilaire Belloc once capped a line by Isaac Watts thus.

7 **Earth has not anything to show more fair
Than Auntie Mabel since she bleached her hair.**
And Harold Ollerenshaw, a listener to BBC Radio *Quote ... Unquote*, contributed
this (with apologies to Wordsworth).

POETRY
1 **Roses are red
Violets are blue,
Some poems rhyme,
But this one doesn't.**
In Haan & Hammerstrom *Graffiti in the Southwest Conference* (1981).

2 **Roses are red,
Violets are blue,
And rhododendrons are
All kinds of peculiar colours.**
By the late 1950s.

See also ROSES 1, 2.

3 **Publishing a volume of verse is like dropping a rose petal
down the Grand Canyon and waiting for the echo.**
Don Marquis, American humorist (1878–1937), quoted in *The Treasury of
Humorous Quotations*, ed. by Evan Esar & Nicolas Bentley (1951).

POLICE
1 **Q. What did the three-headed policeman say to the burglar?
A. Ullo-ullo-ullo!**
Told by Jack de Manio on the BBC Radio *Today* programme (19 July 1968),
having just been told it by me!

2 **When the little boy opened the front door, he found a police-man on the step. 'Do you know who I am, sonny?' said the policeman. The little boy came and told his parents: 'There's a man here who doesn't know who he is.'**
Contributed by Spike Milligan to BBC Radio *Quote ... Unquote* (1 January 1979).

3 **If pigs could fly, Scotland Yard would be the third London airport.**
Graffito contributed to BBC Radio *Quote ... Unquote* (5 January 1982) by Richard Evans of Hertford.

4 **A: Would you like to buy a ticket for the Policeman's Ball?**
B: Why, certainly, I love to dance.
A: This isn't a dance, dearie, it's a raffle.

5 **Help the police — beat yourself up.**
Graffito photographed by Chris Furby and contributed to Granada TV *Cabbages and Kings* (6 June 1979).

POLISH JOKES

There are two types of Polish joke: the ones told by Americans about the Polish minority in the US and the political ones told by Poles in Poland about themselves. The latter are generally sardonic and fatalistic, very much along the lines of RUSSIAN JOKES and have survived the fall of Communism. The American-Polish jokes were very popular in the early 1980s but have largely been driven underground now by the march of political correctness. Some examples of both types:

1 **For my birthday Boris gave me a Polish goldfish. It drowned.**
An early example of the genre? Performed on CBS TV *Rowan and Martin's Laugh-In* and included on the record album *Laugh-In '69* (1969).

2 **Two Poles were on their way home from a Communist Party meeting. One asked the other, 'Comrade Nowak, why weren't you at the last party meeting?' Comrade Nowak answered: 'If I'd known it was the last one, I would certainly have gone.'**
Told in the *Economist* (23 October 1982).

3 **What is the difference between the Polish zloty and the US dollar?**
The dollar is worth a lot in the States and in Poland, the zloty is worth nothing in the States and in Poland.
Told in the *Guardian* (30 January 1989).

4   The Polish Arts Minister (a woman) told this joke. Mother Mouse
    saw her little ones being threatened by a cat. 'Don't worry,'
    she said, 'I'll deal with it.' She drew herself up to her full size
    and came out with: 'Bow wow wow!' At this, the cat fled in
    terror. 'That's the value,' Mother Mouse told the baby mice, 'of
    learning foreign languages.'
    Recounted in the *Financial Times* (6 November 1989).

5   A joke circulated in Warsaw that there were two solutions to
    the Polish crisis: one rational, the other requiring a miracle. The
    rational solution was that the Virgin of Czestochowa should
    appear at the Central Bank with a cheque for 50 billion dollars.
    The one needing a miracle was that the Poles go back to work.
    Told in the *Sunday Telegraph* (12 November 1989).

6   In the present economic conditions we, the workers, have made
    a satisfactory arrangement with the bosses. It is this: we pre-
    tend to work and they pretend to pay us.
    Told in the *Guardian* (4 January 1990).

7   A Pole in a bar is watching television. He bets the bartender
    fifty dollars that the man on the ledge featured on the eight
    o'clock news will not jump to his death. The bartender takes
    the money and the man jumps. The bartender is ashamed to
    take the Pole's money, confessing, 'I saw him jump already on
    the six o'clock news.' 'So did I,' says the Pole, 'but I didn't think
    he'd do it again.'
    Told in *The Times* (20 January 1990).

8   Here's some good news: Lenin's mother is still alive. Now the
    bad news: she's pregnant.
    A joke told by the Polish President, Lech Walesa, at an election meeting in
    Lublin, recorded by the *Sunday Times* (25 November 1990).

9   Lech Walesa was often the subject of jokes about his idiosyn-
    cratic abuse of the Polish language. He is reported to have
    countered these with the remark: 'Foreigners all understand
    what I say and no one corrects my Polish.'
    Told in the *Observer* (21 April 1991).

10 Why do Polish policemen go around in threes?
    One reads, one writes, and one keeps his eye on those two
    bloody intellectuals.
    Told in the *Guardian* (22 March 1993). Compare SOVIET JOKES 1.

11 The Polish airline LOT chose as its 50th anniversary slogan, 'Half a century in the sky'. This was explained as a comment on just how long it took to get anywhere when you flew with them.
Told in the *European* (24 September 1992).

12 There were two trains, one going from Paris to Moscow, and the other from Moscow to Paris. They met in Warsaw and everybody got out. The Parisians because they thought it was Moscow. And the Muscovites because they thought it was Paris.
Told in the *Independent* (3 November 1994).

And finally two puns on the word 'Polish' which don't really belong in this category, but still . . .

13 Hitler's dilemma in 1939 was what to do first, finish off Poland or polish off Finland.

14 When the Polish singers Jan Kiepura and Marta Eggerth opened in a New York production of *The Merry Widow* in the 1940s, an anxious Kiepura asked a fan after one performance whether he should polish up his English? 'No,' replied the fan, 'you should English up your Polish.'
Both of these were told in *The Times* (9 September 1989).

See also LIGHT-BULB JOKES 19.

POLITICAL CORRECTNESS

1 Is there not something quaintly politically correct about the graffito seen sprayed on a North London wall: 'Ethnics out'?
Reported in the *Guardian* (9 November 1991).

2 There is a story told of a (white) American female TV reporter interviewing either Bishop Desmond Tutu or Nelson Mandela in South Africa. She was apparently so intent on being politically correct and on avoiding use of the word 'black' that she asked the interviewee what it really felt like being an 'African-American'.
Included in *The Politically Correct Phrasebook* (1993).

POLLUTION

1 **Pollution is cirrhosis of the river.**
From Australia, in *Graffiti 4* (1982).

POPES

1 **Q. Why does the Pope wear his underpants in the bath?**
A. Because he hates to see the unemployed.
Graffito, quoted in Rachel Bartlett (ed.), *Off the Wall* (1982).

2 *After the sudden death of Pope John Paul I:* **'What lasts longer: a pope or a wine gum?'**
From Glasgow, included in *Graffiti 2* (1980).

3 **'Dave Allen for Pope' was a slogan written up in Wolverhampton when Pope Paul died in 1978. Pope John Paul I got the job but died shortly afterwards. Hence the further graffito: 'Dave Allen for Pope – *this* time?'**
Contributed to BBC Radio *Quote ... Unquote* (31 July 1979) by Thelma Shardlow, E.W. Brookes and John Gilder, all of Wolverhampton. (It was in 1978 that a British newspaper is reported to have printed the headline POPE DIES AGAIN.)

4 **Q. What do you think of the Pope's attitude to birth control?**
A. He no play-a da game. He no make-a da rules!
The American politician Earl Butz (1909–) told this joke publicly in 1974. He lost his job as President Ford's Secretary of Agriculture after making another similar but racist remark.

5 **NO POPE IN NORTHERN IRELAND**
– lucky old Pope.
Graffito from a wall in Belfast. Contributed to BBC Radio *Quote ... Unquote* (31 May 1978) by Derek Parker. Also recorded in Londonderry in 1977.

6 **Why should we take advice on sex from the Pope? If he knows anything about it, he shouldn't.**
Attributed to George Bernard Shaw, but untraced.

POSTAL SERVICES

1 **A *Quote ... Unquote* listener told of receiving a card on his wedding anniversary which the British Post Office had franked**

with the slogan, 'NOT GETTING ON? Telephone the Marriage Guidance Council.'

Contributed to *Foot in Mouth* (1982).

2 **Someone once received a letter from the Race Relations Board franked with the slogan, 'KEEP BRITAIN GREEN'.**

Ditto.

3 **NEITHER SNOW NOR RAIN NOR HEAT NOR GLOOM OF NIGHT STAYS THESE COURIERS FROM THE SWIFT COMPLETION OF THEIR APPOINTED ROUNDS.
– well, what is it then?**

The text inscribed on the stone face of the New York City Post Office is from Herodotus. The graffitoed comment was contributed to BBC Radio *Quote ... Unquote* (9 February 1982) by Malcolm Judelson of London W6.

4 **On the outside of the envelope was written 'PHOTOGRAPHS – DO NOT BEND.' But that was no use. Someone had written underneath: 'OH YES THEY DO!'**

Contributed by Dr Dick Richards of Deal to Granada TV *Cabbages and Kings* (11 August 1979).

5 **A: What's the difference between a postbox and an elephant?
B: I don't know.
A: Well, I'm not going to ask you to post my letters.**

POSTCARD HUMOUR

Comic postcards, featuring brightly-coloured cartoons with double entendres for captions, and on sale especially at the seaside, are unquestionably a great British tradition. The great provider of this form of entertainment was the artist Donald McGill (1875–1962) who was celebrated in a famous essay by George Orwell in 1942. McGill drew his first comic postcard in 1905 and, judging by the style and appearance of his most famous card, it probably dates from within the next ten to fifteen years.

1 **The card shows a fat man with an enormous stomach (or 'corporation') which prevents him from seeing the small boy seated at his feet. The caption is the *double entendre*, 'Can't see my little Willy.'**

Benny Green used the title *I've Lost My Little Willie!* for a 'celebration of comic

postcards' published in 1976 but that version rather obscures the joke. It may
have been taken from the caption to a re-drawing by another cartoonist.

POVERTY

1 **Poverty is an anomaly to rich people; it is very difficult to
make out why people who want dinner do not ring the bell.**
Walter Bagehot, English political writer (1826–77), quoted in *The Treasury of
Humorous Quotations*, ed. by Evan Esar & Nicolas Bentley (1951).

POWER

1 **Power corrupts — absolute power is even more fun.**
Included in *Graffiti 3* (1981).

2 **All power tends to be an aphrodisiac and absolute power
leaves you feeling rotten by Wednesday.**
Alan Coren's version of Lord Acton's famous dictum, on BBC Radio *Quote ...
Unquote* (18 January 1976).

PREDESTINATION

1 **Predestination was doomed to failure from the start.**
Graffito from a wall of the philosophy department, Vanbrugh College, York
University. Contributed to BBC Radio *Quote ... Unquote* (26 April 1978) by David
Palfreyman.

PREGNANCY

1 *On going into hospital for an abortion:* **'It serves me right for
putting all my eggs in one bastard.'**
Dorothy Parker, quoted in John Keats, *You Might As Well Live* (1970).

PRESIDENCY, THE

1 **When I was a boy I was told that anybody could become
President. I'm beginning to believe it.**
Clarence Darrow, American lawyer (1857–1938), quoted in Irving Stone,
Clarence Darrow for the Defence (1941).

2 **The pay is good and I can walk to work.**
John F. Kennedy, American Democratic President (1917–63), attributed.

PRESLEY, ELVIS
American popular singer (1935–77).

1 **ELVIS LIVES!**
– and they've buried the poor bugger!
Graffito and addition from Holborn Underground Station, London. Contributed to BBC Radio Quote ... *Unquote* (17 July 1979) by Mr K. Carter of Ash, Aldershot.

2 **ELVIS IS DEAD**
– good career move.
Graffito and addition, related in *Time* Magazine (8 April 1985.

PRESUMPTION
1 **I and my rhinoceros, said the tick-bird.**
Sotho proverb, quoted in Ruth Finnegan, *Oral Literature in Africa* (1970).

PRICKS
1 **The difference between this place and a hedgehog is that the hedgehog has all the pricks on the outside.**
Graffito contributed by P.S. Smith, Harston, Cambridgeshire (1981). Another version:

2 **Q. What's the difference between BP and a cactus?**
A. On a cactus the pricks are on the outside.
Graffito from Sullom Voe, Shetlands (1981) contributed by James Hawkett of London NW3 to *Graffiti 4* (1982).

3 **Being employed by this firm is like making love to a hedgehog – one prick working against thousands.**
From Birmingham, included in *Graffiti 2* (1980). Compare HOLLYWOOD 3.

PRINCES
1 **Some day my prince will come. However, I'll have nothing to do with it.**
Included in *Graffiti 3* (1981).

2 **Before you meet your handsome prince you have to kiss a lot of toads.**
From Chorlton-cum-Hardy, Manchester, included in *Graffiti Lives OK* (1979).

PROFESSIONALS

1 **A professional is a man who can do his job when he doesn't feel like it; an amateur is one who can't [do his job] when he does feel like it.**

James Agate, English drama critic (1877–1947) in *Ego* (1935) (entry for 17 September 1933). The context was a lunch with the actor Cedric Hardwicke, who said: 'My theory of acting is that it is so minor an art that the only self-respect attaching to it is to be able to reproduce one's performance with mathematical accuracy.' The above was Agate's concurrence. Hardwicke added: 'It shouldn't make a hair's breadth of difference to an actor if he has a dead baby at home and a wife dying.'

There have been several other attempts to define the difference between amateurs and professionals, beyond the acting profession:

2 **[Amateur musicians] practise until they can get it right; professionals practise until they can't get it wrong.**

Quoted by Harold Craxton, one-time professor at the Royal Academy of Music).

3 **Professionals built the *Titanic*; amateurs built the Ark.**

PROFESSORS

1 **Q. Where do professors come from?**
A. From the West. Because the wise men came from the East.

From Leuven University, Belgium. Contributed by Jan Bastiaenssens to *Graffiti 4* (1982).

2 **Martin Routh (1755–1854) was President of Magdalen College, Oxford – not exactly a professor, but near enough. He was man of great composure – so much so that when an excitable Fellow rushed up to announce that a member of the college had killed himself, Routh replied: 'Pray, don't tell me who. Allow me to guess!'**

Told in Dacre Balsdon, *Oxford Life* (1957).

PROMISCUITY

1 **What is a promiscuous person? It's usually someone who is getting more sex than you are.**

Victor Lownes, Playboy Club manager, quoted in Bob Chieger, *Was It Good For You Too?* (1983).

PROSTITUTION

1 **A notice outside a church declared, 'If you are tired of sin, step inside'. Underneath had been added: 'And if you're not, then phone Paddington ****.'**
Contributed by Brian Johnston to BBC Radio Quote ... Unquote (21 August 1979). Bids fair to be the oldest graffiti joke. It made an appearance in Pass the Port (1976). Could one put a date on it? Whatever the case, Sir David Frost is still (1995) using it in his TV warm-ups.

2 **I am bi-sexual. If I can't get it, I buy it.**
Included in Graffiti 3 (1981).

3 **It is better to have loved and lost, than to have paid for it and not liked it.**
From Minnesota, in Haan & Hammerstrom Graffiti in the Big Ten (1981).

PROVERBS
Perverted proverbs, that is:

1 **A bird in the hand does it on your wrist.**
Contributed to HTV All Kinds of Everything (7 May 1981). Earlier in Reisner & Wechsler, Encyclopedia of Graffiti (1974) had been 'A bird in the hand can be messy'.

2 **A bird in the hand makes it difficult to tie your shoelaces.**

3 **The early bird gets the DDT.**

4 **You can lead a horticulture but you can't make her think.**
Dorothy Parker, quoted in John Keats, You Might As Well Live (1970).

5 **Great oafs from little icons grow.**
A fake Russian-style proverb concerning Nikita Khruschev, contributed to BBC Radio Quote ... Unquote (1 June 1977) by Benny Green. Richard Boston attributed to S.J. Perelman the similar 'Great oafs from little infants grow.'

6 **'My dear Norwegian mother spoke quite fluent English but occasionally became a little confused over proverbs. Her best effort, I think, was when she reprimanded me for being ungrateful about a present I had received: "Never, never, cast your teeth in a gift-horse's face!"'**
Contributed by Mrs. E.S.B. Pashley of Cottingham to Foot in Mouth (1982).

7 **You can't find a needle if you haven't got a haystack.**
Contributed to BBC Radio *Quote ... Unquote* (24 July 1980). Said to come from a 'BBC engineer', as also: 'He's getting on like a horse on fire.'

8 **Don't get your pants in a muddle.**
Contributed by Rula Lenska to BBC Radio *Quote ... Unquote* (24 July 1980) — one of her Polish mother's versions of English proverbs. As also: 'Out of the frying pan and into the Serpentine.'

9 **The visiting missionary was delighted that the head of the Wangiboko tribe had decided to embrace Christianity to such an extent that he had dispensed with all the trappings of kingship that hitherto had been his. He had even decided to remove the ceremonial chair in which he had previously held court and put it out of the way up in the roof of the hut — which was, of course, the largest hut in the African village.**

   Unfortunately, when the missionary was calling on the head of the tribe in his hut for tea and cucumber sandwiches (a tradition recently introduced from England) he found that he was required to sit cross-legged on the floor.

   Halfway through the tea — and even more unfortunately — the ceremonial chair detached itself from its moorings up in the roof of the hut and fell to earth flattening the missionary (with fatal consequences) in the process.

   The moral of this story is: 'People in grass houses shouldn't stow thrones.'
Current by the 1950s.

10 **Do not tie your shoes in a melon field or adjust your hat under a plum tree if you wish to avoid suspicion.**
Given as a genuine Chinese proverb by Claud Cockburn in *I, Claud* (1967). On the other hand Cockburn admitted to inventing proverbs in the 1930s and this might well have been one of them.

PSYCHIATRISTS

1 **Psychology is producing habits out of a rat.**
Included in *Graffiti Lives OK* (1979).

2 **A man went to see a psychiatrist for help with his problems. After much consultation and carrying out several tests, the psychiatrist summed up his findings: 'You haven't got an inferiority complex,' he said. 'You really are inferior.'**
Recounted by Valerie Grosvenor Meyer in *Folk Review* (November 1974),

adding: 'I remember seeing [it] in *Everyman's* about 30 years ago. I am told it was originally a *New Yorker* cartoon.'

3 **A man went to a psychiatrist complaining of his dominating mother. The psychiatrist asks him to describe a typical day. 'I got up, had breakfast . . . .'**
   'What did you have for breakfast?' 'Oh, just coffee!' The psychiatrist exploded: 'You call *that* breakfast?!'
   Recounted by Valerie Grosvenor Meyer in *Folk Review* (November 1974), as also the following:

4 **And then there is the story of the psychiatrist who hid under the bed because he thought he was a little potty.**

5 **Two psychiatrists meet in the street. One says to the other, 'I know that you are feeling fine, but tell me, please – how am I feeling?'**

6 **A man rushed into a psychiatrists's consulting room saying he thought he had a 'split personality'. 'All right,' said the psychiatrist. 'That'll be five dollars each.'**

7 **A man who thought he was a dog went to a psychiatrist. When he was invited to lie down he said: 'I'm not allowed on the couch.'**

8 **A patient tells her psychiatrist that she can't resist picking things up in shops and putting them in her pocket. 'Don't worry,' says the psychiatrist. 'I've sorted out your problem straight away. You're a thief.'**

PUBLICITY

1 **Publicity is easy to get. Just be so successful you don't need it, and then you'll get it.**
   Anonymous (American).

2 **Some are born great, some achieve greatness and some hire public relations officers.**

3 **Will somebody please explain to me why public relations people are almost invariably 'associates'? Whom do they**

associate with, and who can stand it?

Attributed to George Dixon (American).

PUNKS

1 **Q. Why did the punk cross the road?**
A. Because he was stapled to the chicken.

Told by Sascha Waring, Plymouth (1986).

PUNS

1 **Hanging is too good for a man who makes puns. He should be drawn and quoted.**

Attributed to Fred Allen, American comedian (1894–1956).

2 **A good pun is its own reword.**

3 **Puns don't kill people, people kill people.**

4 **Are you a spy?**
Yes.
Then why are you covered in mint?
I'm a mint-spy!

From 'The Jet-Propelled Guided NAAFI' in BBC radio's *The Goon Show* (24 January 1956), script by Spike Milligan.

5 **A bird in the Strand is worth two in Shepherd's Bush.**

Spike Milligan. Contributed to BBC Radio *Quote ... Unquote* (19 April 1978) by Roy Hudd.

6 **I told the solitary pedestrian**
He had BO
And he replied
'That's why I wore cologne'.

By Alan F.G. Lewis and included in *A Pun My Soul* (1977).

7 **LOVE LETTER**
You have the kind of XXX
That I cipher.

Same source.

8 **He's a bit of a quiet fish**
I'm told he's a piano tuna.

Same source.

9 **VALENTINE RHYME**
My heart and I
Call to you
But you're too deaf
To Eros.
Same source.

10 **Weight-lifting**
Is a hard way
To hernia living.
Same source.

11 **I can't decide whether to ask Kate or Edith to marry me.**
Well, you can't have your Kate and Edith too.

12 **Camping store — now is the winter offer — discount tents.**

13 **'Explorer's Sale! Now is the discount of our winter tents.'**

14 **There are seventy stanzas in the Uruguay national anthem,**
which fact may account for the Uruguay standing army.
Franklin Pierce Adams, American humorist (1881–1960), quoted in *The Treasury of Humorous Quotations*, ed. by Evan Esar & Nicolas Bentley (1951).

15 **Our story starts on the 21st floor of a New York apartment**
building. It would have started on the 22nd floor — but that's
another storey . . . .
Recalled by A.M. Barnes of Cambridge (1994) from the BBC radio show *Bedtime with Braden* (1950s) when this was spoken by the announcer Ronald Fletcher.

16 **Confucius say: man with no front garden look forlorn.**

QUESTION AND ANSWER JOKES

1 **What's worse than biting into an apple and finding a worm?**
Biting into an apple and finding half a worm.

2   What's the difference between a disappointed audience and
     a sick cow?
     One boos madly and the other moos badly.

3   What's the difference between a sick horse and a dead bee?
     One is a seedy beast and the other is a bee deceased.

4   What's the difference between a pigeon and a yuppie?
     A pigeon can still lay a deposit on a Porsche.

5   What's a cross between a bell and a bee?
     A real humdinger.

6   Why did the fox cross the road?
     Because the chicken was in its mouth.

7   What do you get if you cross a kangaroo with a sheep?
     A woolly jumper.

8   What did the Leaning Tower of Pisa say to Big Ben?
     If you've got the time, I've got the inclination.

9   What goes along the bottom of a river at a hundred miles an
     hour?
     A motor pike and side carp.

10 Why did the lobster blush?
     Because the sea weed.

11 How do you save a drowning mouse?
     By mouse to mouse resuscitation.

12 What do you get if you cross a mouse with an elephant?
     Great big holes in the skirting board.

13 What's made of plastic and hangs around French cathedrals?
     The lunch-pack of Notre Dame.

14 What has four wheels, five doors and hangs around French
     cathedrals?
     The hatch-back of Notre Dame.

15 Why did the hedgehog cross the road?
     To see his flat mate.

16 What's green, hairy and zooms across the water at 50 miles
     an hour?
     A gooseberry with an outboard motor.

17 What did the man who had a jelly in one ear and custard in the other say?
'You'll have to speak up a bit, I'm a trifle deaf.'

18 What is that men do standing up, ladies do sitting down, and dogs do on three legs?
Shake hands.

19 What happened to the earl who was given an OBE?
He has turned into an earlobe.

20 What did the earwig say as he fell down the stairs?
'Ere we go.

21 What did the egg in the monastery say?
'Ah, well, out of the frying pan and into the friar.'

22 Why do bears have fur coats?
Because they'd look like idiots standing around in plastic macs.

23 Why do birds fly south in the winter?
Because it's too far to walk.

24 What's black and white and red all over?
A sunburned zebra.

25 What's black and white and goes round and round?
A zebra stuck in a revolving door.

26 Why does Prince Philip wear red, white and blue braces?
To keep his trousers up.

27 What do you call a camel that has three humps?
Humphrey.

28 What do cannibals do at a wedding?
They toast the bride and groom.

29 What do you call snakes on your car windscreen?
Windscreen vipers.

30 What goes 99-thump, 99-thump, 99-thump?
A centipede with a wooden leg.

31 What's yellow, brown and hairy?
Cheese on toast dropped on the carpet.

32 Where do you find a cheetah?
Depends where you leave him.

33 **Why did the chicken go half-way across the road?**
    Because it wanted to lay it on the line.

34 **Why is it true that children brighten a home?**
    Because they never turn the lights off.

35 **What's made of iron, has a funnel and quivers on the bottom**
    of the ocean?
    A nervous wreck.

36 **What did the digital watch say to its mother?**
    Look, Ma — no hands!

37 **Why is a sheet of foolscap like a lazy dog?**
    A sheet of foolscap is an ink lined plain. An inclined plain is a
    slope up. A slow pup is a lazy dog.

38 **Which are more popular — chickens or owls?**
    Chickens. Have you ever heard of Kentucky Fried Owls?
    Included in *Graffiti 5* (1986).

39 **What's pink and hard and comes in the morning?**
    The FT crossword.
    Included in *Graffiti 5* (1986).

40 **Where does the Pink Panther live?**
    Durham. ('Dum, Dur-r-r-ham, Dur-r-r-rham, Dur-r-r-rham . . .')
    British schoolchildren, quoted by Caroline St John-Brooks in *New Society* (2
    June 1983).

41 **How does Batman's mum call him in for dinner?**
    Dinner, dinner, dinner, dinner, dinner, dinner, dinner, dinner,
    BATMAN!'
    As for the previous joke.

See also DOORS.

QUOTATIONS

1 *When asked for his favourite quotation on BBC Radio* Quote ...
   Unquote *(1 January 1979), Spike Milligan instantly replied:* 'My
   favourite quotation is £8.10 for a second-hand suit.'

RABBITS

1 Did you hear about the rabbit who was caught playing with himself? He explained, 'I washed my thing this morning – and I can't do a hare with it.'
Heard in 1969.

RACE

1 Is racial prejudice a pigment of the imagination?
From Southampton, included in *Graffiti Lives OK* (1979).

RADIO ARMENIA JOKES

In the days of the Soviet Union, say from the late 1950s onwards, the mythical Radio Armenia was given as the source of any number of droll jokes critical of the Communist regime. Radio Armenia was also quoted as the source of any number of jokes about life in other countries behind the Iron Curtain. See also RUSSIAN JOKES and SOVIET JOKES.

1 'Have you heard? The Director of Radio Armenia has committed suicide.'
'No! Why?'
'Well, he read on the front page of *Pravda* that Russia was overtaking America, and he turned to the middle page and read that America is standing at the edge of an abyss and . . . .'
As recounted by Caryl Brahms in a piece called 'Radio Armenia' from BBC TV *That Was the Week That Was* (1962-3 series).

Compare SOVIET JOKES 10; THATCHER, MARGARET 2.

2 The Director of Radio Armenia was tremendously impressed by the production chart on the wall of a Soviet factory. '5,000 the first year, 50,000 the next, 500,000 this year, you'll be up to a million soon! What do you make?'
'Out-of-order notices.'
Same source.

Compare NOTICES AND SIGNS 16.

3 The Director of Radio Armenia called on Major Gagarin, the astronaut. He was told, 'Major Gagarin is in orbit and won't be back for another hour.'
　'Can I speak to Mrs Gagarin, then?'
　'She's buying meat – she won't be back for four hours.'
Same source.

4 An Armenian schoolboy wrote an essay about three new-born kittens. They were round, fluffy, and two were communists.
　'Why only two?'
　'Well, the third one opened its eyes yesterday.'
Same source.

5 'My radio tells me there is plenty of food in the shops, but my refrigerator is empty. What do I do?'
　'Put your radio in the refrigerator.'
Same source.

6 What is the difference between capitalism and communism?
Capitalism is the exploitation of man by man.
　And communism?
　That's the other way round.
This made an early appearance in Daniel Bell, The End of Ideology (1960) in the form, 'Capitalism, it is said, is a system wherein man exploits man. And communism – is vice versa.' Laurence J. Peter in Quotations for Our Time (1977) describes it as a 'Polish proverb' and another source has it 'reported from Warsaw'.

7 An old Radio Armenia joke concerns the competition for a statue to commemorate the centenary of the death of the great Russian poet Lermontov (which actually fell in 1941). Thousands of entries poured in. The winning design was a huge statue of Stalin, with a volume of Lermontov in his hand.
Reported in The Times (16 June 1988).

8 'Excuse me,' asked a listener to Radio Armenia, when it was a mainstay of anti-Brezhnev jokes, 'is it true that you can die as a result of throat cancer?'. The radio replied solemnly: 'Yes, but unfortunately he does not have it.'
Reported in The Times (16 January 1990).

9 A caller-in asks the Radio Armenia commentator what is the average wage of an industrial worker in the United States. After a very long pause comes the answer: 'They kill negroes.'
Reported in the Daily Telegraph (13 April 1990).

10 **Q.** Will there be war?
A. No, there will be such peace that not one stone will be left standing upon another.
Reported in *The Times* (15 December 1990).

RAILWAYS/RAILROADS *See BRITISH RAIL.*

READING

1 I've read so much about the dangers of drinking and smoking that I've decided to give up reading.
From Mudeford, included in *Graffiti 5* (1986).

2 People say that life is the thing, but I prefer reading.
Logan Pearsall Smith, US writer (1865–1946) in *Afterthoughts* (1931).

3 A man in a considerable state of excitement came running up to his friend waving a telegram. 'Charlie,' he said, 'tell me what you think: is that letter an "i" or an "o"?'
     Charlie had a look and replied, 'I think it's an "i".'
     'Thank God for that. I thought for a moment my brother had shot himself.'
An Oxford undergraduate revue 'quickie', c. 1964.

REAGAN, RONALD
American Republican President, Governor and actor (1911–).

1 You could walk through Governor Reagan's deepest thoughts and not get your ankles wet.
Included in *Graffiti 3* (1981).

2 Ronald Reagan has two books on economics, but he hasn't finished colouring the first one yet.
Graffito from Railway Square, Sydney, Australia, reported in 1982.

3 A triumph of the embalmer's art.
Gore Vidal, quoted in the *Observer* (26 April 1981).

4 It's true hard work never killed anybody, but I figure, why take the chance?
Said by Reagan in a speech, 28 March 1987.

REALITY

1 **Reality is for people who can't cope with drugs.**
Included in *Graffiti Lives OK* (1979). Has been ascribed to John Lennon.

2 **Reality is an illusion produced by alcohol deficiency.**
Included in *Graffiti Lives OK* (1979).

RECESSION

1 **Due to the present financial situation, the light at the end of the tunnel will be turned off at the weekends.**
Graffito from Dublin (1987), collected by Darren Hickey, Leixlip, Co. Kildare.

RECORDS

1 **Dear Sir, I have a circular piece of black plastic about twelve inches across with a hole in the middle of it. Is this a record?**

RED ARROWS

1 *On a poster advertising a display by the Red Arrows aerobatic team had been scrawled the helpful information:* 'If wet, in the town hall.'
Contributed to BBC Radio *Quote ... Unquote* (9 February 1982) by Bernard A. Finding of Fowey.

REINCARNATION

1 **Is reincarnation making a comeback?**
Contributed by Liza Goddard to Granada TV *Cabbages and Kings* (29 July 1979).

RELIGION

1 **Religion is man's attempt to communicate with the weather.**
Included in *Graffiti Lives OK* (1979).

2 **My church welcomes all denominations — but my favourite is the five-dollar bill.**
Performed on CBS TV *Rowan and Martin's Laugh-In* and included on the record album *Laugh-In '69* (1969).

RESTAURANTS

1 *When a new restaurant opened near Bromley in Kent, a critic wrote:* **'Geographically, it is halfway between Elmer's End and Pratt's Bottom. Gastronomically, it is about the same.'**
Contributed to BBC Radio Quote ... Unquote (24 July 1980) by J.J. Small of Halstead.

2 **For bad service – ask for the manager.**
Notice in the Rex Inn, Kericho, Kenya. Contributed to BBC Radio Quote ... Unquote (14 June 1978) by David Etheridge of Stirchley, Birmingham.

3 *Diner:* **I'd complain about the service if I could find a waiter to complain to.**
Caption to cartoon in Mel Calman, How to Survive Abroad (1971).

4 **Avoid approaching horses and restaurants from the rear.**
Wise saw contributed by Miss O.E. Burns of Stourbridge (1994).

REVOLUTIONS

1 **Revolution is the opium of the intellectual.**
Graffito featured in the film O, Lucky Man (1971).

2 **Come the revolution, everyone will eat strawberries and cream.
But, Comrade, I don't *like* strawberries and cream.
Come the revolution, *everyone* will eat strawberries and cream!**
Ascribed to the American vaudeville comedian, Willis Howard. Hence, the phrase 'come the revolution', used as the preliminary to some prediction (often ironic) of what life would hold when (usually Communist) revolution swept the world. Also included as a Jewish joke in Leo Rosten, The Joys of Yiddish (1968).

Compare ROLLS-ROYCE MOTORS 2.

ROAD SIGNS

1 **TO MAVIS ENDERBY AND OLD BOLINGBROKE
– the gift of a son.**
An old road sign in Lincolnshire with addition. Included in Graffiti Lives OK (1979).

2 **GOLDERS GREEN 2
– but to you 1½.**
Road sign and addition on the North Circular Road, London. In Graffiti 4 (1982).

3 **Ignore this sign.**
Graffito seen on a bridge over a California freeway. Contributed to BBC
Radio *Quote ... Unquote* (3 July 1979) by Peter Slade of Farnham, Surrey.

ROLLS-ROYCE MOTORS
1 *Sticker on Mini*: **'This was a Rolls before it went through the
carwash.'**
Included in *Graffiti 5* (1986).

2 **When the revolution comes we'll drive Rolls-Royces.
What if we don't want to drive Rolls Royces?
When the Revolution comes you won't have any choice.**
Included in *Graffiti 3* (1981).

Compare REVOLUTIONS 2.

ROMANCE
1 **I could dance with you till the cows come home. On second
thoughts, I'd rather dance with the cows till you came home.**
Groucho Marx in the film *Duck Soup* (US, 1933). Script by various.

ROME
1 **She said that all the sights in Rome were called after London
cinemas.**
Nancy Mitford, British writer (1904–73) in *Pigeon Pie* (1940).

ROSES
1 **Roses are reddish
Violets are blueish
If it wasn't for Jesus
We'd all be Jewish.**
From Amsterdam, included in *Graffiti Lives OK* (1979).

2 **Rose's are red,
Violet's are blue,
And mine are white.**
Included in *Graffiti 2* (1980).

See also POETRY 1, 2.

ROTARIANS

1 **The first Rotarian was the first man to call John the Baptist Jack.**

H.L. Mencken, American writer and editor (1880–1956), quoted in *The Treasury of Humorous Quotations*, ed. by Evan Esar & Nicolas Bentley (1951).

ROYALTY

1 **Let them eat Corgi.**

Graffito on the Hammersmith flyover during a bread strike in Jubilee Year (1977). Described on Granada TV *Cabbages and Kings* (22 July 1979).

2 **A crown is no more than a hat that lets in the rain.**

Frederick the Great, King of Prussia (1712–86) – a remark made in declining a formal coronation in 1740. Included in A. & V. Palmer, *Quotations in History* (1976).

3 **I think it's time they let George VII have a go.**

Graffito contributed by Alan Coren to Granada TV *Cabbages and Kings* (6 June 1979).

—— RULES OK

This curious affirmative of sloganeering is said to have begun in gang-speak of the late 1960s in Scotland and Northern Ireland, though some would say it dates back to the 1930s. Either a gang or a football team or the Provisional IRA would be said to 'rule OK'. Later, around 1976, this was turned into a joke with numerous variations. It soon became an all but unstoppable cliché. In 1981, Virginian rubbed tobacco was advertised beneath the slogan, 'Virginian Rolls OK' and a French cigarette beneath 'Gauloises à rouler, OK'. With luck these marked the end of a gruesome phrase, but while it lasted some of the jokes upon it were quite ingenious:

1 **Acorns rule oak, eh!?**

2 **Amnesia rules O.**

3 **Anagrams – or luke?**

Contributed to BBC Radio *Quote ... Unquote* (12 June 1979) by Phil Glenister of Crowthorne, Berkshire.

4 **Anarchy – no rules OK?**

5 **Apathy rul . . .**

6   **Apathy rules, oh dear . . . .**

7   **ASTIGMATISM RULES OK.**
Written in letters five feet tall — contributed to BBC Radio *Quote ... Unquote* (21 June 1978).

8   **Barad-dûr boot boys rule Middle Earth OK.**

9   **Brunel rules I.K.**
Graffito written in the dust of a Western region Class 50 locomotive. Contributed to BBC Radio *Quote ... Unquote* (31 July 1980) by Richard Porter, writing from the Netherlands.

10   **Bureaucracy rules OK OK OK.**

11   **Chelsea rule OK — whereas Cambridge United exhibit traits indicative of inherent superiority.**

12   **Community dancing rules OK KO K.**

13   **Computers rule 10110101 11100101.**

14   **Consideration rules, if that's OK.**

15   **Cowardice rules — if that's OK with you.**

16   **David Frost drools OK.**

17   **Democracy rules 40% OK, 45% NO, 15% Don't know.**

18   **Dyslexia lures KO.**

19   **Einstein rules relatively OK — well, in theory anyway.**

20   **Examples rule, e.g.**
Contributed to BBC Radio *Quote ... Unquote* (28 August 1980) by Paul Thompson of Southport.

21   **Flower power rules bouquet.**
Contributed to BBC Radio *Quote ... Unquote* (5 February 1979) by Carole Arrenberg of Beckenham, Kent.

22   **French diplomats rule au Quai.**

23   **French dockers rule au quai.**

24   **Geordies rule K.K.K.**

25   **Heisenberg probably rules OK.**
Werner Karl Heisenberg was the German physicist who proposed the uncertainty principle (1927).

26   **Horse power rules neigh neigh.**

27 **Hungarian wines rule Tokay.**

28 **Hurlingham rules, croquet.**

29 **Interflora rules, bouquet.**

30 **Irish drama rules O'Casey.**
Graffito from the Aldwych Theatre, London. Contributed to BBC Radio *Quote* ... *Unquote* (12 January 1982) by Sonia Fraser of Woodbridge, Suffolk.

31 **James Bond rules OOK.**
Contributed to BBC Radio *Quote* ... *Unquote* (12 June 1979) by Anthony C. Evans at University College, Swansea.

32 **Jargon rules, ongoing agreement situation.**

33 **Judaism rules Oy vey!**

34 **The King of Siam rules Bangk OK.**

35 **Llanfairpwllgwyngyllgogerychwryndrobwllllandysiliogogogoch – OK.**
Addition to the station sign in Anglesey. Contributed to BBC Radio *Quote* ... *Unquote* (8 December 1981) by Joseph Meijers of Maastricht in the Netherlands.

36 **Lord Denning rules – OK**
To which was added 'House of Lords over-rules OK.'

37 **Lord Kelvin rules O°K.**
Also 'Absolute zero OK' – 0°Kelvin is absolute zero.

38 **Magic rules – hocus pocus.**

39 **Manuel rules O ¿Qué?**
Contributed to BBC Radio *Quote* ... *Unquote* (5 June 1980) by Miss Lynne M. Tay of King's Langley.

40 **Morse code rules . . . .-.**

41 **Dear George – Moscow Rules, OK.**

42 **My wife wears black rubber gear and whips me – Ohhh Kay!**

43 **Nostalgia rules, hokey cokey.**

44 **OK sauce rules HP.**

45 **Oral sex drools OK.**

46 **P-P-Patrick Campbell Ru-Ru-Ru-Rules (that's all we've got time for, I'm afraid).**

47 **Pavlov's Dogs Rule.**

48 **Pedants rule OK – or, more accurately, exhibit certain of the trappings of the traditional leadership.**
Contributed to BBC Radio *Quote ... Unquote* (19 February 1979) by Nick Cornford of Shendish, Hemel Hempstead.

49 **Personal problems rule, BO.**
Contributed by Prunella Gee to BBC Radio *Quote ... Unquote* (21 August 1979).

50 **Persuasion rules OK. Just this once.**

51 **Pope Innocent is Pious OK.**

52 **Potassium ethoxide rules C2H5OK.**

53 **Procrastination will rule one day, OK?**

54 **Queen Elizabeth Rules UK.**

55 **Queensberry Rules KO/TKO.**

56 **Rizla Skins Roll OK.**

57 **Rodgers and Hammerstein rule OK lahoma.**

58 **George Gershwin rule 'Oh, Kay!'**

59 **Roget's Thesaurus rules administers governs control OK all right adequately.**

60 **Rooner spules OK.**

61 **Royce Rolls KO.**
Contributed to BBC Radio *Quote ... Unquote* (12 June 1979) by Paul Jacobson of Leeds.

62 **The Rubaiyat Rules – OK?**
Written up in the University Library in Cambridge. Contributed by Roger Osborne to Granada TV *Cabbages and Kings* (22 July 1979).

63 **Sausage rolls, OK.**

64 **Sceptics may or may not rule OK.**

65 **Schizophrenia rules OK OK.**

66 **Scotland rules OK the noo!**

67 **Slide rules OK.**

68 **Sloane Rangers rule OK, yah!**

69 **Spanish punks rule olé!**

70 **S-s-s-stutterers r-r-r-rule rule OK.**
Quoted in Bruce Ridley (ed.), *Wall Flowers: A Collection of Australian Graffiti*
(1981).

71 **Steve McGarret rules Hawaii 5OK.**

72 **Sycophancy rules – if it's OK by you.**

73 **Synonyms govern all right.**

74 **Town criers rule okez okez okez.**

75 **12 inch rule OK.**

76 **Typographers rule OQ.**

77 **Voyeurs drool OK.**
Quoted in Bruce Ridley (ed.), *Wall Flowers: A Collection of Australian Graffiti*
(1981).

78 **Women rule, obey.**

79 **Wyatt Earp rules OK corral.**

RUSSIAN JOKES
1 **Russia produces more history than it can consume locally.**
Described as an 'old joke' in *The Times* (31 July 1986).

2 **Being Russian means never saying you're sorry.**

See also SOVIET JOKES.

SADISTS
1 **A sadist is someone who is terribly kind to a masochist.**
Graffito from St Bartholomew's Hospital, London. Contributed to BBC Radio
Quote ... Unquote (17 May 1978) by Richard Gordon.

See also FLOGGING and MASOCHISM.

SAFE PERIOD

1 Make love during the safe period — when her husband's away.

Quoted in Bruce Ridley (ed.), *Wall Flowers: A Collection of Australian Graffiti* (1981).

SAILORS

1 Napoleon, having been captured after Waterloo, was taken aboard the frigate *Bellerophon* for shipment to St Helena. As he stepped on the deck to begin his long voyage into exile, he murmured dreamily, '*Alors, c'est l'heure . . .*'

The bosun's mate, an impressionable youth, heard this and in amazement remarked to the quarter-master, 'His Royal Highness spoke to me . . . in English!'

An apocryphal story, told in this form by Peter Webb in *Oxford Today* (Hilary, 1994). A similar joke about a French naval academy having the motto '*A l'eau, c'est l'heure*' [to the water, it is time] was told by Roy Kinnear on BBC Radio *Quote . . . Unquote* (1986).

SAN FRANCISCO

1 San Francisco — the only city where a man of modest means can live like a queen.

Contributed by Glenn Rankine of Bishops Stortford to *Graffiti 4* (1982).

See also LIGHT-BULB JOKES 2.

SCHEDULES

1 There cannot be a crisis next week. My schedule is already full.

Henry Kissinger, American Secretary of State (1923-), quoted in *Time* Magazine (24 January 1977).

SCHIZOPHRENIA

1 Two people in every one who works for the BBC is schizophrenic.

Included in *Graffiti Lives OK* (1979).

2 OK — so I'm cured of schizophrenia, but where am I now when I need me.

From Manchester University, in *Graffiti 2* (1980).

3 *Notice of meeting*: **YOU'RE NEVER ALONE WITH SCHIZOPHRENIA**
– I've half a mind to attend.
Slogan and addition contributed to BBC Radio *Quote ... Unquote* (7 June 1978) by Celia Haddon.

4 **Roses are red**
Violets are blue,
I'm a schizophrenic
And so am I.

SCHOLARSHIP
1 **Here's to pure scholarship. May it never be of any use to anyone!**
A bravura toast, reported in 1993 as having been given at the centenary of a college. John Julius Norwich comments that his father, Duff Cooper, used to quote it as being a toast to Higher Mathematics.

SCHOOLBOY HOWLERS
1 **'My wife Sally, a school librarian, was amused by the request of a rather small boy, obviously sent by his teacher, who came into the library and asked for a copy of: "She Stoops to Conga".'**
Contributed to BBC Radio *Quote ... Unquote* (15 December 1981) by David Allsopp of Long Eaton.

2 **A schoolboy came home complaining that he had to do drama: 'It's a horrid play, but I've got the best bit. I have to say, "Bubble, bubble, toilet trouble".'**
Contributed to BBC Radio *Quote ... Unquote* (22 June 1977) by Norma Shepherd. Probably a touch 'traditional'.

3 **It is wrong to commit adultery because it breaks the vase you took when you were married.**
Contributed to BBC Radio *Quote ... Unquote* (23 July 1983) by Marion Chumbley of Twickenham.

4 **Salome danced in front of Harrods.**

5 **In a mathematics class, a teacher asked, 'Does anybody know what a ratio is?' A voice piped up: 'Please, miss, I think he was a sailor.'**
Contributed to BBC Radio *Quote ... Unquote* (16 February 1982) by Derek Lamb of Potters Bar.

6 At Christmas, the five-year-old girl liked to sing: 'Oh, come all ye grapefruit . . .'.

7 St Paul's Cathedral was designed by Christopher Robin.

8 The poor Irish had rough mating on the floor.
Contributed to BBC Radio Quote ... Unquote (30 July 1983) by Edward J. Riley of Little Waltham in Essex.

9 In answer to the question, 'What did knights of old use before windows were invented?', a pupil wrote: 'Before widows were invented, knights used slits in the wall.'

10 Q. What did William Harvey discover?
A. Sherry.

11 Completing a biology paper on human reproduction, a fourteen-year-old schoolgirl wrote in answer to the question 'What is a secondary sexual characteristic?' – 'When it doesn't hurt the second time.'

12 Vesuvius is a volcano. You can walk to the top, lean over the edge and see the creator smoking.
Contributed to BBC Radio Quote ... Unquote (14 September 1985) by Mrs T. Lewis of Harpenden.

13 A four-year-old Roman Catholic child used to pray: 'Hail, Mary, full of grace . . . blessed art thou swimming . . . '.
Contributed to BBC Radio Quote ... Unquote (4 June 1986) by Margaret Drake of Nelson, Lancashire.

14 A nine-year-old's answer to a scripture question: 'There were ten bridesmaids and five were virgins and five were careful.'
Traditional? Included in Babes and Sucklings (1983).

15 If Mrs Jones doesn't have her baby soon, I expect she'll have to be seduced.
'Two girls in the dinner queue discussing a member of the teaching staff who was about to have a baby' – contributed to BBC Radio Quote ... Unquote (6 August 1983) by Roger Walkinton of Lewes, East Sussex, whose wife – a teacher – overheard it.

16 Lot's wife was a pillar of salt by day . . . but a ball of fire by night.

17 When Mary heard she was to be the mother of Jesus she went off and sang the *Magna Carta*.

18 Our Lady and all the angels have lilos over their heads.

19 Christopher Columbus circumcised the world with forty-foot clippers.

20 A kangaroo keeps its baby in the porch.

21 Last weekend, the Bishop came to our school and turned some of the Sisters into Mothers in a short, but interesting, ceremony.

22 I know that my reindeer liveth.

From an exchange between two boys at a school's Easter concert. Contributed to BBC Radio *Quote ... Unquote* (1 December 1981) by N. Williamson of Wilmslow, Cheshire.

23 A cuckoo is a bird which lays other birds' eggs in its own nest, and *viva voce*.

From a girl's O-level biology exam paper. Contributed to BBC Radio *Quote ... Unquote* (9 March 1982) by Roger Butterfield of Sandwith near Whitehaven, Cumbria.

24 An orchestra has a man called a conductor who stands out in front with a piece of paper which tells him what music the orchestra is playing.

Contributed to BBC Radio *Quote ... Unquote* (26 January 1982) by Leonard Matthews of Paignton.

25 From a vocabulary test in an Eleven Plus examination paper: 'Write a word which describes a man who keeps on despite all the difficulties.' An eleven-year-old girl gave the answer: 'Passionate'.

Contributed to BBC Radio *Quote ... Unquote* (2 March 1982) by Norman Wordsworth of Norwich (who was marking the paper in question).

26 Macbeth's courage failed him at the last minuet.

Contributed to BBC Radio *Quote ... Unquote* (26 May 1982) by Mrs Eileen Turner of Bridge of Allan, Stirling. Committed by one of her pupils.

27 Pins have saved many lives by people not swallowing them.

The rest of the howlers in this section were collected by Mr D.F. of the
University of Manchester School of Education (December 1990):

28 A sincere friend is one who says nasty things to your face, instead of saying them behind your back.

29 All brutes are imperfect animals. Man alone is a perfect beast.

30 Rural life is found mostly in the country.

31 The reason you feel cool in a bathing-suit is because the suit evaporates.

32 He was dressed in the garbage of a monk.

33 **Q.** What is the Kohinoor?
    A. A Jewish prostitute.

34 Robinson Caruso was a great singer who lived on an island.

35 Brotherly love can be extended to sisters, indeed the Bible recommends it.

36 The woman's brain weighs almost as much as the human brain.

37 An adult is a man who has stopped growing at both ends but not in the middle.

38 Ali Baba means being away when the crime was committed.

39 A bamboo is an Italian baby.

40 An epistle is the wife of an apostle.

41 Heredity means if your grandfather didn't have any children then your father probably wouldn't have any, and neither would you, probably.

42 A mosquito is a child of black and white parents.

43 An octopus is a person who hopes for the best.

44 An omelet is a charm worn around the neck.

45 Paraffin is the next order of angels over seraphims.

46 The psalms and psalter are words the minister uses for spasms and plaster.

47 Psychology is the science of diseases that don't exist.

48 A senator is half a horse and half a man.

49 Spaghetti is thrown on people at weddings.

50 A spinster is a bachelor's wife.

51 Strategy is when you don't let the enemy know that you are out of ammunition but keep on firing.

52 Tantrum is a bicycle for a man and his wife.

53 A theme is a thing that runs down the side of your trousers.

54 Transparent means something you can see through e.g. a keyhole.

55 If you want to understand animals, you should think of Eskimos. They are very fond indeed of their reindeer, in fact they love their reindeer more than their wives. But then, they are very useful to them.

56 The soil is fertile, sir, because it is full of micro-orgasms.
Thirteen-year-old pupil at Cranleigh, reported by 1978.

57 A skeleton is a man with his inside out and his outside off.

58 Digestion is carried out in the stomach by aid of acrobatic juices.

59 Lack of vitamins will give rise to crickets.

60 There are four symptoms of a cold. Two I forget and the other two are too well known to mention.

61 If anyone should faint in church, put her head between the knees of the nearest medical man.

62 Respiration is a handy thing to know how to do especially if you live far from a doctor.

63 Cure for a toothache: take a mouthful of cold water and sit on the stove till it boils.

64 In case of asphyxiation apply artificial respiration until the patient is dead.

65 Natural immunity is being able to catch a disease without the aid of a physician.

66 The air contains more than 100% carbolic acid, it is very dangerous to health.

67 When there are no fresh vegetables, you can always get canned.

68 One of the essentials for a sanitory home is not more than two people in one bed.

69 The doctor felt his patient's purse.

70 When two children are born together they are called twins. When there are three, they are culprits.

71 A person should take a bath once in the summer-time and not quite so often in the winter-time.

72 Reproduction is the life process by which an orgasm produces others of its kind.

73 The average man is rather below normal.

74 To keep milk from turning sour, you should keep it in the cow.

75 A cat is a quadruped – the legs, as usual, being at the four corners.

76 Bach, the composer, wrote music for the organ. He had three wives and twenty children, and in his spare time he practised in the attic on a spinster.

77 Three times Achilles chased the lifeless body of Hector around the walls of Troy.

78 The Greeks wore scandals on their feet.

79 The Trojans rode a wooden horse that said: 'Beware the Greeks asking for lifts.'

80 And as the angels appeared to the shepherds in the fields, they fell on their faces and were sore afterwards.

81 Name a five-letter word meaning a heavenly body with a long luminous tail.
Angel.

82 Shakespeare was born in the year 1569, supposedly on his birthday.

83 Gorreth rode along a high cliff and fell into the jaws of a yawning abbess.

84 An active word shows action as 'he kissed her' and a passive verb shows passion as 'she kissed him'.

85 Letters in shopping type are in hysterics.

86 Every sentence and the name of God must begin with a caterpillar.

87 *Il se met à y aller*: 'he met himself going there.'

88 *Salle à manger*: 'sales manager.'

89 *Caveat emptor*: 'caviare for the Emperor.'

90 *Bonae legiones Caesaris*: 'the bony legs of Caesar.'

91 *O si sic omnes*: 'everybody was seasick.'

92 *Stante litora puppes*: 'there stands a litter of puppies.'

See also GEOGRAPHY and HISTORY.

SCOTS

1 The hairy-arsed Scotsman invited the young lassie to inspect just what exactly he did or didn't have beneath his kilt.
    'Och,' declared the young lassie, having taken a peep, 'it's gruesome!'
    'Aye,' replied the man, 'and if you bide a min longer it'll have grue some more!'
Current by the 1960s.

2 *Tourist*: 'Is anything worn under that kilt you're wearing?'
Scotsman: 'No, madam, I can assure you it is all in perfect working order.'

3 *Fat man to Scot*: 'Would it be any use trying to borrow a fiver off you?'
'Aye, the exercise'll do you good.'

4 *Policeman at Mrs Macpherson's door*: 'Does Mr Macpherson live here?'
'Just carry him in.'

5 A ghillie was slightly wounded in a grouse-shooting accident and was given 'a wee dram' to bring him round. His first — horrified — words on coming round were: 'Is that whisky you're giving me, and me unconscious?'

See also DEATH 10.

SEDUCTION

1 **A man called Skinner took a girl out to dinner.**
At half-past eight, it was in her — not Skinner, but the dinner.
A man called Tupper took the girl out to supper.
At half-past ten, it was up her — not Tupper, or the supper.
It was that bastard Skinner again.

Told by Mr E.R. Kermode of Bristol in 1987. G. Legman in *The Limerick* (1964/9) has limerick versions of this, involving both Skinner and Tupper, and dating back to 1911.

SEX

1 **Sex — the poor man's polo.**

Attributed to Clifford Odets, American playwright (1903–63). See also OPERA 3.

2 **Prostitutes for pleasure, concubines for service, wives for breeding.**

Attributed to Sir Richard Burton, English explorer and writer (1821–90), though unverified. He may have been quoting Demosthenes. 'And a melon for ecstasy' is sometimes added.

3 **At certain times I like sex. Like after a cigarette.**

Rodney Dangerfield, quoted in Bob Chieger, *Was It Good For You Too?* (1983).

4 **I am always looking for meaningful one-night stands.**

Dudley Moore in 1982 — quoted in Bob Chieger, *Was It Good For You Too?* (1983).

5 **Sex between a man and a woman can be wonderful — provided you get between the right man and the right woman.**

Attributed to Woody Allen, US film actor, writer and director (1937–). Compare 'I believe that sex is a beautiful thing between two people. Between five, it's fantastic . . .' on Allen's record album *The Nightclub Years 1964–1968,* 1972).

6 **Q. Why is sex like maths?**
A. You subtract the clothes, divide the legs, and multiply.

Traditional, by 1988.

7 **Sex is like a bank account. After you withdraw you lose interest.**

Traditional, in *Graffiti 4* (1982).

8 **Sex is all right, but it's not as good as the real thing.**
From Hexham, included in *Graffiti 2* (1980).

9 **The thing that takes the least amount of time and causes the most amount of trouble is sex.**
Attributed to John Barrymore, American actor (1882–1942).

10 **Sex is just one damp thing after another.**
Included in *Graffiti 5* (1986).

11 **The three ages of man — tri-weekly, try weekly, try weakly.**
From Sorens Bistro ceiling, Woolloomooloo, NSW, Australia — signed 'Clive' and dated '1/12/73' — in Rennie Elis, *Australian Graffiti Revisited* (1979).

12 **What's the difference between the erotic and the kinky? Erotic is when you do something sensitive and imaginative with a feather. Kinky is when you use the whole chicken.**
Attributed to Elmore Leonard, American novelist (1925–), by William Rushton in 1987. However, in a BBC TV *Moving Pictures* profile of Roman Polanski (reviewed in the *Guardian*, 25 November 1991), Peter Coyote ascribed the remark to Polanski in the form: 'Eroticism is using a feather, while pornography is using the whole chicken.' Another version uses 'perverted' instead of 'kinky'.

13 **Is sex dirty? Only when it is being done right.**
Woody Allen, in his screenplay for the film *Everything You Always Wanted To Know About Sex* (1972).

14 **Sex is bad for one — but it's very good for two.**
Contributed by Eileen Kirby of Croydon to BBC Radio *Quote ... Unquote* (29 January 1979).

15 **Never miss a chance to have sex or appear on television.**
Gore Vidal, quoted in Bob Chieger, *Was It Good For You Too?* (1983).

16 **Do you save fallen women? Well, save one for me.**

17 **What does a paedophile have after dinner?
Under Eights.**

18 **My dad told me, 'Anything worth having is worth waiting for.' I waited until I was fifteen.**
Zsa Zsa Gabor, 1981, quoted in Bob Chieger, *Was It Good For You Too?* (1983).

19 **A married woman was bemoaning to fellow dinner guests that she had been extremely naïve before her marriage. To illustrate the extent of her innocence she remarked: 'I didn't even know what a homosexual was until I met my husband.'**
Contributed by Mary Drury of Plymouth to *Foot in Mouth* (1982).

20 **On Caroline of Brunswick's behaviour with the dey (governor) of Algiers: 'She was happy as the dey was long.'**
Attributed to Lord Norbury (1820).

21 **Mad men and lame men copulate best.**
A peculiar English proverb — quoted in Champion, *Racial Proverbs* (1938).

22 **I met my love in the graveyard**
I did her before we were wed
I laid her on top of the tombstone
We did it to cheer up the dead.
Attributed to Brendan Behan, Irish playwright (1923–64).

23 **My girlfriend's got sex on the brain.**
I only love her for her mind.
Quoted in Bruce Ridley (ed.), *Wall Flowers: A Collection of Australian Graffiti* (1981).

24 *On Henry Kissinger:* **'Henry's idea of sex is to slow down to thirty miles an hour when he drops you off at the door.'**
Barbara Howar, quoted in Barbara Rowes, *The Book of Quotes* (1979).

25 **I like to wake up feeling a new man.**
Attributed to Jean Harlow, American film actress (1911–37).

26 **A hard man is good to find.**
Attributed to Mae West, American film actress (1892–1980).

27 **Thanks, I enjoyed every inch of it.**
Attributed to Mae West.

28 **A man with an erection is in no need of advice.**
Italian proverb.

29 **I like it and him in that order.**
Female graffito, included in *Graffiti 2* (1980). Another version is 'I like it but not them.'

30 **She is a very fascinating woman and he is very fond of fascinating with her.**

Samuel Butler, English writer (1835–1902), quoted in *The Treasury of Humorous Quotations*, ed. by Evan Esar & Nicolas Bentley (1951).

31 **She offered her honour,**
I honoured her offer,
So all night long
It was on her and off her.

Anonymous, described as a 'classic on all campuses' in Haan & Hammerstrom *Graffiti in the Big Ten* (1981).

32 **Do you think that sex ought to take place before the wedding? No, not if it delays the ceremony . . .**

This had an airing in an uncredited quickie sketch called 'Sex' in the Kenneth Williams revue *One Over the Eight* (London, 1961).

33 **Confucius he say no such thing as rape. Lady with skirt up run faster than man with trousers down.**

From London, in *Graffiti 4* (1982).

34 **Some things can't be ravished. You can't ravish a tin of sardines.**

D.H. Lawrence, *Lady Chatterley's Lover* (1928).

35 **It's time we got all this rape and violence off the streets and back in the home – where it really belongs.**

Source not known. Compare: Jonathan Miller as a trendy vicar in *Beyond the Fringe* (1961): 'It is my aim to get the violence off the streets and into the churches where it belongs'. Also 'Television has brought back murder into the home – where it belongs' – Alfred Hitchcock, quoted in the *Observer* (19 December 1965). Also 'Get Bingo out of the supermarkets and into the churches where it really belongs' – performed on CBS TV *Rowan and Martin's Laugh-In* and included on the record album *Laugh-In '69* (1969).

36 **College warden: 'Are you entertaining a woman in your room?' Student: 'Just a minute, I'll ask her.'**

SEXISM

1 **WOMEN'S RIGHTS NOW!**
– yes, dear!

Graffito.

2 **END VIOLENCE TO WOMEN NOW.**
– yes, dear.

Included in *Graffiti 2* (1980). This addition was to a slogan visible on a wall near Wandsworth prison, London, in 1979.

SEX MANIACS

1 **You're never alone if you're a sex maniac.**

From Hatfield, Herts. in *Graffiti 2* (1980).

2 **A man asked his friend where he was working. 'Oh,' said the friend, 'I'm practising as a psychiatrist.'**
   'Never knew that was your ambition,' said the first man.
   'It wasn't,' said the psychiatrist bitterly. 'I wanted to be a sex maniac, but I failed the practical.'

Recounted by Valerie Grosvenor Meyer in *Folk Review* (November 1974).

SHAGGY DOG STORIES

Space – and patience – does not allow more than one of these to be trotted out, but it is certainly a mode of joke that should be registered. The term was in use (in the US) by 1945.

1 **A vicar is walking through the forest one sunny morning when he sees a glum-looking frog perched on a rock in the middle of a pond. 'Why are you so unhappy?' he asks. Replies the frog, 'Well, I wasn't always like this, you see. I used to be a happy normal boy of eleven, a choirboy at the local parish church, in fact. But one day I was walking through the forest when I met a wicked witch, who stood in my way and would not let me pass. "Get out of my way, wicked witch," I said, but she replied, "How dare you, you rude child," and turned me in an instant into the frog you see before you now.'**
   'But my poor child,' said the vicar, 'this is a terrible state of affairs. Is there no way the witch's act can be reversed, or are you to remain a frog forever?'
   'Well,' began the frog, 'there *is* a way of turning me back into a boy again and it is this: if a very nice, kind person were to take me home with him, give me a hot meal, put me in a nice warm bed and make sure I was kept as warm as possible all night long, then in the morning I would wake up a boy once more.'
   On hearing him, the vicar puts the frog in his pocket, takes

him home and puts him into his bed. When the vicar wakes up the next morning, beside him in the bed is an eleven-year-old choirboy.

Er . . . and that, my Lord, is the case for the defence.

SHEEP

1 Why do white sheep eat more than black sheep?
Because there are more of them.
Told by Ben Waring, Plymouth (1986).

See also AUSTRALIA 2.

SHE WAS ONLY THE ——'S DAUGHTER

A series of mildly bawdy jokes – presented as though the first line of a song. Perhaps suggested by an original which escapes me . . . .

1 She was only the road-maker's daughter, but she liked her asphalt.
Included in *Graffiti 5* (1986).

2 She was only the Town Clerk's daughter, but she let the Borough Surveyor.

3 She was only a Red Indian's daughter, but she certainly knew how.

4 She was only a fisherman's daughter, but when she saw my rod she reeled.
Included in John S. Crosbie, *Crosbie's Dictionary of Puns* (1977).

SHORTAGES

1 THERE IS A SHORTAGE OF GIRLS IN OXFORD
– I don't care how short they are, there just aren't enough of them.
Graffito from an Oxford college, contributed to BBC Radio *Quote ... Unquote* (28 August 1980) by Andrew Dalwood of Paddock Wood, Kent.

SINCERITY *See ACTORS AND ACTING 2.*

SIXTY-NINE

1 Personally I have always felt [*soixante-neuf*] to be madly
confusing, like trying to pat your head and rub your stomach
at the same time.

Helen Lawrenson, in *Esquire* (1977) — quoted in Bob Chieger, *Was It Good For You Too?* (1983).

SMILES

1 Smile, they said, life could be worse. So I did and it was.

From the Thatcher's Arms, Norton Heath, Essex, included in *Graffiti 2* (1980).

SMIRNOFF JOKES

*The common advertising notion of a way of life or a belief being swept
away by some sudden revelation – 'I was/thought/did ——— until I
discovered/bought ———' was used memorably in Britain from 1970 to
1975 in a series of slogans for Smirnoff vodka. The original advertising
lines included: 'I thought St Tropez was a Spanish monk . . . /accountancy
was my life . . . /I was the mainstay of the public library . . . /the Kama
Sutra was an Indian restaurant . . . until I discovered Smirnoff.' An
extraordinary number of variations followed, mostly in graffiti form:*

1 I thought the AA was a car club until I discovered Smirnoff.

2 I used to think A10 was the road to Cambridge until I
discovered a crate of Smirnoff in my locker.

From Knightsbridge Crown Court, in *Graffiti 2* (1980). A10 is the section of
Scotland Yard that investigates complaints against the police.

3 I used to play football for Scotland until I discovered Smirnoff.

4 I thought Muhammad Ali was a street in Cairo until I
discovered Smirnoff.

5 I thought cirrhosis was a type of cloud, until I discovered
Smirnoff.

6 I thought clap was a form of applause until I discovered
Smirnoff.

7 I used to think Fellatio was a character from Hamlet until I
discovered Smirnoff.

8 I thought that innuendo was an Italian suppository until I
discovered Smirnoff.

9 I thought Midge Ure was an insect repellent until I discovered Smirnoff.

10 I thought Mother Goose was a textbook by Freud until I discovered Smirnoff.

11 I thought Wanking was a town in China until I discovered Smirnoff.

12 I thought Smirnoff was a tank commander until I discovered Zhukov.

13 I thought Hertz Van Rentals was a Dutch painter until I discovered Smirnoff.

Contributed to BBC Radio Quote ... Unquote (5 June 1979) by Mr D. Lawrence of Heaton Norris, Cheshire.

14 I thought, until I discovered Professor ——.

15 I was a professional journalist until I discovered the Tonight programme.

From the BBC TV studios at Lime Grove, December 1975.

16 I used to think that nightingales sang in tune until I discovered Stravinsky.

17 I thought 7-Up was a drink until I discovered Snow White.

18 I thought UDI was a contraceptive until I discovered Ian Smith.

19 I thought Plato was a Greek washing-up liquid.

20 I thought nausea was a novel by Jean-Paul Sartre until I discovered scrumpy.

21 I thought a sell-out was the end of a special offer until I discovered the NUR.

22 I thought Smirnoff was exciting until I discovered wanking.

Graffito, quoted in Rachel Bartlett (ed.), Off the Wall (1982).

23 I thought graffiti was a kind of pasta until I discovered Nigel Rees.

Graffito from Wells, Somerset, contributed to BBC Radio Quote ... Unquote (31 July 1980) by Les Killip of Camberley.

SMOKING

1 **Does your wife smoke after sexual intercourse?
I don't know, I've never looked.**
Sufficiently well known by the early 1960s to be included in a close-down
sketch on BBC TV *That Was The Week That Was* (1962–3 season).

2 **It is now beyond any doubt that cigarettes are the biggest
single cause of statistics.**
Graffito contributed to BBC Radio *Quote ... Unquote* (19 June 1980) by Mr R.F.
Crosher of London N4.

3 **'Young man,' said the woman to the Aggie seated next to her
on the jet flight, 'Smoking makes me sick.'**
    **'Well, lady,' said the Aggie blowing smoke rings. 'If I were
you I'd give it up.'**
Included in *The Best of 606 Aggie Jokes* (1988).

4 **The Aggie read the Surgeon General's report which said that
studies proved tar and nicotine caused cancer in mice. So he
put his cigarettes up high where the mice couldn't get at them.**
In the same book also.

5 **Cancer cures smoking.**
Included in Reisner & Wechsler, *Encyclopedia of Graffiti* (1974).

6 **Never smoke when asleep; never refrain when awake.**
Attributed to Mark Twain.

See also CIGARETTES.

SOCIOLOGY

1 **Sociology degrees, please take one.**
Written beside by a paper towel dispenser, York. Contributed by Hilary
Pritchard to BBC Radio *Quote ... Unquote* (17 May 1978).

2 **What do you say to a sociology student with a job?
A big Mac, please.**
Graffito, Cambridge University library. Reported in the *Independent* (30 June
1993).

SONG TITLE JOKES
Slightly scrambled versions of well-known songs . . . .

1 **They Tried To Sell Us Egg Foo Young.**

2 **You Make Me Egg Foo Young.**
In BBC radio *Round the Horne* (8 May 1966).

3 **My Funny Heseltine.**

4 **Corgi and Bess.**
A show title, rather, about the British Royal family, suggested by Larry Adler on BBC Radio *Quote ... Unquote* (13 July 1977). By 1984, it was also a nickname in broadcasting circles for the Christmas message given annually on radio and TV by Queen Elizabeth II (noted for her canine pets).

5 **Don't Cry for Me, Marge and Tina.**

6 **Don't Cry for Me, Arthur Negus.**
Contributed to BBC Radio *Quote ... Unquote* (31 May 1978).

7 **I'm So Miserable Without You, It's Almost Like Having You Here.**
An actual song title.

8 **You Are the Scrambled Eggs in My Love Nest.**
And another one.

9 **Plant a Watermelon on My Grave, and Let the Juice Soak Through.**
Even.

10 **How Could You Believe Me When I Said I Love You When You Know I've Been a Liar All My Life?**
The title of a Harold Adamson/Burton Lane song in the show *Royal Wedding* (1951).

11 **I Get Along Without Thee H.G. Wells**
Contributed by Benny Green to BBC Radio *Quote ... Unquote* (13 July 1977), as also the following:

12 **I'm a Noel Coward Fan from the Rio Grande.**

13 **They Tried To Sell Us Mao-tse-tung.**

14 **Won't You Come Home, Disraeli.**

15 **I'm Just a Girl — U Thant Say No.**

16 **I've Grown Accustomed To Steve Race.**

17 **The Night They Invented Jack Payne.**

18 **When Chou en Lai Were Young, Maggie.**

SOVIET JOKES

These examples are taken from a large sample of mostly graffiti jokes gathered in the Soviet Union in the early 1980s by Arthur Hawes and Ivan Ivanovitch Zapiskin. They were translated and included in Graffiti 5 *(1986).*

1 **Q. Why do Russians walk around in threes?**
A. So there is one who can read, one who can write, and one who can keep an eye on the two intellectuals.
·Graffito in Moscow, attributed to a visiting Czech.

Compare POLISH JOKES 10.

2 **Q. What's a hundred metres long and eats cabbage?**
A. The queue outside a Moscow butcher's shop.

3 **She can't be hugged, she can't be kissed –**
She's the guide from Intourist.
In a Leningrad hotel.

4 **Q. Why is there no meat in the Soviet Union?**
A. Because the sheep work and the cows govern.

5 **When the end of the world comes the only safe country will be the Soviet Union. The Soviet Union is fifty years behind the rest of the world.**

6 **The reason there is no fish in the Moscow market is so you won't notice there is no meat.**

7 **The Kremlin has just been broken into and next year's election results stolen.**
From a youth hostel in Salzburg, Austria, by 1988.

8 **The first thing a Russian worker does after leaving work is to take his hands from his pockets. That's why the economy has gone to hell.**

Compare BRITISH WORKMEN.

9 If you have any requirements, contact Reception. We'll explain why you can't have them.
Graffito in English, in lavatory of the Hotel Russia, Moscow.

10 'Within five years communism will overtake the capitalist west which now stands on the edge of a precipice' – Brezhnev.

Compare THATCHER, MARGARET 2.

11 Things may be bad but they're better than next year.

12 By 1985, one Soviet citizen in every five will have a car, one in three will have a television and one in two will own a pair of socks.

13 The Soviet economy is a planned economy. When there's no ham, there's no eggs.

14 New-style Russian roulette: a man goes to bed with six women – one of them is a cannibal.
Compare this with a joke told by Rodney Dangerfield on NBC-TV's *Tonight Show* in 1979: 'I went to a wild party, we played a new version of Russian roulette. We passed around six girls and one of them had VD' – quoted in Bob Chieger, *Was It Good For You Too?* (1983).

15 Russian roulette for women: six birth control pills – one of them is an aspirin.

16 The pollution is terrible. If we were allowed to breathe we'd be in trouble.
Outside Leningrad chemical factory.

17 If it were not necessary to eat and wear clothing, the Soviet Union would be the best in the world.

18 When there's food in the villages and none in the cities – that's right-wing deviationism. When there's food in the cities and none in the villages – that's left-wing deviationism. When there's food in the cities and in the villages – that's capitalist propaganda.

19 When Brezhnev visits, everyone can show their unbridled joy by rattling their chains.
Kaliningrad, Lithuania (prior to a visit by the then Soviet leader).

See also RADIO ARMENIA and LIGHT-BULB JOKES 15.

SPAM
1 **I'm pink therefore I'm spam.**
Graffito contributed by J. O'Grady of Longford, Coventry, to Granada TV
Cabbages and Kings (18 November 1979).

SPENDTHRIFT
1 **Q. How can a jazz musician end up with one million dollars?
A. Start out with two million.**
In *Jazz Anecdotes* (ed. Bill Crow, 1991).

SPINACH
1 **The best way to serve spinach — in my opinion — is to someone else.**

SPOONERISMS
*Spoonerisms – the accidental transposing of the beginnings of words –
are named after the Revd William Spooner (1844–1930), Warden of
New College, Oxford, who was allegedly much given to the process
himself. I am not qualified to say why it is that some people are
prone to this form of word-blindness, and many of the Revd Spooner's
most famous utterances are probably apocryphal, but plenty of people
do do it. They would probably describe their complaint as 'bird
watching':*

1 **Which of us has not felt in his heart a half-warmed fish?**
Attributed to Spooner himself, but unverified.

2 **'My favourite Spoonerism was alleged to have been
originated by the Station Commander at an RAF station in
the Canal Zone round about 1952 when I was there. At
church parade, the order was given: "Roam out the fallen
Catholics!"'**
Contributed by Jack Evans of Wimborne, Dorset, to *Foot in Mouth* (1982).

3 **And almost a Spoonerism: at a luncheon given by Mervyn
Hayt, sometime Bishop of Coventry, a nervous curate said to**

Cosmo Lang, Archbishop of Canterbury: 'Have another piece of Grace, your Cake.'

Contributed to BBC Radio *Quote ... Unquote* (24 July 1979) by W.A. Payne of Kettering.

4   **'I am a Lay Reader. When taking evensong soon after my licensing I called on the congregation to: "Come with me unto the Groan of Thrace".'**

Contributed by Bryan Owen of Deal to the same.

5   **'One afternoon during the long hot summer of '76, a group of us were digesting a large lunch. A large well-endowed lady with a penchant for wearing loose thick woolly jumpers complained that the heat was overbearing. I said: "That's hardly surprising. What do you expect with your big sweaty floppers . . . ?"'**

Contributed to BBC Radio *Quote ... Unquote* (9 March 1982) by John Carter of Cardiff.

6   **'A canticle is a sacred song used in church services and a New Testament canticle would be such a song deriving from the New Testament, e.g. "My soul doth magnify the Lord". One day at theological college some years ago, a lecturer marched in and announced he would address us on the subject of: "New Cantament Testicles".'**

Contributed by the Revd A.C. Betts of Leeds to *Foot in Mouth* (1982).

7   **'We were passing through the village where Gray's "Elegy" was written when a lady at the rear of the bus remarked to her companion: "I have always wanted to go to Poke Stoges".'**

Contributed by Nancy Redfern of Cambridge to the same.

8   **'I had entered the wrong time in my diary for a Harvest Festival Supper at my church and consequently arrived an hour late. Wanting to apologize in a light-hearted way, I heard myself say: "Ladies and gentlemen, I cannot remember ever being late for such a function as a Harvest Supper before, but it seems that tonight I have well and truly clotted my bottybook . . . .'**

Contributed to BBC Radio *Quote ... Unquote* (26 June 1980) by the Revd John E. Bourne, Stroud.

See also DEATH 2.

SPORT

1 **Our local football team's doing really badly.**
How badly?
Well, to give you an idea — every time they win a corner,
they do a lap of honour.
This appeared as a graffito, contributed by Rod Cartner of Bristol to *Graffiti 4*
(1982): 'When City win a corner, they do a lap of honour — That's nothing.
Rovers do a lap of honour when they win the toss.'

SQUIRRELS

1 **A squirrel's home Is really a nutcracker's suite.**

STATISTICIANS

1 **A statistician is someone who is good with figures but who**
doesn't have the personality to become an accountant.
Told by Roy Hyde (April 1994). Another version: 'An actuary is someone who is
too boring to be an accountant.'

2 **A statistician Is a person who draws a mathematically precise**
line from an unwarranted assumption to a foregone
conclusion.
Source untraced.

3 **He uses statistics as a drunken man uses lampposts — for**
support rather than for illumination.
Andrew Lang, Scottish poet, novelist and scholar (1844–1912), quoted in
The Treasury of Humorous Quotations, ed. by Evan Esar & Nicolas Bentley
(1951).

STEAMROLLER

1 **If you're not part of the steamroller, you're part of the road.**
Michael Eisner, the Walt Disney chairman, said this in 1994. A 'terrific piece of
Hollywood swagger' according to the person who spotted it in *Screen
International*.

STICKERS

Mid-way between the official slogan and the unofficial graffito, there is
the ever-growing craze for promotional phrases emblazoned on T-shirts,

lapel badges, bumper stickers and hand-drawn placards. Some of them not only promote a point of view but also provoke a smile . . .

1 **WE DON'T LIKE ANYONE VERY MUCH.**
Placard during the 1964 US Presidential Election.

2 **BETTY FORD'S HUSBAND FOR PRESIDENT.**
This was the best-selling button of the 1976 campaign in the US, acknowledging the high regard in which the incumbent First Lady was held.

3 **A REACTOR IS A SAFER PLACE THAN TED KENNEDY'S CAR.**
Window sticker in the US (1979). See also KENNEDY, EDWARD 2.

4 **MRS THATCHER HELPS SMALL BUSINESSES (GET SMALLER ALL THE TIME).**
Window sticker in the UK (1981).

5 **Don't ask me; I was hired for my looks.**
Button.

7 **NOW USE YOUR SKIRT.**
Sign on hand drier in women's lavatory, reported in December 1986.

8 **THIS MAY NOT BE THE MAYFLOWER BUT YOUR DAUGHTER CAME ACROSS IN IT.**
Bumper sticker on an old transit van in New York City (1985) by Roy Osborne of London SW15.

9 **WHEN THE GOING GETS TOUGH, THE TOUGH GO SHOPPING.**
On T-shirts in the US by 1982.

10 **IT'S NOT WHETHER YOU WIN OR LOSE. IT'S HOW YOU LOOK PLAYING THE GAME.**
T-shirt, US.

STREAKERS
1 **Streak now or forever hold your piece.**
Graffito on the sea-front at Brighton, described on Granada TV *Cabbages and Kings* (15 July 1979).

SUBMARINES

1 **Q. Why did the submarine blush?**
A. Because it saw the *Queen Mary*'s bottom.
Current by the 1950s (at least).

2 **Q. Why was your brother thrown out of the submarine service?**
A. He liked to sleep with the windows open.

SUCCESS

1 **If at first you don't succeed — so much for sky-diving.**
Contributed to BBC Radio *Quote ... Unquote* (2 March 1982) by Mr J. Cox of
Epping.

SUITS

1 **Nigel's a very snappy dresser. Do you know he has a suit for
every day of the year?**
   Yes, and by the looks of it, he's wearing it now.
I had the questionable honour of having this remark made about me by Ted Ray
and Kenneth Williams in BBC Radio's *The Betty Witherspoon Show* (1973). As Ted
must surely have recognized the joke was probably older than he was. It had
been served up, on this occasion (if memory serves), by a certain Fred Metcalf.

SUMMER

1 **Q. How do you know it's summer in the UK?**
A. The rain's warmer.

SURGERY

1 **I feel like a new woman and I only came in to have my
prostate removed.**
Included in *Graffiti 5* (1986).

SWANS

1 **Q. What happened when Leda was seduced by that swan in
    classical mythology?**
A. Well, for one thing, she got down in the dumps.
A version of this was told on BBC Radio *The Burkiss Way* in c. 1979. Script by
Andrew Marshall and David Renwick.

TALCUM POWDER

1   A man came into the pharmacy and asked the proprietor if he had any talcum powder. 'Certainly, sir,' said the pharmacist, 'walk this way.' And the potential customer said, 'If I walked like that I wouldn't be needing any talcum powder . . .'

See also WAITER JOKES 20.

TAYLOR, ELIZABETH
American film actress (1932–).

1   I knew Elizabeth Taylor when she didn't know where her next husband was coming from.
Included in *Graffiti 5* (1986).

TEACHERS

1

TO
THE MEMBERS
OF
THE MOST RESPONSIBLE
THE LEAST ADVERTISED
THE WORST PAID
AND
THE MOST RICHLY REWARDED
PROFESSION
IN THE WORLD.

Ian Hay's dedication of his book *The Lighter Side of School Life* (1914).

2   Those who can, do – those who can't, teach – those who can't teach, lecture on the sociology of education degrees.
Graffito from Middlesex Polytechnic, contributed to Granada TV *Cabbages and Kings* (6 June 1979). 'He who can, does. He who cannot, teaches' is from George Bernard Shaw's 'Maxims: Education' published with *Man and Superman* (1903).

Yet a further development is encompassed by A.B. Ramsay in 'Epitaph on a Syndic' from his *Frondes Salicis* (1935):

No teacher I of boys or smaller fry,
No teacher I of teachers, no, not I.
Mine was the distant aim, the longer reach,
To teach men how to teach men how to teach.

Compare CONSULTANTS 1.

TEDDY BEARS

1 I wish I were a teddy bear
With hairs upon my tummy.
I'd climb into a honey pot
And get my tummy gummy.
First heard by me in about 1958.

TEENAGERS

1 **Teenagers are God's punishment for having sex.**
Reported from Wellington, New Zealand, November 1994.

TEETH

1 **I wouldn't say her teeth protrude that much, but the other day I *did* catch her eating an apple through a tennis racquet.**
Noël Coward often recycled witticisms from his own conversation in his plays, but there is a firm example of his borrowing from another in *Come Into the Garden, Maud* (1966): 'She could eat an apple through a tennis racquet.' Earlier, a note in his diary for 10 December 1954 had recorded: 'Lunched and dined with Darryl Zannuck who, David Niven wickedly said, is the only man who can eat an apple through a tennis racquet!'

TELEPHONES

1 **A little old lady called the operator almost as soon as her phone had been installed. 'I'm sorry to bother you,' she said, 'but my telephone cord is too long. Could you pull it back a bit from your end, please?'**

2 *When a man asked to be excused to go to the men's room:* 'He really needs to telephone, but he's too embarrassed to say so.'
Dorothy Parker, related in John Keats, *You Might As Well Live* (1970).

3 **'Well, if I called the wrong number, why did you answer the phone?'**
James Thurber, American humorous writer and artist (1894–1961) – the caption to a cartoon in *Men, Women and Dogs* (1943).

TELEVISION

1 **TV . . . is our latest medium – we call it a medium because nothing's well done.**
Goodman Ace, US writer (1899–1982) in a letter (1954) to Groucho Marx included in *The Groucho Letters* (1967).

2 **Television's got so bad they're scraping the top of the barrel.**
Attributed to Gore Vidal, by 1979.

3 **Television is more interesting than people. If it were not, we should have people standing in the corners of our rooms.**
Attributed to Alan Coren, British writer (b.1938).

TERRORIST

1 **Did you hear about the stupid terrorist who tried to blow up a bus?**
He burnt his lips on the exhaust pipe.

TEXANS

1 **Texans are living proof that Indians screwed buffaloes.**
From Fairbanks, Alaska, included in *Graffiti Lives OK* (1979).

2 **Q. What is a Texas virgin?**
A. A girl who can run faster than her brother.
From Dallas-Fort Worth airport, Texas, in Haan & Hammerstrom *Graffiti in the Southwest Conference* (1981).

THATCHER, MARGARET
British Conservative Prime Minister (1925–), later Baroness Thatcher.

1 **A group of Ulstermen came to the Houses of Parliament in Westminster to confer with the Rev Dr Ian Paisley MP. Inevitably voices were raised and Mrs Thatcher (then Prime Minister) asked what all the noise was about. 'It is Dr Paisley**

arguing with some of his constituents,' she was told. 'Well,' she replied, 'ask him to use the telephone like everyone else.'

Recounted by T.A. Dyer (1994), who adds: 'I have no doubt this has referred to other people long before Dr P. and Lady T. were born but that's the form I liked.'

2 **Before the Thatcher Government came to power we were on the edge of an economic precipice – since then we have taken a great step forward.**

Graffito at the Polytechnic of the South Bank, London. Contributed to BBC Radio Quote ... Unquote (25 December 1980) by Graeme Ashford of Hampton Hill.

Compare RADIO ARMENIA JOKES 1; SOVIET JOKES 10.

3 **Does the Iron Lady use Brillo pads? – only her gynometallurgist knows for sure.**

From Newcastle upon Tyne, in *Graffiti 4* (1982).

4 **Why is Mrs Thatcher like a toilet? Because she gets rid of jobs.**

Graffito quoted by Caroline St John-Brooks in *New Society* (2 June 1983).

5 **When the Queen is home they run up a flag. When Mrs Thatcher's home they run up a side street.**

Graffito, Hertford (1981).

6 **First we were a kingdom under a king, then an empire under an emperor, now we're a country under Maggie Thatcher.**

Contributed by Mat Coward to *Graffiti 5* (1986).

7 **Margaret Thatcher does the work of two men – Laurel and Hardy.**

Known by 1981. As I explain in the Introduction, I first encountered this joke concerning Malcolm Fraser in Australia, that same year.

See also STICKERS 4.

THEATRE

1 **You know, I go to the theatre to be entertained ... I don't want to see plays about rape, sodomy and drug addiction ... I can get all that at home.**

Peter Cook, caption for a cartoon by Roger Law in the *Observer* (8 July 1962).

THIEVES

1 Thieves respect property; they merely wish the property to become their property that they may more perfectly respect it.

G.K. Chesterton, English writer (1874–1936), quoted in *The Treasury of Humorous Quotations*, ed. by Evan Esar & Nicolas Bentley (1951).

2 Lady Dorothy Nevill, so Sir Edmund Gosse tells, preserved her library by pasting in each volume the legend: 'This book has been stolen from Lady Dorothy Nevill'.

Quoted in *The Week-End Book* (1955).

TIME

1 A stitch in time would have confused Stephen Hawking.

2 Time flies like knives. Fruit flies like bananas.

Graffito contributed to BBC Radio Quote ... Unquote (28 August 1980) by Graham Goodfellow of Box, Wiltshire.

TITANIC JOKES

1 Q. What did the passenger on the *Titanic* say?
A. Waiter, I know I asked for ice, but this is ridiculous.

Told by Kenneth Williams on BBC Radio Quote ... Unquote (8 June 1977).

2 Rogers Morton was President Gerald Ford's campaign manager when the President was seeking re-election in 1976. He saw that things were not going well but refused any last-ditch attempts to rescue the campaign, and used the words: 'I'm not going to do anything to rearrange the furniture on the deck of the *Titanic*.'

Quoted in *The Times* (London) (13 May 1976).

See also PROFESSIONALS 3.

TOLKIEN, J.R.R.
English scholar and novelist (1892–1973).

1 TOLKIEN IS HOBBIT-FORMING
– so is Dildo Baggins.

The addition was spotted in London in 1981, but the main pun had been known for some time before that. Indeed, in a letter to Roger Lancelyn Green (8

January 1971) and included in *The Letters of J.R. Tolkien* (1981), Tolkien himself noted: 'A review appeared in *The Observer* 16 Jan 1938, signed "*Habit*" (incidentally thus long anticipating [Nevill] Coghill's perception of the similarity of the words in his humorous adj. "hobbit-forming" applied to my books).'

TOMORROW
1 **Owing to lack of interest, tomorrow has been cancelled.**
Included in *Graffiti 2* (1980).

TORTOISE
1 **Q. Where do you find a tortoise with no legs?**
A. Same place you left it.

TOULOUSE-LAUTREC, HENRI DE
French painter (1864–1901).

1 **It is not generally known that a meeting once took place between the diminutive French painter and the well-upholstered American film star, Mae West. T-L said, 'Come down and see me some time.' Mae West replied, 'I've got nothing To Lose'. To which T-L replied: 'Doesn't look like it from where I'm standing.'**
Dialogue submitted by J.E. White of Cheltenham and broadcast in BBC Radio *Quote ... Unquote* (25 January 1976).

TOURISTS
1 **'I was sitting on a coach behind two American tourists. As we passed the Houses of Parliament, one asked the other what it was. The other replied: "Well, I don't know, but it must be either Oxford or Cambridge."'**
Contributed to BBC Radio *Quote ... Unquote* (21 August 1979) by Sally Bigwood of Reading.

2 **'In Canterbury Cathedral, two old ladies were gazing at the spot where Thomas à Becket met his death. As a friend of mine passed by, he heard one lady say to the other, in a tone of patient resignation: "No dear, not *married* — *murdered!*"'**
Contributed to BBC Radio *Quote ... Unquote* (15 December 1981) by the Revd Michael Burgess of Broadstairs.

3 **'Some years ago at Stonehenge, a harassed mother was overheard saying to her small daughter: "Now, Doreen, just you be careful and don't knock anything over . . .".'**
Contributed to BBC Radio Quote ... Unquote (1 January 1979) by Mr L. Markes of Brockenhurst, Hampshire.

4 **Last year I took my wife on a trip around the world. This year she wants to go somewhere else!**

TOWELS
1 **After using this towel, you are advised to wash your hands.**
Graffito written alongside a dirty roller towel. Contributed to BBC Radio Quote ... Unquote (21 August 1980) by Mrs B. Granett of Bingley.

TRADERS
1 **We have come to an arrangement with our bankers. They have agreed not to sell drink. We, on our part, have agreed not to cash cheques.**
Quoted in Flann O'Brien, The Best of Myles — extracts from his Irish newspaper column from the early 1940s.

TRANSCENDENTAL MEDITATION
1 **Transcendental meditation is better than sitting around doing nothing.**
Graffito, Chelsea, quoted in the Financial Times (16 March 1983).

2 **Is a Buddhist monk refusing an injection at the dentist trying to transcend dental medication?**
From Ilkley College, North Yorkshire, contributed by Roger Eve of Leeds to Graffiti 4 (1982).

TRANSLATIONS
1 **In the 1960s, both in the US and UK, government funding was provided for research into machine translation and, since the Cold War was raging, the only languages the goverments were interested in supporting were English and Russian. The chief groups were at MIT and at Cambridge University. The story is told that on one occasion the phrase 'the spirit is willing, but the flesh is weak' was fed into the machine and**

translated into Russian. It was then translated back into English as 'the vodka's all right but the meat is bad'. Similarly, 'hydraulic ram' turned into 'water goat' and 'out of sight, out of mind' was re-translated as 'invisible lunatic'.

The second example (translated as 'invisible maniac') is quoted by Arthur Calder-Marshall and included in Laurence J. Peter's *Quotations for Our Time* (1977). The former is included in Margaret Boden's *Artificial Intelligence and Natural Man* (1977). Indeed, these computer 'urban myths' certainly seem to date from the 1970s, though T.A. Dyer clearly remembers being told the 'invisible lunatic' one at the Mathematical Laboratory at Cambridge University where 'some very brave men were working on the problem of computer translations' in 1961.

2 A British businessman went on a trade visit to Moscow. The high point of his visit was to be a speech he had to give at a dinner of Russian business people. He duly slaved away at his speech and paid to have it translated into Russian. He also had a phonetic transcription made so that he would be able to recite the speech himself, although he did not understand the language.

When he arrived in Moscow, however, the businessman realised that he had neglected to put the greeting 'ladies and gentlemen' at the start of his speech. He had no idea what the Russian for this was. Then he hit upon a plan. He went down to the lavatories in the hotel where he was staying and saw men going in one door and women in the other. He took the appropriate word from over each door and put them at the start of his speech.

It went triumphantly well and, at the conclusion, he was feted by the Russians for having spoken in their language. 'Only one thing puzzled us,' explained his host. 'We weren't terribly sure why you chose to start your speech by addressing us as "water closets" and "urinals" . . .'

I remember hearing this c. 1960.

Some odd French versions of English idioms or odd English translations of French ones:

3 *Elle a des idées au-dessus de sa gare:* She has ideas above her station.

From Terence Rattigan's play *French Without Tears* (1937).

4 *Ça prend le biscuit!:* That takes the biscuit.

5 *Chacun à son gout:* They've all got the gout.

6 *Tant pis, tant mieux*: **Auntie feels much better now she's been to the ladies.**
Contributed to BBC Radio *Quote ... Unquote* (12 June 1986) by Lady Ellenborough of Crowborough, East Sussex.

7 *Caw! Jeter des pierres aux corbeaux qui vont périr*: **Cor! Stone the perishing crows!**

8 *Crudités variées*: **Assorted rudenesses.**

9 *Je n'aurai pas de camion avec vous*: **I'll have no truck with you.**

10 *C'est un Kleenex de mensonges*: **It's a tissue of lies.**
Contributed to BBC Radio *Quote ... Unquote* (12 June 1986) by J. Mackie, Switzerland.

11 *J'y suis, j'y reste*: **I'm Swiss and I'm staying here for the night.**

12 **What does a Frenchman eat for breakfast?**
Huit heures bix.

13 *Hors de combat*: **Camp followers.**
Included in John S. Crosbie, *Crosbie's Dictionary of Puns* (1977).

14 **Q. What does** *pas de deux* **mean?**
A. The father of twins.

TRANSVESTITES

1 **I AM A PRACTISING TRANSVESTITE ON HOLIDAY HERE TILL NEXT WEEK. IF YOU WOULD LIKE TO MEET ME I'LL BE HERE AT 7.30 EACH NIGHT.**
– how will I recognize you?
In gents' lavatory at Welsh seaside resort, included in *Graffiti 2* (1980).

TRAVEL

1 **A motorist asked a country yokel for directions as to how to get to Salisbury. The yokel had a go at describing the way but then stopped in confusion. 'You know,' he said, 'if I was going to Salisbury, I wouldn't start from here at all . . .'**
Often also told of an Irish countryman.

2 'I'm very excited about going to the Gulf,' said the
   holidaymaker. 'But I have absolutely no idea what to expect!'
       'Ah,' replied the experienced traveller, 'Kuwait and
   sea . . . .'
   Current by the 1960s.

3 Did you hear about the tour guide who took visitors 'where the
   hand of man has never before set foot'?

TREPANNING
1 I need trepanning like I need a hole in the head.
   Quoted in Bruce Ridley (ed.), *Wall Flowers: A Collection of Australian Graffiti*
   (1981).

T-SHIRT JOKES *See under STICKERS.*

TURPENTINE
1 Two farmers met and one said to the other: "Ere, you
   remember telling me you gave your 'oss turpentine when 'e
   'ad colic.' The other said: 'Ay!' The first farmer went on: 'Well,
   I gave my 'oss turpentine, an' 'e died.' Said the other: 'Well,
   mine died too!'
   A classic *Punch* joke – from the caption to a cartoon by Craven Hill (published
   24 November 1909).

TUTANKHAMEN
1 Tutankhamen has changed his mind and wants to be buried at
   sea.
   Graffito in a motorway service area on the M1. Contributed to BBC Radio
   Quote ... Unquote (24 May 1978) by Mrs Belinda Huddleson of Surbiton.

TYPHOID
1 Typhoid is a terrible disease; it can kill you or damage your
   brain. I know what I'm talking about, I've had typhoid.
   Marshal MacMahon, French soldier and statesman (1808–93), quoted in Bechtel
   & Carrière, *Dictionnaire de la Bêtise* (1983).

UMBRELLAS

1 All men are born equal – all men that is to say who possess umbrellas.

E.M. Forster, quoted by Michael York in *Travelling Player* (1991).

UNIONS

1 Being a member of a union is like using a rubber – it gives you a false sense of security while being screwed.

Graffito, reported from Paducah, Kentucky, by Dr Stephen J. Rigby (1990).

URNS

1 A man went into a shop selling archaeological discoveries. 'What's a Grecian urn?' he asked the shop assistant. 'Oh, about three drachmas a week,' came the reply.

A hoary old joke, indeed. Certainly known by the 1940s – but any earlier citings?

USED CARS/MOTORS

1 Buy a used car with the same caution a naked man uses to climb a barbed-wire fence.

Wise saw contributed by Miss O.E. Burns, Stourbridge (1994).

VALETS

1 The difference between a man and his valet: they both smoke the same cigars, but only one pays for them.

Robert Frost, American poet (1874–1963), quoted in *The Treasury of Humorous Quotations*, ed. by Evan Esar & Nicolas Bentley (1951).

VAN DER MERWE JOKES

In South Africa, Van Der Merwe is the archetype of bone-headed Afrikaners. Having the ultimate in Afrikaner surnames, he is the man about whom all the Afrikaners-are-stupid jokes are told. They have been in circulation since the 1960s at least.

1 **Policeman Van Der Merwe is taking an exam for promotion, and in the first-aid section one of the questions is: 'What are rabies, and how do you treat them?' Rabies are Jewish priests', says Van Der Merwe, 'and I treat them with contempt'.**
Told in *The Times* (13 June 1988). It sounds better in an Afrikaans accent.

2 **Piet Van Der Merwe was getting old, and sex with his wife was getting to be like hard work. So he got a black to do it.**
Told in *The Times* (13 July 1991).

VASECTOMY

1 **A vasectomy means never having to say you're sorry.**
Larry Adler once said this at a BBC Radio *Quote ... Unquote* recording (20 January 1976) on his way to having a vasectomy. It appears, however, in Reisner & Wechsler, *Encyclopedia of Graffiti* (1974).

2 **A fertile imagination is no compensation for a vasectomy.**
Graffito from London NW1 on Granada TV *Cabbages and Kings* (20 June 1979).

VENEREAL DISEASES

1 *Observation astronomique – trois heures de Venus, trois ans de Mercure.*
Graffito reported from near Lake Geneva in *Graffiti 2* (1980). Compare the aphorism, 'Two minutes with Venus, two years with mercury' ascribed to J. Earle Moore (1892–1957), untraced. Mercury was once widely used as a cure for syphilis.

2 **Moby Dick is a venereal disease.**
Included in Reisner & Wechsler, *Encyclopedia of Graffiti* (1974).

VENETIAN BLINDS

1 **But for Venetian blinds it would be curtains for all of us.**
Graffito from a youth hostel in Ireland. Contributed to BBC Radio *Quote ... Unquote* (24 July 1980) by Andrew West of Ipswich.

VENUS DE MILO

1 **See what'll happen if you don't stop biting your finger-nails.**
Will Rogers, quoted in Bennett Cerf, *Shake Well Before Using* (1948).

VICTORIA, QUEEN
British Sovereign (1819–1901).

1 **No, Queen Victoria never said 'We are not amused'. What she actually said was, 'We are not a *museum* . . . and, Albert, stop making such a Great Exhibition of yourself.'**
Contributed by John Mitcham of Sheffield to BBC Radio *Quote ... Unquote* (25 January 1976).

2 **On 17 June 1882, Mr Gladstone was paying his weekly visit to Queen Victoria. He arrived in a brougham drawn by two bay geldings and asked the Queen respectfully if he might leave the carriage in the Palace yard. Unfortunately, her late majesty was in an irritable mood at the time and made this reply: 'Certainly not. We are not a mews . . . .'**
Contributed by Dick Jordan of Datchet, Buckinghamshire, to BBC Radio *Quote ... Unquote* (14 March 1976).

See also HISTORY 31.

VIENNA

1 **A classic agent/booker of shows story is where an agent phoned the man who booked the attractions for Walthamstow Palace. The agent, desperate to fill in vacant weeks for the tour of a musical comedy he was representing, asked, 'How do you think *Goodnight Vienna* would go in Walthamstow?' Replied the booker, 'About as well as *Goodnight Walthamstow* would go in Vienna!'**
Told in *Roy Hudd's Book of Music-Hall, Variety and Showbiz Anecdotes* (1993).

VIRGINITY

1 **Virginity is like a balloon — one prick and it's gone.**
Included in *Graffiti 2* (1980).

VOTES OF THANKS

1 **I've had a wonderful evening — but this wasn't it.**

Traditional put down, recalled by Sue Limb on BBC Radio *Quote ... Unquote* (15 September 1984).

VOTING

1 **If voting could change things it would be illegal.**

Graffito, Carlton, Victoria. Quoted in Rennie Ellis & Ian Turner, *Australian Graffiti Revisited* (1979).

VULTURES

1 **If there's one thing above all a vulture can't stand, it's a glass eye.**

Attributed to Frank McKinney ('Kin') Hubbard, US humorist (1868–1930).

WAITER JOKES

1 **Waiter, waiter, there's a fly in my soup!
Please keep your voice down, sir, or all the other customers will want one.**

A possible indication of the age of these exchanges is said to be contained in Barbara C. Bowen's anthology *One Hundred Renaissance Jokes*. In a Latin joke told by Sir Thomas More, a guest at a banquet removes flies from a loving-cup before drinking from it and then putting them back in. He remarks: 'I don't like flies myself, but perhaps some of you chaps do.'

2 **Waiter, waiter, there's a fly in my soup!
What's it doing, sir, crawl or breast-stroke?**

Heard in the 1950s?

3 **Waiter, there's a fly in my soup!
Yes, sir, the chef used to be a tailor.**

Told in *Today* (11 January 1993).

4 **Waiter, there's a fly in my soup!**
Don't worry, how much soup can a fly drink?

This and the previous joke are two said to come from Lindy's restaurant in New York, which was founded in 1921 and became famous for the backchat of its waiters. Two more:

5 **Waiter, there's a fly in my soup!**
They don't seem to care what they eat, do they, sir?

6 **Waiter, there's a fly in my soup!**
Looks as if he's trying to get out, sir.

7 **Waiter, there's a fly in my soup!**
Throw him this doughnut, sir, it'll make a good lifebelt.

8 **Waiter, waiter — there's a fly in my soup!**
I'm sorry, sir, I didn't realize you wished to eat alone.

9 **Waiter, there's a *dead* fly in my soup!**
Oh, dear, it must have committed insecticide.

10 **Waiter, there's a *dead* fly in my soup!**
Yes, sir, it's the heat that kills them.

11 **Waiter, there's a *dead* fly in my soup!**
What do you expect for 50p, a live one?

12 **Waiter, there's a *dead* fly in my soup!**
Oh, that's terrible, sir! He was too young to die.

13 **Waiter, waiter — there's a dead fly in my *wine*.**
Well, sir, you did ask for something with a little body to it.

14 **Waiter, what is that fly doing on my sorbet?**
Learning to ski, sir.

15 **Waiter, your thumb is in my soup.**
Don't worry, sir, it's not hot.

16 **Waiter, do you serve shrimps here?**
Sure. We don't care how tall you are. Sit down.

Another version: 'Do you serve crabs here?' — 'We serve anyone, sir.'

17 **Waiter, is there rice pudding on the menu?**
    There was, sir, but I wiped it off.

18 **Waiter, this coffee tastes like tea!**
    Forgive me, sir, I must have given you the hot chocolate.

19 **Waiter, waiter, this lobster's only got one claw.**
    I'm sorry, sir, it must have been in a fight.
    Well, bring me the winner then.

20 **I say, waiter – have you got frogs' legs?**
    No, sir, I always walk this way.

    In the introduction to *The Groucho Letters* (1967), Arthur Sheekman writes: 'If in a mood to parody the small-time comedians, [Marx] might say to a waiter – or waitress – "Have you got frog legs?" And no matter what the reply, Groucho will look painfully disappointed and say, "That's the wrong answer. You were supposed to say, 'No; it's rheumatism that makes me walk this way.'"'

    See also TALCUM POWDER 1.

21 **I say, waiter – have you got frog's legs?**
    Yes, I have, sir.
    Well, could you hop over the counter and get me a cheese sandwich?

    See also EPITAPHS 6.

WALES AND THE WELSH

1 **Come home to a real fire – buy a cottage in Wales.**
   From Swansea (1980), in *Graffiti 3* (1981).

   Compare NORTHERN IRELAND 2.

2 **There are still parts of Wales where the only concession to gaiety is a striped shroud.**
   Gwyn Thomas, Welsh humorist (1913–81), in *Punch* (18 June 1958).

3 **The Welsh are the Italians in the rain.**
   Quoted by the writer Elaine Morgan on BBC Radio *Quote ... Unquote* (16 July 1983). An earlier version spoken, though probably not coined, by the journalist René Cutforth was: 'The Welsh are the Mediterraneans in the rain', which was quoted by Nancy Banks-Smith in the *Guardian* (17 October 1979).

WALLS

1 **Walls have ears – I've just found one in my ice cream.**
Contributed to BBC Radio Quote ... Unquote (11 September 1979) by Dr D.M. Etheridge of Bournville, Birmingham, who saw it on a wall at Lapworth, Warwickshire.

WATER ON THE KNEE

1 **If you've got water on the knee, you're not aiming straight.**
From Circular Quay, Sydney, Australia – reported by Tim Denes (1982).

WATERBEDS

1 **Waterbeds are cutting down the incidence of adultery.**
Why?
Ever tried to crawl under one?
From South Melbourne, Victoria, Australia – quoted in Rennie Ellis & Ian Turner, Australian Graffiti Revisited (1979).

WATERMELON

1 **It is a good fruit. You eat, you drink, you wash your face.**
Attributed to Enrico Caruso, Italian singer (1873–1921).

WATERSHIP DOWN

1 **Watership Down – you've seen the film, you've read the book, now eat the pie.**
Included in Graffiti 3 (1981).

WAYNE, JOHN
American film actor (1907–79).

1 **JOHN WAYNE IS DEAD**
– the hell I am!
Newspaper placard and addition, London, in Graffiti 2 (1980). According to The Oxford Book of Death (1983), the exchange was reported in the Evening Standard in 1980 and came from Bermondsey Antique Market.

WEALTH

1 **My uncle is so rich he even suffers from Perrier on the knee.**

WEATHER

1 **The weather will be cold. There are two reasons for this. One is that the temperatures will be lower.**
Weather forecast on BBC Radio (12 April 1969).

WEIGHT

1 **I whisper your weight.**
Graffito on weighing machine near the Dartford Tunnel. Contributed to BBC Radio *Quote ... Unquote* (11 September 1979) by Mr D. Patch of Maldon, Essex.

WHITLAM, MARGARET

1 **Margaret Whitlam kick starts jumbos.**
Graffito in Adelaide, South Australia. She was the formidably tall wife of Gough Whitlam, the Australian Prime Minister. Quoted in Rennie Ellis & Ian Turner, *Australian Graffiti Revisited* (1979), but known by 1975.

WIDOWS

1 **He had heard that one is permitted a certain latitude with widows, and went in for the whole 180 degrees.**
George Ade, American humorist (1866–1944), quoted in *The Treasury of Humorous Quotations*, ed. by Evan Esar & Nicolas Bentley (1951).

WILDE, OSCAR
Irish-born playwright, poet and wit (1854–1900).

1 **A formidable woman he did not admire encountered Oscar Wilde one evening at a party. 'Ah, Mr Wilde,' she said, beaming at him, 'I passed your house this afternoon.' 'Thank you so much,' replied Wilde.**
Contributed to BBC Radio *Quote ... Unquote* (1 January 1979).

2 **Wilde was once offered a dreadful watercress sandwich. He said, 'Tell the cook of this restaurant with the compliments of Mr Oscar Wilde that these are the very worst sandwiches in the world, and that, when I asked for a watercress sandwich, I do not mean a loaf with a field in the middle of it . . . .'**
Quoted in *The Lyttelton Hart-Davis Letters* (for 3 June 1956).

WISDOM

1 Too bad that all the people who know how to run the country are busy driving taxicabs and cutting hair.

From Vancouver BC, included in *Graffiti 3* (1981). Also attributed to George Burns, American comedian (1896–) by 1977.

WIVES

1 A newly elected mayor was replying to a speech congratulating him on his elevation. He promised that during his year of office, he would lay aside all his political prepossessions and be, 'like Caesar's wife, all things to all men'.

Told by G.W.E. Russell in *Collections and Recollections* (1898).

2 When Jimmy Thomas, the Labour member of parliament and cabinet minister around the 1920s was asked whether his wife would be accompanying him on an official visit to Paris, he replied: 'You don't take a ham sandwich to the Lord Mayor's Banquet, do you?'

Told by Richard Toeman of London N6 (1995).

3 *Wife:* One more word out of you and I am going back to my mother.
Husband: Taxi!

4 A wife lasts as long as a marriage, an ex-wife for ever.

5 I don't know what all this fuss is about weight. My wife lost two stone swimming last year. I don't know how. I tied 'em round her neck tight enough.

Les Dawson, British comedian, quoted in the *Independent* (9 April 1990).

6 I'm into wife-swapping. I'll accept anything in exchange.

Included in *Graffiti 5* (1986).

7 They say a woman should be a cook in the kitchen and a whore in bed. Unfortunately, my wife is a whore in the kitchen and a cook in bed.

Quoted by Peter Porter on BBC Radio *Quote ... Unquote* (31 July 1979).

Compare MARRIAGE 5.

WOMEN

1 **Women were born without a sense of humour – so they could love men, not laugh at them.**
From Amsterdam, included in *Graffiti 2* (1980). In Leslie Robert Missen, *Quotable Anecdotes* (1966) the remark is ascribed to Mrs Patrick Campbell, the British actress (1865-1940).

2 **The female sex has no bigger fan than I, and I have the bills to prove it.**
Alan J. Lerner, *The Street Where I Live* (1978).

3 **A woman's mind is cleaner than a man's; she changes it more often.**
Oliver Herford, American humorist (1863–1935), quoted in *The Treasury of Humorous Quotations*, ed. by Evan Esar & Nicolas Bentley (1951).

4 **WOMEN LIKE THE SIMPLER THINGS IN LIFE – LIKE MEN – simple things please simple minds.**
The original feminist slogan appeared in *Graffiti Lives OK* (1979), the addition in *Graffiti 5* (1986).

5 **Men who do not make advances to women are apt to become victims to women who makes advances to them.**
Walter Bagehot, English political writer (1826–77), quoted in *The Treasury of Humorous Quotations*, ed. by Evan Esar & Nicolas Bentley (1951).

See also FEMINIST JOKES.

WORK AND WORKERS

1 **I go on working for the same reason that a hen goes on laying eggs.**
H.L. Mencken, American writer and editor (1880–1956), quoted in *The Treasury of Humorous Quotations*, ed. by Evan Esar & Nicolas Bentley (1951).

2 **IN PEOPLE'S CHINA THE WORKERS TAKE THE LEAD – in capitalist England the sods also take the iron, copper, floorboards and fillings from your teeth.**
From Euston station, London, before 1975, included in *Graffiti Lives OK* (1979).

3 **Work is the curse of the drinking classes.**
Oscar Wilde, quoted in Hesketh Pearson, *The Life of Oscar Wilde* (1946).

WRESTLING, ALL-IN
1 **If it's all in, why wrestle?**
Attributed to Mae West.

YOGA
1 **Try Yoga. They did, and the judge said: 'How did you get into this awful position, and look me straight in the feet when I'm talking to you.'**
From Exeter, included in *Graffiti 5* (1986).

YOUTH
1 **The barman asked the girl, 'Are you old enough to drink here?' 'Sure,' she replied, 'I've been drinking for years.' 'OK, then, what'll you have to drink?' 'Scotch and wah-wah.'**
Performed on CBS TV *Rowan and Martin's Laugh-In* and included on the record album *Laugh-In '69* (1969).

ZIPS
1 **What has 27 teeth and holds back the Incredible Hulk? My zipper.**
In Haan & Hammerstrom *Graffiti in the Southwest Conference* (1981).

ZOOS
1 **Is the Regents Park toilet a Zulu?**
Included in *Graffiti Lives OK* (1979).

2 **Why did the ant elope? Nobody gnu.**